THE TREASURY

OF

AMERICAN SACRED SONG

The Treasury

of

American Sacred Song

WITH

NOTES EXPLANATORY AND BIOGRAPHICAL

SELECTED AND EDITED BY

W. GARRETT HORDER

Granger Index Reprint Series

BOOKS FOR LIBRARIES PRESS

FREEPORT, NEW YORK

First published 1896
Reprinted 1969

*In seeking for the beautiful, poets meet with more truths
than the philosophers in their researches after the true.*

JOUBERT.

STANDARD BOOK NUMBER:
8369-6019-X

LIBRARY OF CONGRESS CATALOG CARD NUMBER:
74-76944

MANUFACTURED
BY
HALLMARK LITHOGRAPHERS, INC.
IN THE U.S.A.

PREFACE

—◆—

THIS is an attempt to give a fuller presentation of the Sacred Verse of America than has previously existed.

During the progress of my researches I have again and again been reminded of the remark of Colonel Higginson —one of the most delightful of American poets—to Matthew Arnold: 'As I take it, Nature said some years since, "Thus far the English is my best race; but we have had Englishmen enough; we need something with a little more buoyancy than the Englishman; let us lighten the structure, even at some peril in the process. Put in one drop more of nervous fluid, and make the American."'

In much of the sacred verse I have examined I have found 'one drop more of the nervous fluid,' which sometimes, perhaps, has been so quick in its operation as not to produce a structure as perfect as could be desired. My aim has been to select verse with the fullest native force, and at the same time the most finished form.

Readers may perchance, here and there, light on poems which seem scarcely suited for a collection of sacred verse; but in such cases the sacred character, which may at a first glance appear lacking, will nevertheless be found in the thoughts they suggest.

I have not cared to present any of the earliest verse of America, considering that it possesses only an antiquarian interest. Nor have I gone beyond the limits of the United States. If I seem to have omitted certain familiar poems, it has not been from oversight, but after a careful weighing of reasons.

The arrangement of poems is, as nearly as I could make it, chronological : the order being determined by the birth-date of writers.

If I have in any measure succeeded in my difficult task, it is largely due to the effective assistance I have received on both sides of the Atlantic. On this side, mention must first be made of the Rev. Richard Wilton, M.A., Rector of Londesborough and Canon of York — one of our best-known sacred poets *—who has spared neither time nor thought in aiding me to make the collection as choice as possible : to his fine taste I am under the deepest obligation, as well as for the Dedicatory Sonnet, ' To the Sacred Poets of America,' which at my suggestion he wrote. For help of various kinds I am indebted to the late lamented James Ashcroft Noble, an accomplished literary critic ; Norman Gale, author of *A Country Muse* ; Gleeson White, editor of *Ballades and Rondeaux*, whose ample library of American poetry was freely put at my service ; the Rev. Andrew Chalmers, M.A., editor of *Modern Hymns*; the Rev. H. C. Beeching, M.A., editor of *Lyra Christi* ; Coulson Kernahan, author of *A Dead Man's Diary*; the Rev. G. T. Coster, author of *Gloria Christi*; Paul B. Neuman, Author of *The Interpreter's House*; the Rev. Valentine D. Davis, B.A., and Dr. Garnett, who afforded me every facility in consulting books at the British Museum.

On the other side of the Atlantic my helpers have been both numerous and distinguished. Special acknow-ledgments are due to Mrs. Tileston, the editor of *Quiet Hours*, who has been almost an American colleague-

---

* Author of *Wood-Notes and Church Bells*, *Lyrics Sylvan and Sacred*, *Sungleams*, and *Benedicite*.

editor, examining for me the works of American poets in the Boston libraries ; Mrs. Louise Chandler Moulton, to whom I am also indebted for three unpublished sonnets; Richard Watson Gilder, LL.D., editor of *The Century*; Edmund Clarence Stedman, LL.D., author of *American Poets*; Dr. Doane, Bishop of Albany, and Miss Edith Matilda Thomas, who in recent interviews gave me valuable counsel; and Dr. J. M. Whiton, who sought out for me books that could not be obtained in England, and rendered valuable aid in revision of the proofs. To all these I tender my sincere thanks.

From every writer and publisher I have received the most ready response to my application for the use of copyright poems. The only restriction imposed was by Messrs. Houghton, Mifflin, & Co., in the case of a few poets, such as Longfellow, Whittier, and Lowell, that my extracts should not exceed a certain number ; these writers, however, are within the reach of all, so that the restriction has really proved of service by affording me space for the verse of less-known writers, whose works are more difficult of access.

My selections from the authors named below have been taken by permission of, and by special arrangement with, their publishers, to whom I render my most cordial thanks :—

HOUGHTON, MIFFLIN, & Co.—Ralph Waldo Emerson, Henry Wadsworth Longfellow, John Greenleaf Whittier, Oliver Wendell Holmes, Samuel Longfellow, Christopher P. Cranch, Alice and Phœbe Cary, Caroline Atherton Mason, James Russell Lowell, Thomas W. Parsons, Edna Dean Proctor, Lucy Larcom, Harriet Beecher Stowe, Henry David Thoreau, Edmund Clarence Stedman, Margaret E. Sangster, Bayard Taylor, Celia Thaxter, Thomas Bailey Aldrich, Francis Bret Harte, Edgar Fawcett, Edward Rowland Sill, Emma Lazarus, Edith

Matilda Thomas, Henry Augustin Beers, Margaret Deland, Frank Dempster Sherman, James Thomas Fields, Elizabeth Stuart Phelps, Nora Perry, John James Piatt, Sarah M. B. Piatt, John Townsend Trowbridge, Adeline D. Train Whitney, George Edward Woodberry, Harriet Prescott Spofford, William Roscoe Thayer, William Henry Burleigh, John Burroughs, James Freeman Clarke, William Henry Furness, Lizette Woodworth Reese, Louise Imogen Guiney, Saxe Holm, William Dean Howells, Ellen Mackay Hutchinson, Ina Donna Coolbrith.

ROBERTS BROTHERS. — Louisa May Alcott, Charles Timothy Brooks, Sarah Chauncey Woolsey (Susan Coolidge), Emily Dickinson, Frederic Henry Hedge, William Channing Gannett, Thomas Wentworth Higginson, Frederick Lucian Hosmer, Julia Ward Howe, Helen Hunt Jackson, Louise Chandler Moulton, Theodore Parker, John White Chadwick.

THE CENTURY COMPANY.—Richard Watson Gilder, Mary Mapes Dodge, Washington Gladden, Thomas Bailey Aldrich.

G. P. PUTNAM'S SONS.—James Herbert Morse, Sarah Hammond Palfrey, Francis Howard Williams, Danske Dandridge, Charles Henry Crandall.

CASSELL & CO. (New York).—Minnie Gilmore, Charles Munroe Dickinson.

D. APPLETON & CO.—William Cullen Bryant.

HARPER BROTHERS.—Amélie Rives (the Princess Troubetzköy), Horatio Nelson Powers.

CHARLES SCRIBNER'S SONS.—Anne Reeve Aldrich, Julia C. R. Dorr, Eugene Field, Josiah Gilbert Holland, Sidney Lanier, Richard Henry Stoddard, Charles Henry Lüders.

ARMSTRONG & SONS. — Edgar Allan Poe.

BOWEN MERRILL COMPANY.—James Whitcomb Riley.

COPELAND & DAY.—John Banister Tabb, Hannah' Parker Kimball, Alice Brown.

T. Y. CROWELL & Co.—Sarah Knowles Bolton, Nathan Haskell Dole, Charlotte Fiske Bates.

G. H. ELLIS.—Minot Judson Savage.

DAVID McKAY.—Walt Whitman.

LEE & SHEPARD.—David Atwood Wasson.

A. D. F. RANDOLPH & Co.—Harriet McEwen Kimball, Willis Boyd Allen, May Riley Smith.

THE LOTHROP PUBLISHING COMPANY.—Paul Hamilton Hayne, Lydia Maria Child, Katharine Lee Bates, Oscar Fay Adams.

F. A. STOKES & Co.—Frank Dempster Sherman.

J. POTT & Co.—Arthur Cleveland Coxe.

THOMAS WHITTAKER.—Augustus William Muhlenberg.

E. P. DUTTON & Co.—Phillips Brooks, Edmund Hamilton Sears, William Croswell, George Washington Doane.

MORRELL HIGGINSON & Co.—Joaquin Miller.

THE OUTLOOK COMPANY.—Tudor Jenks.

THE INDEPENDENT (New York).—Rose Terry Cooke.

J. B. LIPPINCOTT & Co.—Charles F. Richardson.

GEORGE H. CARR.—W. Hunter Birckhead.

A. S. BARNES & Co.—Ray Palmer.

G. GOTTSBERGER PECK.—Rose Terry Cooke.

To the following I am indebted for permission to use poems of which they hold the British copyright:—

LONGMANS, GREEN & Co.—John James Piatt, Sarah M. B. Piatt, J. Whitcomb Riley, Margaret Deland, Thomas Wentworth Higginson.

OSGOOD, MACILVAINE & Co.—Emily Dickinson, Eugene Field, Margaret Deland.

To the following authors I am indebted for permission to use their poems:—

Louise Chandler Moulton, Amélie Rives (the Princess

Troubetzköy), to both of whom I am indebted for un-published poems, Anna Jane Granniss, Martha Perry Lowe, Maurice Francis Egan, Langdon Elwyn Mitchell (John Philip Varley), Tudor Jenks, Charles Gordon Ames, George McKnight, Arlo Bates, W. Ordway Partridge, Richard Hovey, John Vance Cheney; also to Bishop Doane for a hymn by his father, Charles Ray Palmer for poems by his father, Lydia A. Very for poems by her brother, and Charles T. Weitzel for poems by his wife.

I have taken the greatest pains to reach holders of copyright of the poems included; but if in any case I have unwittingly failed, I trust that the permission I would gladly have sought will be as generously ac-corded as it has been, without exception, by all others.

I now offer this collection — the result of careful research extending over several years—to lovers of sacred verse in all English-speaking lands.

May it tend to strengthen the bond, already so strong, which unites the kindred nations of Great Britain and America!

W. G. H.

EALING, LONDON, W.
August, 1896.

PROLOGUE

———•◆•———

TO THE SACRED POETS OF AMERICA

*A*S *from the East unto the utmost West*
   God bids the banner of His lightning shine,
  The flashing signal of the Face Divine
With whose fair radiance earth may soon be blest;
So speeds the Heavenly Muse, at His behest,
  Across the waters; so the spreading vine
  Of sacred poesy, with clusters fine,
By Western airs is welcomed and caressed.
O ye whose sires our English fields have trod,
  By holy Herbert's feet made hallowed ground,
  His dower of truth and beauty ye have found:
With you still buds and blossoms Aaron's rod,
Proclaiming you the poet-priests of God,
  To wave the incense of His praise around.

RICHARD WILTON.

LONDESBOROUGH RECTORY,
  EAST YORKSHIRE,
    June, 1896.

THE AMERICAN
TREASURY OF SACRED SONG

—·—

John Pierpont

UNIVERSAL WORSHIP

O THOU, to whom in ancient time
  The lyre of Hebrew bards was strung;
Whom kings adored in songs sublime,
  And prophets praised with glowing tongue:

Not now on Zion's height alone
  Thy favoured worshippers may dwell,
Nor where at sultry noon Thy Son
  Sat weary, by the patriarch's well:

From every place below the skies,
  The grateful song, the fervent prayer,
The incense of the heart, may rise
  To heaven, and find acceptance there.

To Thee shall age with snowy hair,
  And strength and beauty, bend the knee;
And childhood lisp, with reverent air,
  Its praises and its prayers to Thee.

O Thou, to whom, in ancient time
  The lyre of prophet-bards was strung,—
To Thee, at last, in every clime,
  Shall temples rise. and praise be sung.

HYMN OF THE LAST SUPPER

THE winds are hushed; the peaceful moon
  Looks down on Zion's hill;
The city sleeps; 'tis night's calm noon,
  And all the streets are still.

Save when, along the shaded walks,
  We hear the watchman's call,
Or the guard's footsteps, as he stalks
  In moonlight on the wall.

How soft, how holy is this light!
  And hark! a mournful song,
As gentle as these dews of night,
  Floats on the air along.

Affection's wish, devotion's prayer,
  Are in that holy strain;
'Tis resignation, not despair,
  'Tis triumph, though 'tis pain.

'Tis Jesus and His faithful few
  That pour that hymn of love;
O God! may we the song renew,
  Around Thy board above!

MORNING HYMN FOR A CHILD

O GOD, I thank Thee that the night
  In peace and rest hath passed away;
And that I see, in this fair light,
  My Father's smile, that makes it day.

Be Thou my Guide, and let me live
  As under Thine all-seeing eye;
Supply my wants, my sins forgive,
  And make me happy when I die.

EVENING HYMN FOR A CHILD

ANOTHER day its course hath run,
　And still, O God, Thy child is blest;
For Thou hast been by day my sun,
　And Thou wilt be by night my rest.

Sweet sleep descends, my eyes to close;
　And now, when all the world is still,
I give my body to repose,
　My spirit to my Father's will.

Andrews Norton

THE DEDICATION OF A CHURCH

WHERE ancient forests round us spread,
　Where bends the cataract's ocean-fall,
On the lone mountain's silent head,
　There are Thy temples, God of all!

Beneath the dark-blue midnight arch,
　Whence myriad suns pour down their rays,
Where planets trace their ceaseless march,
　Father! we worship as we gaze.

The tombs Thy altars are; for there,
　When earthly loves and hopes have fled,
To Thee ascends the spirit's prayer,
　Thou God of the immortal dead!

All space is holy; for all space
　Is filled by Thee; but human thought
Burns clearer in some chosen place,
　Where Thy own words of love are taught.

Here be they taught; and may we know
　That faith Thy servants knew of old,
Which onward bears through weal and woe,
　Till Death the gates of heaven unfold.

Nor we alone : may those whose brow
    Shows yet no trace of human cares,
Hereafter stand where we do now,
    And raise to Thee still holier prayers.

Charles Sprague

THE WINGED WORSHIPPERS

(TO TWO SWALLOWS IN A CHURCH)

GAY, guiltless pair !
    What seek ye from the fields of heaven ?
Ye have no need of prayer,
Ye have no sins to be forgiven.

    Why perch ye here,
Where mortals to their Maker bend ?
    Can your pure spirits fear
The God ye never could offend ?

    Ye never knew
The crimes for which we come to weep,
    Penance is not for you,
Bless'd wanderers of the upper deep !

    To you 'tis given
To wake sweet Nature's untaught lays ;
    Beneath the arch of heaven
To chirp away a life of praise.

    Then spread each wing,
Far, far above, o'er lakes and lands,
    And join the choirs that sing
In yon blue dome not rear'd with hands :

    Or, if ye stay,
To note the consecrated hour,
    Teach me the airy way,
And let me try your envied power !

Above the crowd
On upward wings could I but fly,
    I'd bathe in yon bright cloud,
And seek the stars that gem the sky.

    'Twere heaven indeed,
Through fields of trackless light to soar,
    On Nature's charms to feed,
And Nature's own great God adore.

Nathaniel Langdon Frothingham

COMMUNION HYMN

'REMEMBER ME,' the Saviour said
        On that forsaken night,
When from His side the nearest fled,
    And death was close in sight.

Through all the following ages' track
    The world remembers yet;
With love and worship gazes back,
    And never can forget.

But who of us has seen His face,
    Or heard the words He said?
And none can now His look retrace
    In breaking of the bread.

Oh, blest are they who have not seen,
    And yet believe Him still!
They know Him, when His praise they mean,
    And when they do His will.

We hear His word along our way;
    We see His light above;
Remember when we strive and pray,
    Remember when we love.

THE CHURCH

O LORD of life, and truth, and grace,
  Ere Nature was begun!
Make welcome to our erring race
  Thy Spirit and Thy Son.

We hail the Church, built high o'er all
  The heathen's rage and scoff;
Thy Providence its fenced wall,
  'The Lamb the light thereof.'

Thy Christ hath reached His heavenly seat
  Through sorrows and through scars;
The golden lamps are at His feet,
  And in His hand the stars.

Oh, may He walk among us here,
  With His rebuke and love,—
A brightness o'er this lower sphere,
  A ray from worlds above!

A LAMENT *

A WAIL from beyond the desert!
  A wail from across the sea!
    The home he left,
    Bereft, bereft,
For evermore must be.

As spread the heavy tidings,
  How many a heart grows sore
    That the eloquent grace
    Of that pensive face
And that mellow voice is o'er.

Alas for thee, O our brother!
  And for this we sorrow most,
    That a spirit so fair
    Must be breathed out there,
On that stern Arabian coast:—

* See Note.

That a life so all unforeign,
    To faith and his country bound,
        Turned dying eyes
        Upon Asian skies,
And dropped on Moslem ground.

Away for the Holy City
    With pilgrim soul he trod ;
        But nearer at hand
        Must the pearl gates expand
Of the city new of God.

The judgment-peak of Sinai
    Rose now in the homeward West,
        Its shadows grim
        Had no terror for him,
As he sank to his Christian rest.

But, oh, that the thoughtful scholar,—
    His mind at its fullest noon,—
        That the preacher's tongue
        And the poet's song
Should pass away so soon !

William Cullen Bryant

THANATOPSIS

TO him who in the love of Nature holds
    Communion with her visible forms, she speaks
A various language ; for his gayer hours
She has a voice of gladness, and a smile
And eloquence of beauty, and she glides
Into his darker musings, with a mild
And healing sympathy, that steals away
Their sharpness, ere he is aware. When thoughts
Of the last bitter hour come like a blight
Over thy spirit, and sad images
Of the stern agony, and shroud, and pall,
And breathless darkness, and the narrow house,
Make thee to shudder, and grow sick at heart ;—

Go forth, under the open sky, and list
To Nature's teachings, while from all around—
Earth and her waters, and the depths of air—
Comes a still voice—Yet a few days, and thee
The all-beholding sun shall see no more
In all his course; nor yet in the cold ground,
Where thy pale form was laid, with many tears,
Nor in the embrace of ocean, shall exist
Thy image.   Earth, that nourished thee, shall claim
Thy growth, to be resolved to earth again,
And, lost each human trace, surrendering up
Thine individual being, shalt thou go
To mix for ever with the elements,
To be a brother to the insensible rock
And to the sluggish clod, which the rude swain
Turns with his share, and treads upon.   The oak
Shall send his roots abroad, and pierce thy mould.

Yet not to thine eternal resting-place
Shalt thou retire alone, nor couldst thou wish
Couch more magnificent.   Thou shalt lie down
With patriarchs of the infant world—with kings,
The powerful of the earth—the wise, the good,
Fair forms, and hoary seers of ages past,
All in one mighty sepulchre.   The hills
Rock-ribbed and ancient as the sun,—the vales
Stretching in pensive quietness between;
The venerable woods—rivers that move
In majesty, and the complaining brooks
That make the meadows green; and, poured round all,
Old Ocean's gray and melancholy waste,—
Are but the solemn decorations all
Of the great tomb of man.   The golden sun,
The planets, all the infinite host of heaven,
Are shining on the sad abodes of death,
Through the still lapse of ages.   All that tread
The globe are but a handful to the tribes
That slumber in its bosom.—Take the wings
Of morning, pierce the Barcan wilderness,
Or lose thyself in the continuous woods
Where rolls the Oregon, and hears no sound,
Save his own dashings—yet the dead are there:

And millions in those solitudes, since first
The flight of years began, have laid them down
In their last sleep—the dead reign there alone.
So shalt thou rest, and what if thou withdraw
In silence from the living, and no friend
Take note of thy departure? All that breathe
Will share thy destiny. The gay will laugh
When thou art gone, the solemn brood of care
Plod on, and each one as before will chase
His favorite phantom; yet all these shall leave
Their mirth and their employments, and shall come
And make their bed with thee. As the long train
Of ages glide away, the sons of men,
The youth in life's green spring, and he who goes
In the full strength of years, matron and maid,
The speechless babe, and the gray-headed man—
Shall one by one be gathered to thy side,
By those, who in their turn shall follow them.

So live, that when thy summons comes to join
The innumerable caravan, which moves
To that mysterious realm, where each shall take
His chamber in the silent halls of death,
Thou go not, like the quarry-slave at night,
Scourged to his dungeon; but, sustained and soothed
By an unfaltering trust, approach thy grave,
Like one who wraps the drapery of his couch
About him, and lies down to pleasant dreams.

TO A WATERFOWL

WHITHER, midst falling dew,
     While glow the heavens with the last
          steps of day,
Far, through their rosy depths, dost thou pursue
     Thy solitary way?

     Vainly the fowler's eye
Might mark thy distant flight to do thee wrong,
As, darkly seen against the crimson sky,
     Thy figure floats along.

Seek'st thou the plashy brink
Of weedy lake, or marge of river wide,
Or where the rocking billows rise and sink
On the chafed ocean-side?

There is a Power whose care
Teaches thy way along that pathless coast—
The desert and illimitable air—
Lone wandering, but not lost.

All day thy wings have fanned,
At that far height, the cold, thin atmosphere,
Yet stoop not, weary, to the welcome land,
Though the dark night is near.

And soon that toil shall end;
Soon shalt thou find a summer home, and rest,
And scream among thy fellows; reeds shall bend,
Soon, o'er thy sheltered nest.

Thou'rt gone, the abyss of heaven
Hath swallowed up thy form; yet, on my heart
Deeply hath sunk the lesson thou hast given,
And shall not soon depart.

He who, from zone to zone,
Guides through the boundless sky thy certain flight,
In the long way that I must tread alone,
Will lead my steps aright.

HYMN OF THE CITY

NOT in the solitude
Alone may man commune with Heaven, or see,
Only in savage wood
And sunny vale, the present Deity;
Or only hear His voice
Where the winds whisper and the waves rejoice.

Even here do I behold
Thy steps, Almighty!—here, amidst the crowd
Through the great city rolled,
With everlasting murmur deep and loud—
Choking the ways that wind
'Mongst the proud piles, the work of human kind.

Thy golden sunshine comes
From the round heaven, and on their dwellings lies
   And lights their inner homes;
For them Thou fill'st with air the unbounded skies,
   And givest them the stores
Of ocean, and the harvests of its shores.

Thy Spirit is around,
Quickening the restless mass that sweeps along;
   And this eternal sound —
Voices and footfalls of the numberless throng —
   Like the resounding sea,
Or like the rainy tempest, speaks of Thee.

And when the hour of rest
Comes, like a calm upon the mid-sea brine,
   Hushing its billowy breast—
The quiet of that moment too is thine;
   It breathes of Him who keeps
The vast and helpless city while it sleeps.

THE TIDES

THE moon is at her full, and, riding high,
   Floods the calm fields with light;
The airs that hover in the summer sky
   Are all asleep to-night.

There comes no voice from the great woodlands round
   That murmured all the day;
Beneath the shadow of their boughs the ground
   Is not more still than they.

But ever heaves and moans the restless Deep;
   His rising tides I hear,
Afar I see the glimmering billows leap;
   I see them breaking near.

Each wave springs upward, climbing toward the fair
   Pure light that sits on high—
Springs eagerly, and faintly sinks, to where
   The mother-waters lie.

Upward again it swells; the moonbeams show
    Again its glimmering crest;
Again it feels the fatal weight below,
    And sinks, but not to rest.

Again and yet again; until the Deep
    Recalls his brood of waves;
And, with a sudden moan, abashed, they creep
    Back to his inner caves.

Brief respite! they shall rush from that recess
    With noise and tumult soon,
And fling themselves, with unavailing stress,
    Up toward the placid moon.

O restless Sea, that, in thy prison here,
    Dost struggle and complain;
Through the slow centuries yearning to be near
    To that fair orb in vain;

The glorious source of light and heat must warm
    Thy billows from on high,
And change them to the cloudy trains that form
    The curtains of the sky.

Then only may they leave the waste of brine
    In which they welter here,
And rise above the hills of earth, and shine
    In a serener sphere.

THE MOTHER'S HYMN

LORD, who ordainest for mankind
    Benignant toils and tender cares!
We thank Thee for the ties that bind
    The mother to the child she bears.

We thank Thee for the hopes that rise
    Within her heart, as, day by day,
The dawning soul, from those young eyes,
    Looks, with a clearer, steadier ray.

And grateful for the blessing given
  With that dear infant on her knee,
She trains the eye to look to heaven,
  The voice to lisp a prayer to Thee.

Such thanks the blessed Mary gave,
  When, from her lap, the Holy Child,
Sent from on high to seek and save
  The lost of earth, looked up and smiled.

All-Gracious! grant, to those who bear
  A mother's charge, the strength and light
To lead the steps that own their care
  In ways of Love, and Truth, and Right.

THE STAR OF BETHLEHEM

AS shadows, cast by cloud and sun,
  Flit o'er the summer grass,
So, in Thy sight, Almighty One!
  Earth's generations pass.

And while the years, an endless host,
  Come pressing swiftly on,
The brightest names that earth can boast
  Just glisten, and are gone.

Yet doth the Star of Bethlehem shed
  A lustre pure and sweet;
And still it leads, as once it led,
  To the Messiah's feet.

O Father, may that holy Star
  Grow every year more bright,
And send its glorious beams afar
  To fill the world with light.

OUR CHILDREN

STANDING forth on life's rough way,
  Father, guide them;
Oh! we know not what of harm
  May betide them;

'Neath the shadow of Thy wing,
   Father, hide them;
Waking, sleeping, Lord, we pray,
   Go beside them.

When in prayer they cry to Thee,
   Thou wilt hear them:
From the stains of sin and shame
   Thou wilt clear them;
'Mid the quicksands and the rocks,
   Thou wilt steer them;
In temptation, trial, grief,
   Be Thou near them.

Unto Thee we give them up,
   Lord, receive them;
In the world we know must be
   Much to grieve them—
Many striving oft and strong
   To deceive them:
Trustful, in Thy hands of love
   We must leave them.

Henry Ware, jun.

RESURRECTION OF CHRIST

LIFT your glad voices in triumph on high,
   For Jesus hath risen, and man cannot die;
Vain were the terrors that gathered around Him,
   And short the dominion of death and the grave;
He burst from the fetters of darkness that bound Him,
   Resplendent in glory to live and to save;
Loud was the chorus of angels on high,
The Saviour hath risen, and man shall not die.

Glory to God, in full anthems of joy;
The being He gave us death cannot destroy;
Sad were the life we must part with to-morrow,
   If tears were our birthright and death were our end;
But Jesus hath cheered the dark valley of sorrow,
   And bade us, immortal, to heaven ascend.
Lift, then, your voices in triumph on high,
For Jesus hath risen, and man shall not die!

CHRISTMAS GATHERING

IN this glad hour, when children meet,
    And home with them their children bring,
Our hearts with one affection beat,
    One song of praise our voices sing.

For all the faithful, loved and dear,
    Whom Thou so kindly, Lord, hast given,
For those who still are with us here,
    And those who wait for us in heaven;

For every past and present joy,
    For honour, competence, and health,
For hopes which time may not destroy,
    Our soul's imperishable wealth;—

For all, accept our humble praise;
    Still bless us, Father, by Thy love;
And when are closed our mortal days,
    Unite us in one home above.

William Augustus Muhlenberg

THE SOUL'S HOME

LIKE Noah's weary dove,
    That soared the earth around,
But not a resting-place above
    The cheerless waters found;

Oh cease, my wandering soul,
    On restless wing to roam;
All the wide world, to either pole,
    Has not for thee a home.

Behold the Ark of God,
    Behold the open door;
Hasten to gain that dear abode,
    And rove, my soul, no more.

There, safe thou shalt abide,
    There, sweet shall be thy rest,
And every longing satisfied,
    With full salvation blest.

William Bourne Oliver Peabody

THE AUTUMN EVENING

BEHOLD the western evening light!
It melts in deepening gloom;
So calmly Christians sink away,
Descending to the tomb.

The winds breathe low; the withering leaf
Scarce whispers from the tree:
So gently flows the parting breath
When good men cease to be.

How beautiful on all the hills
The crimson light is shed!
'Tis like the peace the Christian gives
To mourners round his bed.

How mildly on the wandering cloud
The sunset beam is cast!
'Tis like the memory left behind
When loved ones breathe their last.

And now above the dews of night
The yellow star appears!
So faith springs in the hearts of those
Whose eyes are bathed in tears.

But soon the morning's happier light
Its glories shall restore;
And eyelids that are sealed in death
Shall wake to close no more.

George Washington Doane

THE BANNER OF THE CROSS

FLING out the banner! let it float
Skyward and seaward, high and wide;
The sun shall light its shining folds,
The Cross on which the Saviour died.

Fling out the banner! angels bend
  In anxious silence o'er the sign;
And vainly seek to comprehend
  The wonder of the Love Divine.

Fling out the banner! heathen lands
  Shall see from far the glorious sight,
And nations, crowding to be born,
  Baptize their spirits in its light.

Fling out the banner! sin-sick souls
  That sink and perish in the strife,
Shall touch in faith its radiant hem,
  And spring immortal into life.

Fling out the banner! let it float
  Skyward and seaward, high and wide:
Our glory, only in the Cross;
  Our only hope, the Crucified!

Fling out the banner! wide and high,
  Seaward and skyward, let it shine:
Nor skill, nor might, nor merit ours;
  We conquer only in that Sign.

Lydia Maria Child

THE CLOISTER

THOUGHT never knew material bound or place,
  Nor footsteps may the roving fancy trace:
Peace cannot learn beneath a roof to house,
Nor cloister hold us safe within our vows.

The cloistered heart may brave the common air,
And the world's children breathe the holiest prayer:
Build for us, Lord, and in Thy temple reign!
Watch with us, Lord, our watchman wakes in vain!

Louisa Jane Hall

GROWING OLD

NEVER, my heart, wilt thou grow old!
  My hair is white, my blood runs cold,
And one by one my powers depart,
But youth sits smiling in my heart.

Downhill the path of age! oh, no;
Up, up with patient steps I go;
I watch the skies fast brightening there,
I breathe a sweeter, purer air.

Beside my road small tasks spring up,
Though but to hand the cooling cup,
Speak the true word of hearty cheer,
Tell the lone soul that God is near.

Beat on, my heart, and grow not old!
And when thy pulses all are told,
Let me, though working, loving still,
Kneel as I meet my Father's will.

THE LORD'S PRAYER

WHEN Jesus trod by thy blue sea,
  How blest wert thou, O Galilee!
While there He walked His gracious way,
And taught us how to live and pray.

In sweet and solemn tones His prayer
Still lingers on the waving air;
Where suns may rise, or suns may set,
All wants in that one prayer are met.

From lips of childish innocence,
From weary age with failing sense,
Still mounts to heaven that wondrous prayer,
To find a loving 'Father' there.

The listening stars more brightly shine,
The morning glows with love divine,
When human hearts, in pain or ease,
Use these dear words on bended knees.

William Henry Furness

REMEMBRANCE OF GOD

THOU who dost all things give,
  Be not Thyself forgot!
No longer may Thy children live
  As if their God were not!

But every day and hour,
  Since Thou dost bless us thus,
In still increasing light and power
  Reveal Thyself to us;

Until our faith shall be
  Stronger than words can tell,
And we shall live beholding Thee,
  O Thou Invisible!

NIGHTFALL

SLOWLY, by Thy hand unfurled,
  Down around the weary world
Falls the darkness; oh, how still
Is the working of Thy will!

Mighty Maker, here am I,
Work in me as silently;
Veil the day's distracting sights;
Show me heaven's eternal lights.

From the darkened sky come forth
Countless stars,—a wondrous birth!
So may gleams of glory start
From this dim abyss, my heart.

Living worlds to view be brought
In the boundless realms of thought;
High and infinite desires,
Flaming like those upper fires!

Holy Truth, eternal Right—
Let them break upon my sight;
Let them shine serenely still,
And with light my being fill.

Thou who dwellest there, I know,
Dwellest here within me too ;
May the perfect love of God
Here, as there, be shed abroad.

Let my soul attunèd be
To the heavenly harmony
Which, beyond the power of sound,
Fills the universe around.

Ralph Waldo Emerson

DIRGE

KNOWS he who tills this lonely field
  To reap its scanty corn,
What mystic fruit his acres yield
  At midnight and at morn?

In the long sunny afternoon
  The plain was full of ghosts ;
I wandered up, I wandered down,
  Beset by pensive hosts.

The winding Concord gleamed below,
  Pouring as wide a flood
As when my brothers, long ago,
  Came with me to the wood.

But they are gone,—the holy ones
  Who trod with me this lovely vale ;
The strong, star-bright companions
  Are silent, low and pale.

My good, my noble, in their prime,
  Who made this world the feast it was,
Who learned with me the lore of time,
  Who loved this dwelling-place !

They took this valley for their toy,
　They played with it in every mood;
A cell for prayer, a hall for joy,—
　They treated nature as they would.

They colored the horizon round;
　Stars flamed and faded as they bade,
All echoes hearkened for their sound,—
　They made the woodlands glad or mad.

I touch this flower of silken leaf,
　Which once our childhood knew;
Its soft leaves wound me with a grief
　Whose balsam never grew.

Hearken to yon pine-warbler
　Singing aloft in the tree!
Hearest thou, O traveller,
　What he singeth to me?

Not unless God made sharp thine ear
　With sorrow such as mine,
Out of that delicate lay could'st thou
　Its heavy tale divine.

' Go, lonely man,' it saith;
　' They loved thee from their birth;
Their hands were pure, and pure their faith,—
　There are no such hearts on earth.

' Ye drew one mother's milk,
　One chamber held ye all;
A very tender history
　Did in your childhood fall.

' You cannot unlock your heart,
　The key is gone with them;
The silent organ loudest chants
　The master's requiem.'

THRENODY

THE South wind brings
    Life, sunshine and desire,
And on every mount and meadow
Breathes aromatic fire;
But over the dead he has no power,
The lost, the lost, he cannot restore,
And, looking over the hills, I mourn
The darling who shall not return.

I see my empty house,
I see my trees repair their boughs;
And he, the wondrous child,
Whose silver warble wild
Outvalued every pulsing sound
Within the air's cerulean round,—
The hyacinthine boy, for whom
Morn well might break and April bloom,—
The gracious boy, who did adorn
The world whereinto he was born,
And by his countenance repay
The favor of the loving Day,—
Has disappeared from the Day's eye;
Far and wide she cannot find him;
My hopes pursue, they cannot bind him.
Returned this day, the south wind searches,
And finds young pines and budding birches;
But finds not the budding man;
Nature, who lost, cannot remake him;
Fate let him fall, Fate can't retake him;
Nature, Fate, men, him seek in vain.

And whither now, my truant wise and sweet,
O, whither tend thy feet?
I had the right, few days ago,
Thy steps to watch, thy place to know:
How have I forfeited the right?
Hast thou forgot me in a new delight?
I hearken for thy household cheer,
O eloquent child!
Whose voice, an equal messenger,

Conveyed thy meaning mild.
What though the pains and joys
Whereof it spoke were toys
Fitting his age and ken,
Yet fairest dames and bearded men,
Who heard the sweet request,
So gentle, wise and grave,
Bended with joy to his behest
And let the world's affairs go by,
Awhile to share his cordial game,
Or mend his wicker wagon-frame,
Still plotting how their hungry ear
That winsome voice again might hear.

*   *   *   *   *   *   *

O child of paradise,
Boy who made dear his father's home,
In whose deep eyes
Men read the welfare of the times to come,
I am too much bereft.
The world dishonored thou hast left.
O truth's and nature's costly lie!
O trusted broken prophecy!
O richest fortune sourly crossed!
Born for the future, to the future lost!

The deep Heart answered, 'Weepest thou?
Worthier cause for passion wild
If I had not taken the child.
And deemest thou as those who pore,
With aged eyes, short way before,—
Think'st Beauty vanished from the coast
Of matter, and thy darling lost?
Taught he not thee—the man of eld,
Whose eyes within his eyes beheld
Heaven's numerous hierarchy span
The mystic gulf from God to man?
To be alone wilt thou begin
When worlds of lovers hem thee in?
To-morrow, when the masks shall fall
That dizen Nature's carnival,
The pure shall see by their own will,
Which overflowing Love shall fill,

'Tis not within the force of fate
The fate-conjoined to separate.
But thou, my votary, weepest thou?
I gave thee sight—where is it now?
I taught thy heart beyond the reach
Of ritual, bible, or of speech;
Wrote in thy mind's transparent table,
As far as the incommunicable;
Taught thee each private sign to raise
Lit by the supersolar blaze.
Past utterance, and past belief,
And past the blasphemy of grief,
The mysteries of Nature's heart;
And though no Muse can these impart,
Throb thine with Nature's throbbing breast,
And all is clear from east to west.

' I came to thee as to a friend;
Dearest, to thee I did not send
Tutors, but a joyful eye,
Innocence that matched the sky,
Lovely locks, a form of wonder,
Laughter rich as woodland thunder,
That thou might'st entertain apart
The richest flowering of all art:
And, as the great all-loving Day
Through smallest chambers takes its way,
That thou might'st break thy daily bread
With prophet, savior and head;
That thou might'st cherish for thine own
The riches of sweet Mary's Son,
Boy-Rabbi, Israel's paragon.
And thoughtest thou such guest
Would in thy hall take up his rest?
Would rushing life forget her laws,
Fate's glowing revolution pause?
High omens ask diviner guess;
Not to be conned to tediousness.
And know my higher gifts unbind
The zone that girds the incarnate mind.
When the scanty shores are full
With Thought's perilous, whirling pool;

When frail Nature can no more,
Then the Spirit strikes the hour:
My servant Death, with solving rite,
Pours finite into infinite.

   *   *   *   *   *   *

Wilt thou not ope thy heart to know
What rainbows teach, and sunsets show?
Verdict which accumulates
From lengthening scroll of human fates,
Voice of earth to earth returned,
Prayers of saints that inly burned,—
Saying, *What is excellent,*
As God lives, is permanent;
Hearts are dust, hearts' loves remain;
Heart's love will meet thee again.
Revere the Maker; fetch thine eye
Up to His style, and manners of the sky.
Not of adamant and gold
Built He heaven stark and cold;
No, but a nest of bending reeds,
Flowering grass and scented weeds;
Or like a traveller's fleeing tent,
Or bow above the tempest bent;
Built of tears and sacred flames,
And virtue reaching to its aims;
Built of furtherance and pursuing,
Not of spent deeds, but of doing.
Silent rushes the swift Lord
Through ruined systems still restored,
Broadsowing, bleak and void to bless,
Plants with worlds the wilderness;
Waters with tears of ancient sorrow
Apples of Eden ripe to-morrow.
House and tenant go to ground,
Lost in God, in Godhead found.'

THE PROBLEM

 *   *   *   *   *   *   *

NOT from a vain or shallow thought
   His awful Jove young Phidias brought;
Never from lips of cunning fell
The thrilling Delphic oracle;

Out from the heart of nature rolled
The burdens of the Bible old;
The litanies of nations came,
Like the volcano's tongue of flame,
Up from the burning core below,—
The canticles of love and woe:
The hand that rounded Peter's dome
And groined the aisles of Christian Rome
Wrought in a sad sincerity;
Himself from God he could not free;
He builded better than he knew;—
The conscious stone to beauty grew.

*   *   *   *   *   *   *

These temples grew as grows the grass;
Art might obey, but not surpass.
The passive Master lent his hand
To the vast soul that o'er him planned;
And the same power that reared the shrine
Bestrode the tribes that knelt within.
Ever the fiery Pentecost
Girds with one flame the countless host,
Trances the heart through chanting choirs,
And through the priest the mind inspires.
The word unto the prophet spoken
Was writ on tables yet unbroken;
The word by seers or sibyls told,
In groves of oak, or fanes of gold,
Still floats upon the morning wind,
Still whispers to the willing mind.
One accent of the Holy Ghost
The heedless world hath never lost.

*   *   *   *   *   *   *

THE RHODORA

ON BEING ASKED, WHENCE IS THE FLOWER?

IN May, when sea-winds pierced our solitudes,
    I found the fresh Rhodora in the woods,
Spreading its leafless blooms in a damp nook,
To please the desert and the sluggish brook;
The purple petals, fallen in the pool,
Made the black water with their beauty gay;

Here might the red-bird come his plumes to cool,
And court the flower that cheapens his array.
Rhodora! If the sages ask thee why
This charm is wasted on the marsh and sky,
Dear, tell them that if eyes were made for seeing,
Then beauty is its own excuse for being:
Why thou wert there, O rival of the rose!
I never thought to ask, I never knew;
But, in my simple ignorance, suppose
The self-same power that brought me there brought you.

THE CELESTIAL LOVE

AND they serve men austerely,
  After their own genius, clearly,
Without a false humility;
For this is Love's nobility,—
Not to scatter bread and gold,
Goods and raiment bought and sold;
But to hold fast his simple sense,
And speak the speech of innocence,
And with hand and body and blood,
To make his bosom-counsel good.
He that feeds men serveth few;
He serves all who dares be true.

THE HOUSE OF GOD

WE love the venerable house
  Our fathers built to God:—
In heaven are kept their grateful vows,
  Their dust endears the sod.

Here holy thoughts a light have shed
  From many a radiant face,
And prayers of tender hope have spread
  A perfume through the place.

And anxious hearts have pondered here
  The mystery of life,
And prayed the eternal Light to clear
  Their doubts, and aid their strife.

From humble tenements around
  Came up the pensive train,
And in the Church a blessing found,
  That filled their homes again;

For faith, and peace, and mighty love,
  That from the Godhead flow,
Showed them the life of heaven above
  Springs from the life below.

They live with God, their homes are dust;
  Yet here their children pray,
And in this fleeting life-time trust
  To find the narrow way.

On him who by the altar stands,
  On him Thy blessing fall!
Speak through his lips Thy pure commands,
  Thou Heart, that lovest all.

William Croswell

SONG OF FAITH

THE lilied fields behold;
  What king in his array
Of purple pall and cloth of gold
  Shines gorgeously as they?
Their pomp, however gay,
  Is brief, alas! as bright;
It lives but for a summer's day,
  And withers in a night.

If God so clothe the soil,
  And glorify the dust,
Why should the slave of daily toil
  His providence distrust?
Will He, whose love has nursed
  The sparrow's brood, do less
For those who seek His kingdom first,
  And with it righteousness?

The birds fly forth at will;
    They neither plough nor sow:
Yet theirs the sheaves that crown the hill,
    Or glad the vale below.
While through the realms of air
    He guides their trackless way,
Will man, in faithlessness, despair?
    Is he worth less than they?

Frederic Henry Hedge

THE MORNING STAR

A SINGLE star how bright,
        From earth-mists free,
In heaven's deep shrine its image burns!
Star of the morn, my spirit yearns
        To be with thee.

Lord of the desert sky :
        Night's last, lone heir,
Benign thou smilest from on high,
Pure, calm, as if an angel's eye
        Were watching there.

Nor wholly vain I deem
        The Magian plan,
That, sphered in thee, a spirit reigns
Who knows this earth, and kindly deigns
        To succor man.

Gone are thy glittering peers!
        Quenched each bright spark;
Save where some pale sun's lingering ghost,
Dull remnant of a scattered host,
        Still spots the dark.

But thou, propitious star,
        Night's youngest born,
Wilt not withdraw thy steady light
Till bursts on yonder snow-clad height
        The rosy morn.

Fair orb! I love to watch
Thy tranquil ray;
Emblem thou art of hope that springs
When joys are fled, and dreaming brings
The better day.

So, when from my life's course
Its stars are riven,
Dawn on my soul, prophetic light,
That gilds old age's winter night
With hope of heaven!

THE CRUCIFIXION

*   *   *   *   *   *

IT is finished! Man of Sorrows!
From Thy cross our nature borrows
Strength to bear and conquer thus.

While exalted there we view Thee,
Mighty Sufferer! draw us to Thee,
Sufferer victorious!

Not in vain for us uplifted,
Man of Sorrows, wonder-gifted!
May that sacred symbol be.

Eminent amid the ages,
Guide of heroes and of sages,
May it guide us still to Thee!

Still to Thee! whose love unbounded,
Sorrow's deep for us hath sounded,
Perfected by conflicts sore.

Glory to Thy cross for ever!
Star that points our high endeavor
Whither Thou hast gone before.

Henry Wadsworth Longfellow

THE REAPER AND THE FLOWERS

THERE is a Reaper, whose name is Death,
　And with his sickle keen,
He reaps the bearded grain at a breath,
　And the flowers that grow between.

'Shall I have nought that is fair?' saith he;
　'Have nought but the bearded grain?
Though the breath of these flowers is sweet to me,
　I will give them all back again.'

He gazed at the flowers with tearful eyes,
　He kissed their drooping leaves;
It was for the Lord of Paradise
　He bound them in his sheaves.

'My Lord has need of these flowerets gay,'
　The Reaper said, and smiled;
'Dear tokens of the earth are they,
　Where He was once a child.

'They shall all bloom in fields of light,
　Transplanted by my care,
And saints, upon their garments white,
　These sacred blossoms wear.'

And the mother gave, in tears and pain,
　The flowers she most did love;
She knew she should find them all again
　In the fields of light above.

O, not in cruelty, not in wrath,
　The Reaper came that day;
'Twas an angel visited the green earth,
　And took the flowers away.

FOOTSTEPS OF ANGELS

WHEN the hours of Day are numbered,
  And the voices of the Night
Wake the better soul, that slumbered,
  To a holy, calm delight;

Ere the evening lamps are lighted,
  And, like phantoms grim and tall,
Shadows from the fitful fire-light
  Dance upon the parlor wall;

Then the forms of the departed
  Enter at the open door;
The beloved, the true-hearted,
  Come to visit me once more;

He, the young and strong, who cherished
  Noble longings for the strife,
By the road-side fell and perished,
  Weary with the march of life!

They, the holy ones and weakly,
  Who the cross of suffering bore,
Folded their pale hands so meekly,
  Spake with us on earth no more!

And with them the Being Beauteous,
  Who unto my youth was given,
More than all things else to love me,
  And is now a saint in heaven.

With a slow and noiseless footstep
  Comes that messenger divine,
Takes the vacant chair beside me,
  Lays her gentle hand in mine.

And she sits and gazes at me
  With those deep and tender eyes,
Like the stars, so still and saint-like,
  Looking downward from the skies.

Uttered not, yet comprehended,
   Is the spirit's voiceless prayer,
Soft rebukes, in blessings ended,
   Breathing from her lips of air.

O, though oft depressed and lonely,
   All my fears are laid aside,
If I but remember only
   Such as these have lived and died!

RESIGNATION

THERE is no flock, however watched and tended,
   But one dead lamb is there!
There is no fireside, howsoe'er defended,
   But has one vacant chair!

The air is full of farewells to the dying,
   And mournings for the dead;
The heart of Rachel, for her children crying,
   Will not be comforted!

Let us be patient! These severe afflictions
   Not from the ground arise,
But oftentimes celestial benedictions
   Assume this dark disguise.

We see but dimly through the mists and vapors,
   Amid these earthly damps;
What seem to us but sad, funereal tapers,
   May be heaven's distant lamps.

There is no Death! What seems so is transition;
   This life of mortal breath
Is but a suburb of the life elysian,
   Whose portal we call Death.

She is not dead,—the child of our affection,—
   But gone unto that school
Where she no longer needs our poor protection,
   And Christ himself doth rule.

In that great cloister's stillness and seclusion,
  By guardian angels led,
Safe from temptation, safe from sin's pollution,
  She lives, whom we call dead.

Day after day we think what she is doing
  In those bright realms of air;
Year after year, her tender steps pursuing,
  Behold her grown more fair.

Thus do we walk with her, and keep unbroken
  The bond which Nature gives,
Thinking that our remembrance, though unspoken,
  May reach her where she lives.

Not as a child shall we again behold her;
  For when with raptures wild
In our embraces we again enfold her,
  She will not be a child;

But a fair maiden, in her Father's mansion,
  Clothed with celestial grace;
And beautiful with all the soul's expansion
  Shall we behold her face.

And though at times impetuous with emotion
  And anguish long suppressed,
The swelling heart heaves moaning like the ocean,
  That cannot be at rest,—

We will be patient, and assuage the feeling
  We may not wholly stay;
By silence sanctifying, not concealing,
  The grief that must have way.

HYMN FOR MY BROTHER'S ORDINATION

CHRIST to the young man said: 'Yet one thing
      more:
  If thou wouldst perfect be,
Sell all thou hast and give it to the poor,
  And come and follow Me!'

Within this temple Christ again, unseen,
　　Those sacred words hath said,
And His invisible hands to-day have been
　　Laid on a young man's head.

And evermore beside him on his way
　　The unseen Christ shall move,
That he may lean upon His arm and say,
　　'Dost Thou, dear Lord, approve?'

Beside him at the marriage-feast shall be,
　　To make the scene more fair;
Beside him in the dark Gethsemane
　　Of pain and midnight prayer.

O holy trust! O endless sense of rest!
　　Like the beloved John
To lay his head upon the Saviour's breast,
　　And thus to journey on!

NATURE

As a fond mother, when the day is o'er,
　　Leads by the hand her little child to bed,
Half willing, half reluctant to be led,
And leave his broken playthings on the floor,
Still gazing at them through the open door,
　　Nor wholly reassured and comforted
　　By promises of others in their stead,
　　Which, though more splendid, may not please him more;
So Nature deals with us, and takes away
　　Our playthings one by one, and by the hand
　　Leads us to rest so gently, that we go
Scarce knowing if we wished to go or stay,
　　Being too full of sleep to understand
How far the unknown transcends the what we know.

THE CHAMBER OVER THE GATE

Is it so far from thee
　　Thou canst no longer see,
In the Chamber over the Gate,
That old man desolate,

Weeping and wailing sore
For his son, who is no more?
  O Absalom, my son!

Is it so long ago
That cry of human woe
From the walled city came,
Calling on his dear name,
That it has died away
In the distance of to-day?
  O Absalom, my son!

There is no far nor near,
There is neither there nor here,
There is neither soon nor late,
In that Chamber over the Gate,
Nor any long ago
To that cry of human woe,
  O Absalom, my son!

From the ages that are past
The voice sounds like a blast,
Over seas that wreck and drown,
Over tumult of traffic and town;
And from ages yet to be
Come the echoes back to me,
  O Absalom, my son!

Somewhere at every hour
The watchman on the tower
Looks forth, and sees the fleet
Approach of the hurrying feet
Of messengers, that bear
The tidings of despair.
  O Absalom, my son!

He goes forth from the door,
Who shall return no more.
With him our joy departs;
The light goes out in our hearts;
In the Chamber over the Gate
We sit disconsolate.
  O Absalom, my son!

That 'tis a common grief
Bringeth but slight relief;
Ours is the bitterest loss,
Ours is the heaviest cross;
And for ever the cry will be,
' Would God I had died for thee,
  O Absalom, my son !'

Saraß Elizaßetß Miles

LOOKING UNTO JESUS

THOU who didst stoop below
  To drain the cup of woe,
Wearing the form of frail mortality;
  Thy blessèd labors done,
  Thy crown of victory won,
Hast passed from earth, passed to Thy home on high.

Our eyes behold Thee not,
  Yet hast Thou not forgot
Those who have placed their hope, their trust in Thee;
  Before Thy Father's face
  Thou hast prepared a place,
That where Thou art, there they may also be.

It was no path of flowers,
  Which, through this world of ours,
Belovèd of the Father, Thou didst tread;
  And shall we in dismay
  Shrink from the narrow way,
When clouds and darkness are around it spread?

O Thou, who art our life,
  Be with us through the strife;
Thy holy head by earth's fierce storms was bowed:
  Raise Thou our eyes above,
  To see a Father's love
Beam, like the bow of promise, thro' the cloud.

And O, if thoughts of gloom
Should hover o'er the tomb,
That light of love our guiding star shall be:
Our spirits shall not dread
The shadowy path to tread,
Friend, Guardian, Saviour, which doth lead to Thee.

Nathaniel Parker Willis

DEDICATION HYMN

THE perfect world by Adam trod
  Was the first temple—built by God;
His fiat laid the corner-stone,
And heaved its pillars one by one.

He hung its starry roof on high—
The broad illimitable sky;
He spread its pavement green and bright,
And curtain'd it with morning light.

The mountains in their places stood—
The sea—the sky—and 'all was good';
And when its first pure praises rang,
The 'morning stars together sang.'

Lord! 'tis not ours to make the sea
And earth and sky a house for Thee;
But in Thy sight our offering stands—
A humbler temple, 'made with hands.'

Ray Palmer

FAITH

'*Behold the Lamb of God.*'—John i. 29.

MY faith looks up to Thee,
  Thou Lamb of Calvary:
Saviour divine:

Now hear me while I pray,
Take all my guilt away,
O let me from this day
    Be wholly Thine.

May Thy rich grace impart
Strength to my fainting heart,
    My zeal inspire:
As Thou hast died for me,
O may my love to Thee,
Pure, warm, and changeless be,
    A living fire.

While life's dark maze I tread,
And griefs around me spread,
    Be Thou my guide ;
Bid darkness turn to day,
Wipe sorrow's tears away,
Nor let me ever stray
    From Thee aside.

When ends life's transient dream,
When death's cold, sullen stream
    Shall o'er me roll ;
Blest Saviour, then, in love,
Fear and distrust remove,
O bear me safe above—
    A ransomed soul.

UNSEEN, NOT UNKNOWN

'*Whom not having seen, ye love.*'—1 Pet. i. 8.

JESUS, these eyes have never seen
    That radiant form of Thine;
The veil of sense hangs dark between
    Thy blessèd face and mine.

I see Thee not, I hear Thee not,
    Yet art Thou oft with me ;
And earth has ne'er so dear a spot,
    As where I meet with Thee.

Like some bright dream, that comes unsought,
  When slumbers o'er me roll,
Thine image ever fills my thought,
  And charms my ravished soul.

Yea, though I have not seen, and still
  Must rest in faith alone,
I love Thee, dearest Lord, and will,
  Unseen but not unknown.

When death these mortal eyes shall seal,
  And still this throbbing heart;
The rending veil shall Thee reveal,
  All-glorious as Thou art.

UNFALTERING TRUST

'How unsearchable are His judgments.'—Rom. xi. 33.

LORD, my weak thought in vain would climb
  To search the starry vault profound;
In vain would wing her flight sublime,
  To find creation's utmost bound.

But weaker yet that thought must prove
  To search Thy great eternal plan,—
Thy sovereign counsels, born of love
  Long ages ere the world began.

When my dim reason would demand
  Why that, or this, Thou dost ordain,
By some vast deep I seem to stand,
  Whose secrets I must ask in vain.

When doubts disturb my troubled breast,
  And all is dark as night to me,
Here, as on solid rock, I rest,
  That so it seemeth good to Thee.

Be this my joy, that evermore
  Thou rulest all things at Thy will;
Thy sovereign wisdom I adore,
  And calmly, sweetly, trust Thee still.

John Greenleaf Whittier

MY PSALM

I MOURN no more my vanished years;
    Beneath a tender rain,
An April rain of smiles and tears,
    My heart is young again.

The west winds blow, and, singing low,
    I hear the glad streams run;
The windows of my soul I throw
    Wide open to the sun.

No longer forward nor behind
    I look in hope or fear;
But, grateful, take the good I find,
    The best of now and here.

I plough no more a desert land,
    To harvest weed and tare;
The manna dropping from God's hand
    Rebukes my painful care.

I break my pilgrim staff, I lay
    Aside the toiling oar;
The angel sought so far away
    I welcome at my door.

The airs of spring may never play
    Among the ripening corn,
Nor freshness of the flowers of May
    Blow through the autumn morn;

Yet shall the blue-eyed gentian look
    Through fringèd lids to heaven,
And the pale aster in the brook
    Shall see its image given; —

The woods shall wear their robes of praise,
    The south wind softly sigh,
And sweet, calm days in golden haze
    Melt down the amber sky.

Not less shall manly deed and word
   Rebuke an age of wrong;
The graven flowers that wreathe the sword
   Make not the blade less strong.

But smiting hands shall learn to heal,—
   To build as to destroy;
Nor less my heart for others feel
   That I the more enjoy.

All as God wills, who wisely heeds
   To give or to withhold,
And knoweth more of all my needs
   Than all my prayers have told!

Enough that blessings undeserved
   Have marked my erring track;
That wheresoe'er my feet have swerved,
   His chastening turned me back;—

That more and more a Providence
   Of love is understood,
Making the springs of time and sense
   Sweet with eternal good;—

That death seems but a covered way
   Which opens into light,
Wherein no blinded child can stray
   Beyond the Father's sight;—

That care and trial seem at last,
   Through Memory's sunset air,
Like mountain-ranges overpast,
   In purple distance fair;

That all the jarring notes of life
   Seem blending in a psalm,
And all the angles of its strife
   Slow rounding into calm.

And so the shadows fall apart,
   And so the west winds play;
And all the windows of my heart
   I open to the day.

THE ETERNAL GOODNESS

O FRIENDS! with whom my feet have trod
    The quiet aisles of prayer,
Glad witness to your zeal for God
    And love of man I bear.

I trace your lines of argument;
    Your logic linked and strong
I weigh as one who dreads dissent,
    And fears a doubt as wrong.

But still my human hands are weak
    To hold your iron creeds:
Against the words ye bid me speak
    My heart within me pleads.

Who fathoms the Eternal Thought?
    Who talks of scheme and plan?
The Lord is God! He needeth not
    The poor device of man.

I walk with bare, hushed feet the ground
    Ye tread with boldness shod;
I dare not fix with mete and bound
    The love and power of God.

Ye praise His justice; even such
    His pitying love I deem:
Ye seek a king; I fain would touch
    The robe that hath no seam.

Ye see the curse which overbroods
    A world of pain and loss;
I hear our Lord's beatitudes
    And prayer upon the cross.

More than your schoolmen teach, within
    Myself, alas! I know:
Too dark ye cannot paint the sin,
    Too small the merit show.

I bow my forehead to the dust,
  I veil mine eyes for shame,
And urge, in trembling self-distrust,
  A prayer without a claim.

I see the wrong that round me lies,
  I feel the guilt within;
I hear, with groan and travail-cries,
  The world confess its sin.

Yet, in the maddening maze of things,
  And tossed by storm and flood,
To one fixed trust my spirit clings;
  I know that God is good!

Not mine to look where cherubim
  And seraphs may not see,
But nothing can be good in Him
  Which evil is in me.

The wrong that pains my soul below
  I dare not throne above,
I know not of His hate —I know
  His goodness and His love.

I dimly guess from blessings known
  Of greater out of sight,
And, with the chastened Psalmist, own
  His judgments too are right.

I long for household voices gone,
  For vanished smiles I long,
But God hath led my dear ones on,
  And He can do no wrong.

I know not what the future hath
  Of marvel or surprise,
Assured alone that life and death
  His mercy underlies.

And if my heart and flesh are weak
  To bear an untried pain,
The bruised reed He will not break,
  But strengthen and sustain.

No offering of my own I have,
  Nor works my faith to prove ;
I can but give the gifts He gave,
  And plead His love for love.

And so beside the Silent Sea
  I wait the muffled oar ;
No harm from Him can come to me
  On ocean or on shore.

I know not where His islands lift
  Their fronded palms in air ;
I only know I cannot drift
  Beyond His love and care.

O brothers ! if my faith is vain,
  If hopes like these betray,
Pray for me that my feet may gain
  The sure and safer way.

And Thou, O Lord ! by whom are seen
  Thy creatures as they be,
Forgive me if too close I lean
  My human heart on Thee !

OUR MASTER

IMMORTAL Love, for ever full,
  For ever flowing free,
For ever shared, for ever whole,
  A never-ebbing sea !

Our outward lips confess the name
  All other names above ;
Love only knoweth whence it came,
  And comprehendeth love.

Blow, winds of God, awake and blow
  The mists of earth away !
Shine out, O Light Divine, and show
  How wide and far we stray !

Hush every lip, close every book,
    The strife of tongues forbear;
Why forward reach, or backward look,
    For love that clasps like air?

We may not climb the heavenly steeps
    To bring the Lord Christ down:
In vain we search the lowest deeps,
    For Him no depths can drown.

Nor holy bread, nor blood of grape,
    The lineaments restore
Of Him we know in outward shape
    And in the flesh no more.

He cometh not a king to reign;
    The world's long-hope is dim;
The weary centuries watch in vain
    The clouds of heaven for Him.

Death comes, life goes; the asking eye
    And ear are answerless;
The grave is dumb, the hollow sky
    Is sad with silentness.

The letter fails, and systems fall,
    And every symbol wanes;
The Spirit over-brooding all
    Eternal Love remains.

And not for signs in heaven above
    Or earth below they look,
Who know with John His smile of love,
    With Peter His rebuke.

In joy of inward peace, or sense
    Of sorrow over sin,
He is His own best evidence,
    His witness is within.

No fable old, nor mythic lore,
    Nor dream of bards and seers,
No dead fact stranded on the shore
    Of the oblivious years;—

But warm, sweet, tender, even yet
  A present help is He;
And faith has still its Olivet,
  And love its Galilee.

The healing of His seamless dress
  Is by our beds of pain;
We touch Him in life's throng and press,
  And we are whole again.

Through Him the first fond prayers are said
  Our lips of childhood frame,
The last low whispers of our dead
  Are burdened with His name.

O Lord and Master of us all!
  Whate'er our name or sign,
We own Thy sway, we hear Thy call,
  We test our lives by Thine.

Thou judgest us; Thy purity
  Doth all our lusts condemn;
The love that draws us nearer Thee
  Is hot with wrath to them.

Our thoughts lie open to Thy sight;
  And, naked to Thy glance,
Our secret sins are in the light
  Of Thy pure countenance.

Thy healing pains, a keen distress
  Thy tender light shines in;
Thy sweetness is the bitterness,
  Thy grace the pang of sin.

Yet, weak and blinded though we be,
  Thou dost our service own;
We bring our varying gifts to Thee,
  And Thou rejectest none.

To Thee our full humanity,
  Its joys and pains, belong;
The wrong of man to man on Thee
  Inflicts a deeper wrong.

Who hates, hates Thee, who loves becomes
   Therein to Thee allied;
All sweet accords of hearts and homes
   In Thee are multiplied.

Deep strike Thy roots, O heavenly Vine,
   Within our earthly sod,
Most human and yet most divine,
   The flower of man and God!

O Love! O Life! Our faith and sight
   Thy presence maketh one,
As through transfigured clouds of white
   We trace the noon-day sun.

So, to our mortal eyes subdued,
   Flesh-veiled, but not concealed,
We know in Thee the fatherhood
   And heart of God revealed.

We faintly hear, we dimly see,
   In differing phrase we pray;
But, dim or clear, we own in Thee
   The Light, the Truth, the Way!

The homage that we render Thee
   Is still our Father's own;
No jealous claim or rivalry
   Divides the Cross and Throne.

To do Thy will is more than praise,
   As words are less than deeds,
And simple trust can find Thy ways
   We miss with chart of creeds.

No pride of self Thy service hath,
   No place for me and mine;
Our human strength is weakness, death
   Our life, apart from Thine.

Apart from Thee all gain is loss,
   All labor vainly done;
The solemn shadow of Thy Cross
   Is better than the sun.

Alone, O Love ineffable!
  Thy saving name is given;
To turn aside from Thee is hell,
  To walk with Thee is heaven!

How vain, secure in all Thou art,
  Our noisy championship!
The sighing of the contrite heart
  Is more than flattering lip.

Not Thine the bigot's partial plea,
  Nor Thine the zealot's ban:
Thou well canst spare a love of Thee
  Which ends in hate of man.

Our Friend, our Brother, and our Lord,
  What may Thy service be?—
Nor name, nor form, nor ritual word,
  But simply following Thee.

We bring no ghastly holocaust,
  We pile no graven stone;
He serves Thee best who loveth most
  His brothers and Thy own.

Thy litanies, sweet offices
  Of love and gratitude;
Thy sacramental liturgies,
  The joy of doing good.

In vain shall waves of incense drift
  The vaulted nave around,
In vain the minster turret lift
  Its brazen weights of sound.

The heart must ring Thy Christmas bells,
  Thy inward altars raise;
Its faith and hope Thy canticles,
  And its obedience praise!

MY BIRTHDAY

BENEATH the moonlight and the snow
  Lies dead my latest year;
The winter winds are wailing low
  Its dirges in my ear.

I grieve not with the moaning wind
   As if a loss befell;
Before me, even as behind,
   God is, and all is well!

His light shines on me from above,
   His low voice speaks within,—
The patience of immortal love
   Outwearying mortal sin.

Not mindless of the growing years
   Of care and loss and pain,
My eyes are wet with thankful tears
   For blessings which remain.

If dim the gold of life has grown,
   I will not count it dross,
Nor turn from treasures still my own
   To sigh for lack and loss.

The years no charm from Nature take;
   As sweet her voices call,
As beautiful her mornings break,
   As fair her evenings fall.

Love watches o'er my quiet ways,
   Kind voices speak my name,
And lips that find it hard to praise
   Are slow, at least, to blame.

How softly ebb the tides of will!
   How fields, once lost or won,
Now lie behind me green and still
   Beneath a level sun!

How hushed the hiss of party hate,
   The clamor of the throng!
How old, harsh voices of debate
   Flow into rhythmic song!

Methinks the spirit's temper grows
   Too soft in this still air;
Somewhat the restful heart foregoes
   Of needed watch and prayer.

The bark by tempest vainly tossed
  May founder in the calm,
And he who braved the polar frost
  Faint by the isles of balm.

Better than self-indulgent years
  The outflung heart of youth,
Than pleasant songs in idle years
  The tumult of the truth.

Rest for the weary hands is good,
  And love for hearts that pine,
But let the manly habitude
  Of upright souls be mine.

Let winds that blow from heaven refresh,
  Dear Lord, the languid air;
And let the weakness of the flesh
  Thy strength of spirit share.

And, if the eye must fail of light,
  The ear forget to hear,
Make clearer still the spirit's sight,
  More fine the inward ear!

Be near me in mine hours of need,
  To soothe, or cheer, or warn,
And down these slopes of sunset lead
  As up the hills of morn!

CHURCH DEDICATION

ALL things are Thine : no gift have we,
  Lord of all gifts! to offer Thee;
And hence with grateful hearts to-day,
Thy own before Thy feet we lay.

Thy will was in the builders' thought;
Thy hand unseen amidst us wrought;
Through mortal motive, scheme and plan,
Thy wise eternal purpose ran.

No lack Thy perfect fulness knew;
From human needs and longings grew
This house of prayer, this home of rest
In the fair garden of the West.

In weakness and in want we call
On Thee for whom the heavens are small;
Thy glory is Thy children's good,
Thy joy Thy tender Fatherhood.

O Father! deign these walls to bless;
Fill with Thy love their emptiness:
And let their door a gateway be
To lead us from ourselves to Thee!

THE VOICE OF CALM

DEAR Lord and Father of mankind,
  Forgive our foolish ways!
Reclothe us in our rightful mind,
In purer lives Thy service find,
  In deeper reverence, praise.

In simple trust like theirs who heard
  Beside the Syrian sea
The gracious calling of the Lord,
Let us, like them, without a word,
  Rise up and follow Thee.

O Sabbath rest by Galilee!
  O calm of hills above,
Where Jesus knelt to share with Thee
The silence of eternity
  Interpreted by love!

With that deep hush subduing all
  Our words and works that drown
The tender whisper of Thy call,
As noiseless let Thy blessing fall
  As fell Thy manna down.

Drop Thy still dews of quietness,
  Till all our strivings cease;
Take from our souls the strain and stress,
And let our ordered lives confess
  The beauty of Thy peace.

Breathe through the heats of our desire
  Thy coolness and Thy balm ;
Let sense be dumb, let flesh retire ;
Speak through the earthquake, wind, and fire,
  O still, small voice of calm !

THE FRIEND'S BURIAL

MY thoughts are all in yonder town,
    Where, wept by many tears,
To-day my mother's friend lays down
  The burden of her years.

True as in life, no poor disguise
  Of death with her is seen,
And on her simple casket lies
  No wreath of bloom and green.

O, not for her the florist's art,
  The mocking weeds of woe ;
Dear memories in each mourner's heart
  Like heaven's white lilies blow.

And all about the softening air
  Of new-born sweetness tells,
And the ungathered May-flowers wear
  The tints of ocean shells.

The old, assuring miracle
  Is fresh as heretofore ;
And earth takes up its parable
  Of life from death once more.

Here organ-swell and church-bell toll
  Methinks but discord were,—
The prayerful silence of the soul
  Is best befitting her.

No sound should break the quietude
  Alike of earth and sky ;
O wandering wind in Seabrook wood,
  Breathe but a half-heard sigh !

Sing softly, spring-bird, for her sake;
  And thou not distant sea,
Lapse lightly as if Jesus spake,
  And thou wert Galilee!

For all her quiet life flowed on
  As meadow streamlets flow,
Where fresher green reveals alone
  The noiseless ways they go.

From her loved place of prayer I see
  The plain-robed mourners pass,
With slow feet treading reverently
  The graveyard's springing grass.

Make room, O mourning ones, for me,
  Where, like the friends of Paul,
That you no more her face shall see
  You sorrow most of all.

Her path shall brighten more and more
  Unto the perfect day;
She cannot fail of peace who bore
  Such peace with her away.

O sweet, calm face that seemed to wear
  The look of sins forgiven!
O voice of prayer that seemed to bear
  Our own needs up to heaven!

How reverent in our midst she stood,
  Or knelt in grateful praise!
What grace of Christian womanhood
  Was in her household ways!

For still her holy living meant
  No duty left undone;
The heavenly and the human blent
  Their kindred loves in one.

And if her life small leisure found
  For feasting ear and eye,
And Pleasure, on her daily round,
  She passed unpausing by,

Yet with her went a secret sense
  Of all things sweet and fair,
And Beauty's gracious providence
  Refreshed her unaware.

She kept her line of rectitude
  With love's unconscious ease;
Her kindly instincts understood
  All gentle courtesies.

An inborn charm of graciousness
  Made sweet her smile and tone
And glorified her farm-wife dress
  With beauty not its own.

The dear Lord's best interpreters
  Are humble human souls;
The Gospel of a life like hers
  Is more than books or scrolls.

From scheme and creed the light goes out,
  The saintly fact survives;
The blessed Master none can doubt
  Revealed in holy lives.

AT LAST

WHEN on my day of life the night is falling,
  And, in the winds from unsunned spaces blown,
I hear far voices out of darkness calling
  My feet to paths unknown,

Thou who hast made my home of life so pleasant,
  Leave not its tenant when its walls decay;
O Love Divine, O Helper ever present,
  Be Thou my strength and stay!

Be near me when all else is from me drifting:
  Earth, sky, home's pictures, days of shade and shine,
And kindly faces to my own uplifting
  The love which answers mine.

I have but Thee, my Father! let Thy spirit
  Be with me then to comfort and uphold;
No gate of pearl, no branch of palm I merit,
  Nor street of shining gold.

Suffice it if – my good and ill unreckoned,
  And both forgiven through Thy abounding grace—
I find myself by hands familiar beckoned
    Unto my fitting place.

Some humble door among Thy many mansions,
  Some sheltering shade where sin and striving cease,
And flows for ever through heaven's green expansions
    The river of Thy peace.

There, from the music round about me stealing,
  I fain would learn the new and holy song,
And find at last, beneath Thy trees of healing,
    The life for which I long.

THE LIGHT THAT IS FELT

A TENDER child of summers three,
    Seeking her little bed at night,
Paused on the dark stair timidly,
'Oh, mother! take my hand,' said she,
'And then the dark will all be light.'

We older children grope our way
  From dark behind to dark before;
And only when our hands we lay,
Dear Lord, in Thine, the night is day,
  And there is darkness nevermore.

Reach downwards to the sunless days,
  Wherein our guides are blind as we,
And faith is small and hope delays;
Take Thou the hands of prayer we raise,
  And let us feel the light of Thee.

Oliver Wendell Holmes

OUR LIMITATIONS

WE trust and fear, we question and believe,
  From life's dark threads a trembling faith to weave,
Frail as the web that misty night has spun,
Whose dew-gemmed awnings glitter in the sun.

While the calm centuries spell their lessons out,
Each truth we conquer spreads the realm of doubt;
When Sinai's summit was Jehovah's throne,
The chosen Prophet knew His voice alone;
When Pilate's hall that awful question heard,
The heavenly Captive answered not a word.

Eternal Truth! beyond our hopes and fears
Sweep the vast orbits of thy myriad spheres!
From age to age, while history carves sublime
On her waste rock the flaming curves of time,
How the wild swayings of our planet show
That worlds unseen surround the world we know.

THE CHAMBERED NAUTILUS

THIS is the ship of pearl, which, poets feign,
    Sails the unshadowed main,—
    The venturous bark that flings
On the sweet summer wind its purpled wings
In gulfs enchanted, where the Siren sings,
    And coral reefs lie bare,
Where the cold sea-maids rise to sun their streaming
        hair.

Its webs of living gauze no more unfurl;
    Wrecked is the ship of pearl!
    And every chambered cell,
Where its dim dreaming life was wont to dwell,
As the frail tenant shaped his growing shell,
    Before thee lies revealed,—
Its irised ceiling rent, its sunless crypt unsealed!

Year after year beheld the silent toil
    That spread his lustrous coil;
    Still, as the spiral grew,
He left the past year's dwelling for the new,
Stole with soft step its shining archway through,
    Built up its idle door,
Stretched in his last-found home, and knew the old no
        more.

Thanks for the heavenly message brought by thee,
   Child of the wandering sea,
   Cast from her lap, forlorn!
From thy dead lips a clearer note is born
Than ever Triton blew from wreathèd horn!
   While on mine ear it rings,
Through the deep caves of thought I hear a voice that
      sings :—

Build thee more stately mansions, O my soul,
   As the swift seasons roll!
   Leave thy low-vaulted past!
Let each new temple, nobler than the last,
Shut thee from heaven with a dome more vast,
   Till thou at length art free,
Leaving thine outgrown shell by life's unresting sea!

THE LIVING TEMPLE

NOT in the world of light alone,
   Where God has built His blazing throne,
Nor yet alone in earth below,
With belted seas that come and go,
And endless isles of sunlit green,
Is all thy Maker's glory seen:
Look in upon thy wondrous frame,—
Eternal wisdom still the same!

The smooth, soft air with pulse-like waves
Flows murmuring through its hidden caves,
Whose streams of brightening purple rush,
Fired with a new and livelier blush,
While all their burden of decay
The ebbing current steals away,
And red with Nature's flame they start
From the warm fountains of the heart.

No rest that throbbing slave may ask,
For ever quivering o'er his task,
While far and wide a crimson jet
Leaps forth to fill the woven net

Which in unnumbered crossing tides
The flood of burning life divides,
Then, kindling each decaying part,
Creeps back to find the throbbing heart.

But warmed with that unchanging flame
Behold the outward moving frame,
Its living marbles jointed strong
With glistening band and silvery thong,
And linked to reason's guiding reins
By myriad rings in trembling chains,
Each graven with the threaded zone
Which claims it as the Master's own.

See how yon beam of seeming white
Is braided out of seven-hued light,
Yet in those lucid globes no ray
By any chance shall break astray.
Hark how the rolling surge of sound,
Arches and spirals circling round,
Wakes the hushed spirit through thine ear
With music it is heaven to hear.

Then mark the cloven sphere that holds
All thought in its mysterious folds,
That feels sensation's faintest thrill,
And flashes forth the sovereign will;
Think on the stormy world that dwells
Locked in its dim and clustering cells!
The lightning gleams of power it sheds
Along its hollow glassy threads!

O Father! grant Thy love divine
To make these mystic temples Thine!
When wasting age and wearying strife
Have sapped the leaning walls of life,
When darkness gathers over all,
And the last tottering pillars fall,
Take the poor dust Thy mercy warms,
And mould it into heavenly forms!

THE PROMISE

NOT charity we ask,
    Nor yet thy gift refuse;
Please thy light fancy with the easy task,
    Only to look and choose.

The little-heeded toy
    That wins thy treasured gold
May be the dearest memory, holiest joy,
    Of coming years untold.

Heaven rains on every heart,
    But there its showers divide,
The drops of mercy choosing as they part
    The dark or glowing side.

One kindly deed may turn
    The fountain of thy soul
To love's sweet day-star, that shall o'er thee burn
    Long as its currents roll!

The pleasures thou hast planned,—
    Where shall their memory be
When the white angel with the freezing hand
    Shall sit and watch by thee?

Living, thou dost not live,
    If mercy's spring run dry;
What heaven has lent thee wilt thou freely give,
    Dying, thou shalt not die!

He promised even so!
    To thee His lips repeat,—
Behold, the tears that soothed thy sister's woe
    Have washed thy Master's feet!

A SUNDAY HYMN

LORD of all being! throned afar,
    Thy glory flames from sun and star;
Centre and soul of every sphere,
    Yet to each loving heart how near!

Sun of our life, Thy quickening ray
Sheds on our path the glow of day;
Star of our hope, Thy softened light
Cheers the long watches of the night.

Our midnight is Thy smile withdrawn;
Our noontide is Thy gracious dawn;
Our rainbow arch Thy mercy's sign;
All, save the clouds of sin, are Thine!

Lord of all life, below, above,
Whose light is truth, whose warmth is love,
Before Thy ever-blazing throne
We ask no lustre of our own.

Grant us Thy truth to make us free,
And kindling hearts that burn for Thee,
Till all Thy living altars claim
One holy light, one heavenly flame!

HYMN OF TRUST

O LOVE Divine, that stooped to share
      Our sharpest pang, our bitterest tear,
On Thee we cast each earth-born care,
   We smile at pain while Thou art near!

Though long the weary way we tread,
   And sorrow crown each lingering year,
No path we shun, no darkness dread,
   Our hearts still whispering, Thou art near!

When drooping pleasure turns to grief,
   And trembling faith is changed to fear,
The murmuring wind, the quivering leaf,
   Shall softly tell us, Thou art near!

On Thee we fling our burdening woe,
   O Love Divine, for ever dear,
Content to suffer while we know,
   Living and dying, Thou art near!

Stephen Greenleaf Bulfinch

THE COMMUNION OF SAINTS

WE gather to the sacred board,
　　Perchance a scanty band;
But with us in sublime accord
　　What mighty armies stand!

In creed and rite howe'er apart,
　　One Saviour still we own,
And pour the worship of the heart
　　Before our Father's throne.

A thousand spires o'er hill and vale
　　Point to the same blue heaven;
A thousand voices tell the tale
　　Of grace through Jesus given.

High choirs, in Europe's ancient fanes,
　　Praise Him for man who died;
And o'er our boundless Western plains
　　His name is glorified.

Around His tomb, on Salem's height,
　　Greek and Armenian bend;
And through all Lapland's months of night
　　The peasants' hymns ascend.

Are we not brethren? Saviour dear!
　　Then may we walk in love,
Joint subjects of Thy kingdom here,
　　Joint heirs of bliss above!

MEDITATION

*' And they said one to another, Did not our heart burn within us,
while He talked with us by the way, and while He opened to us the
Scriptures?'*—Luke xxiv. 32.

HATH not thy heart within thee burned
　　At evening's calm and holy hour,
As if its inmost depths discerned
　　The presence of a loftier power?

Hast thou not heard 'mid forest glades,
    While ancient rivers murmured by,
A voice from forth the eternal shades,
    That spake a present Deity?

And as, upon the sacred page,
    Thine eye in rapt attention turned
O'er records of a holier age,
    Hath not thy heart within thee burned?

It was the voice of God, that spake
    In silence to thy silent heart;
And bade each worthier thought awake,
    And every dream of earth depart.

Voice of our God, O yet be near!
    In low, sweet accents, whisper peace;
Direct us on our pathway here;
    Then bid in heaven our wanderings cease.

THE SABBATH DAY

'I will have mercy, and not sacrifice.'—Matt. xii. 7.

HAIL to the Sabbath Day,
    The day divinely given,
When men to God their homage pay,
    And earth draws near to heaven.

Lord, in this sacred hour,
    Within Thy courts we bend;
And bless Thy love, and own Thy power,
    Our Father and our Friend.

But Thou art not alone
    In courts by mortals trod:
Nor only is the day Thine own
    When crowds adore their God.

Thy Temple is the arch
    Of yon unmeasured sky;
Thy Sabbath the stupendous march
    Of grand Eternity.

Lord, may a holier day
Dawn on Thy servants' sight:
And grant us in Thy courts to pray
Of pure, unclouded light.

Edgar Allan Poe

SILENCE

THERE are some qualities—some incorporate things,
    That have a double life, which thus is made
A type of that twin entity which springs
    From matter and light, evinced in solid and shade.
There is a two-fold *Silence*—sea and shore—
    Body and soul. One dwells in lonely places,
Newly with grass o'ergrown; some solemn graces,
Some human memories and tearful lore,
Render him terrorless: his name 's ' No More.'
He is the corporate Silence: dread him not!
    No power hath he of evil in himself;
But should some urgent fate (untimely lot!)
    Bring thee to meet his shadow (nameless elf,
That haunteth the low regions where hath trod
No foot of man), commend thyself to God!

James Freeman Clarke

CANA

DEAR Friend! whose presence in the house,
    Whose gracious word benign,
Could once, at Cana's wedding-feast,
    Change water into wine,—

Come, visit us, and when dull work
    Grows weary, line on line,
Revive our souls, and make us see
    Life's water glow as wine.

Gay mirth shall deepen into joy,
  Earth's hopes shall grow divine,
When Jesus visits us, to turn
  Life's water into wine.

The social talk, the evening fire,
  The homely household shrine,
Shall glow with angel-visits when
  The Lord pours out the wine.

For when self-seeking turns to love,
  Which knows not mine and thine,
The miracle again is wrought,
  And water changed to wine.

Theodore Parker

JESUS

JESUS, there is no dearer name than Thine,
  Which Time has blazoned on his mighty scroll;
No wreaths nor garlands ever did entwine
  So fair a temple of so vast a soul.

There every virtue set his triumph-seal;
  Wisdom, conjoined with strength and radiant grace,
In a sweet copy Heaven to reveal,
  And stamp perfection on a mortal face.

Once on the earth wert Thou, before men's eyes,
  That did not half Thy beauteous brightness see;
E'en as the emmet does not read the skies,
  Nor our weak orbs look through immensity.

THE ALMIGHTY LOVE

IN darkest days and nights of storm,
  Men knew Thee but to fear Thy form;
And in the reddest lightning saw
Thine arm avenge insulted law.

In brighter days, we read Thy love
In flowers beneath, in stars above;
And in the track of every storm
Behold Thy beauty's rainbow form.

And in the reddest lightning's path
We see no vestiges of wrath,
But always wisdom,—perfect love,
From flowers beneath to stars above.

See, from on high sweet influence rains
On palace, cottage, mountains, plains;
No hour of wrath shall mortals fear,
For their Almighty Love is here.

Chandler Robbins

EVENING HYMN

LO! the day of rest declineth,
    Gather fast the shades of night;
May the Sun that ever shineth
    Fill our souls with heavenly light.

Softly now the dew is falling;
    Peace o'er all the scene is spread;
On His children, meekly calling,
    Purer influence God will shed.

While Thine ear of love addressing,
    Thus our parting hymn we sing,—
Father, give Thine evening blessing;
    Fold us safe beneath Thy wing.

Edmund Hamilton Sears

PEACE ON EARTH

IT came upon the midnight clear,
    That glorious song of old,
From angels bending near the earth,
    To touch their harps of gold—

'Peace on the earth, good will to men,'
   From heaven's all-gracious King;
The world in solemn stillness lay
   To hear the angels sing.

Still through the cloven skies they come,
   With peaceful wings unfurled,
And still their heavenly music floats
   O'er all the weary world;
Above its sad and lowly plains
   They bend on hovering wing,
And ever o'er its Babel-sounds
   The blessèd angels sing.

Yet, with the woes of sin and strife,
   The world has suffered long;
Beneath the angel-strain have rolled
   Two thousand years of wrong;
And man, at war with man, hears not
   The love-song which they bring:
O hush the noise, ye men of strife,
   And hear the angels sing!

And ye, beneath life's crushing load,
   Whose forms are bending low,
Who toil along the climbing way,
   With painful steps and slow,—
Look now; for glad and golden hours
   Come swiftly on the wing:
O rest beside the weary road
   And hear the angels sing!

For lo! the days are hastening on,
   By prophet-bards foretold,
When with the ever-circling years
   Comes round the age of gold:
When peace shall over all the earth
   Its ancient splendors fling,
And the whole world send back the song
   Which now the angels sing.

IDEALS

O BRIGHT Ideals, how ye shine,
    Aloft in realms of air!
Ye pour your streams of light divine
    Above our low despair.

I've climbed, and climbed these weary years
    To come your glories nigh;
I'm tired of climbing, and in tears
    Here on the earth I lie.

As a weak child all vainly tries
    To pluck the evening star,
So vain have been my life-long cries
    To reach up where ye are.

Shine on, shine on, through earth's dark night,
    Nor let your glories pale!
Some stronger soul may win the height
    Where weaker ones must fail.

And this one thought of hope and trust
    Comes with its soothing balm,
As here I lay my brow in dust,
    And breathe my lowly psalm,—

That not for heights of victory won,
    But those I tried to gain,
Will come my gracious Lord's 'Well done!'
    And sweet effacing rain.

Then on your awful heights of blue
    Shine on, for ever shine;
I come! I'll climb, I'll fly to you,
    For endless years of mine.

William Henry Burleigh

BLESSED ARE THEY THAT MOURN

OH, deem not that earth's crowning bliss
　　Is found in joy alone ;
For sorrow, bitter though it be,
　　Hath blessings all its own ;
From lips divine, like healing balm,
　　To hearts oppressed and torn,
This heavenly consolation fell,—
　　' Blessed are they that mourn ! '

As blossoms smitten by the rain
　　Their sweetest odors yield,
As where the ploughshare deepest strikes
　　Rich harvests crown the field,
So, to the hopes by sorrow crushed,
　　A nobler faith succeeds ;
And life, by trials furrowed, bears
　　The fruit of loving deeds.

Who never mourned, hath never known
　　What treasures grief reveals :
The sympathies that humanize,
　　The tenderness that heals,
The power to look within the veil
　　And learn the heavenly lore,
The key-word to life's mysteries,
　　So dark to us before.

How rich and sweet and full of strength
　　Our human spirits are,
Baptized into the sanctities
　　Of suffering and of prayer !
Supernal wisdom, love divine,
　　Breathed through the lips which said,
' Oh, blessed are the souls that mourn—
　　They shall be comforted ! '

TRUST

STILL will we trust, though earth seem dark and dreary,
  And the heart faint beneath His chastening rod,
Though rough and steep our pathway, worn and weary,
    Still will we trust in God!

Our eyes see dimly till by faith anointed,
  And our blind choosing brings us grief and pain;
Through Him alone, who hath our way appointed,
    We find our peace again.

Choose for us, God, nor let our weak preferring
  Cheat our poor souls of good Thou hast designed:
Choose for us, God! Thy wisdom is unerring,
    And we are fools and blind.

So from our sky the night shall furl her shadows,
  And day pour gladness through her golden gates;
Our rough path lead to flower-enamelled meadows,
    Where joy our coming waits.

Let us press on: in patient self-denial,
  Accept the hardship, shrink not from the loss;
Our guerdon lies beyond the hour of trial,
    Our crown beyond the cross.

MATINS

FOR the dear love that kept us through the night,
  And gave our senses to sleep's gentle sway,—
For the new miracle of dawning light
  Flushing the east with prophecies of day,
    We thank Thee, O our God!

For the fresh life that through our being flows
  With its full tide to strengthen and to bless—
For calm sweet thoughts, upspringing from repose
  To bear to Thee their song of thankfulness,
    We praise Thee, O our God!

Day uttereth speech to day, and night to night
   Tells of Thy power and glory. So would we,
Thy children, duly, with the morning light,
   Or at still eve, upon the bended knee
      Adore Thee, O our God!

Thou know'st our needs, Thy fulness will supply
   Our blindness,—let Thy hand still lead us on,
Till, visited by the dayspring from on high,
   Our prayer, one only, 'Let Thy will be done!'
      We breathe to Thee, O God!

GIFTED FOR GIVING

'Freely ye have received, freely give.'—Matt. x. 8.

BE true, O poet, to your gift divine!
   And let your heart go throbbing through your line,
Till it grows vital with the life that burns
In joy and grief, in faith and doubt, by turns,
And full, complete expression gives to these
In the clear ringing of its cadences!
Pour your soul's passion through the tide of song,
Nor ask the plaudits of the changeful throng.
Sing as the bird sings, when the morning beam
With gentlest touch awakes it from its dream,
And life and light, their motion and their glow,
Gush through the song, with flow and overflow;
Sing as the stream sings, winding through the maze
Of woods and meadows with no thought of praise,
Its murmurous music, or in storm or calm,
Blending its low, sweet notes with Nature's psalm;
Sing as the wind sings, when the forest trees
Are vocal with its mystic melodies,
And every leaf lifts up its tiny harp
To answer back in tones distinct and sharp.
Though purblind men, the devotees of greed
To song or singer give but little heed,
And the deaf multitudes refuse to turn
From Mammon's shrines diviner lore to learn,

The angels, in their starry homes, shall know
How true a spirit walks the earth below,
And, pausing in their song, to list your lyre,
Shall whisper through the spaces, '*Come up higher!*'

Samuel Dowse Robbins

BACA

THROUGH Baca's vale my way is cast,—
    Its thorns my feet have trod;
But I have found the well at last,
    And quench my thirst in God.

My roof is but an humble home
    Hid in the wilderness;
But o'er me springs the eternal dome,
    For He my dwelling is.

My raiment rude and lowly seems,
    All travel-stained and old;
But with His brightest morning beams
    He doth my soul infold.

How scantly is my table spread!
    With tears my cup o'erflows:
But He is still my daily bread,—
    No want my spirit knows.

Hard is the stony pillow bed;
    How broken is my rest!
On Him I lean my aching head,
    And sleep upon His breast.

For faith can make the desert bloom;
    And, through the vistas dim,
Love sees, in sunlight or in gloom,
    All pathways lead to Him.

THE COMPASS

THOU art, O God, my East! In Thee I dawned;
  Within me ever let Thy day-spring shine;
Then, for each night of sorrow I have mourned,
  I'll bless Thee, Father, since it seals me Thine.

Thou art, O God, my North! My trembling soul,
  Like a charmed needle, points to Thee alone:
Each wave of time, each storm of life, shall roll
  My trusting spirit forward to Thy throne.

Thou art, O God, my South! Thy fervent love
  Perennial verdure o'er my life hath shed;
And constant sunshine, from Thy heart above,
  With wine and oil Thy grateful child hath fed.

Thou art, O God, my West! Into Thy arms,
  Glad as the setting sun, may I decline;
Baptized from earthly stains and sin's alarms,
  Reborn, arise in Thy new heavens to shine.

Robert Cassie Waterston

CEASELESS ASPIRATIONS

NOT all the beauties of this joyous earth,
  Its smiling valleys or its azure sky,
Or the sweet blossoms that in quiet mirth
  Turn their soft cheeks to winds that wander by,
Can please enough the ear, or satisfy the eye!

The silver fountain, with its misty shower;
  The curling wave, dissolving on the shore;
The clouds that feed with dew each infant flower;
  The small stream's gentle song, the ocean's roar,—
All give the mind delight, and yet it seeks for more!

Thus doth the soul, by its innate desire,
  Give inward prophecy of what shall be !—
The spirit struggling, higher yet, and higher,
  Panting for light and restless to be free,
Foreshadows in itself its immortality

MORTAL AND IMMORTAL

I STAND between the Future and the Past,—
  That which has been and that which is to be ;—
A feeble ray from the Eternal cast ;
  A scanty rill, that seeks a shoreless sea ;
A living soul, treading this earthly sod ;
A finite being, yet a child of God !

A body crumbling to the dust away ;
  A spirit panting for eternal peace ;
A heavenly kingdom in a frame of clay ;
  An infant-angel fluttering for release ;
An erring man, whose race has just begun ;
A pilgrim, journeying on from sun to sun !

Creature of clay, yet heir of future life ;
  Dweller upon a world I shall outlive ;
Soldier of Christ, battling midst earthly strife,
  Yet hoping, by that strength which God may give,
To burst the doors of death, and glorying rise
Triumphant from the grave, to tread the skies !

Harriet Beecher Stowe

THE OTHER WORLD

IT lies around us like a cloud,—
  A world we do not see ;
Yet the sweet closing of an eye
  May bring us there to be.

Its gentle breezes fan our cheek;
  Amid our worldly cares,
Its gentle voices whisper love,
  And mingle with our prayers.

Sweet hearts around us throb and beat,
  Sweet helping hands are stirred,
And palpitates the veil between
  With breathings almost heard.

The silence, awful, sweet, and calm,
  They have no power to break;
For mortal words are not for them
  To utter or partake.

So thin, so soft, so sweet, they glide,
  So near to press they seem,
They lull us gently to our rest,
  And melt into our dream.

And in the hush of rest they bring
  'Tis easy now to see
How lovely and how sweet a pass
  The hour of death may be;—

To close the eye and close the ear,
  Wrapped in a trance of bliss,
And gently dream in loving arms,
  To swoon to that—from this,—

Scarce knowing if we wake or sleep,
  Scarce asking where we are,
To feel all evil sink away,
  All sorrow and all care.

Sweet souls around us! watch us still;
  Press nearer to our side;
Into our thoughts, into our prayers,
  With gentle helpings glide.

Let death between us be as naught,
  A dried and vanished stream:
Your joy be the reality,
  Our suffering life the dream.

THE SOUL'S ANSWER

'Abide in Me, and I in you.'—John xv. 4.

THAT mystic word of Thine, O sovereign Lord,
  Is all too pure, too high, too deep for me;
Weary of striving, and with longing faint,
  I breathe it back again in *prayer* to Thee.

Abide in me, I pray, and I in Thee;
  From this good hour, O, leave me never more;
Then shall the discord cease, the wound be healed,
  The life-long bleeding of the soul be o'er.

Abide in me; o'ershadow by Thy love
  Each half-formed purpose and dark thought of sin;
Quench, ere it rise, each selfish, low desire,
  And keep my soul as Thine, calm and divine.

As some rare perfume in a vase of clay
  Pervades it with a fragrance not its own,
So, when Thou dwellest in a mortal soul,
  All heaven's own sweetness seems around it thrown.

Abide in me; there have been moments blest
  When I have heard Thy voice and felt Thy power,
Then evil lost its grasp, and passion hushed,
  Owned the divine enchantment of the hour.

These were but seasons, beautiful and rare;
  Abide in me, and they shall ever be;
Fulfil at once Thy precept and my prayer—
  Come, and abide in me, and I in Thee!

THE SECRET

*' Thou shalt keep them in the secret of Thy presence from the
strife of tongues.'*

WHEN winds are raging o'er the upper ocean,
  And billows wild contend with angry roar,
'Tis said, far down beneath the wild commotion,
  That peaceful stillness reigneth evermore.

Far, far beneath, the noise of tempests dieth,
    And silver waves glide ever peacefully,
And no rude storm, how fierce soe'er it flieth,
    Disturbs the sabbath of that deeper sea.

So to the soul that knows Thy love, O Purest!
    There is a temple, sacred evermore!
And all the babble of life's angry voices
    Dies in hushed stillness at its peaceful door.

Far, far away, the noise of passion dieth,
    And loving thoughts rise ever peacefully,
And no rude storm, how fierce soe'er it flieth,
    Disturbs that deeper rest, O Lord, in Thee.

O Rest of rests! O Peace serene, eternal!
    Thou ever livest, and Thou changest never;
And in the secret of Thy presence dwelleth
    Fulness of joy, forever and forever.

WHEN I AWAKE I AM STILL WITH THEE.

STILL, still with Thee, when purple morning breaketh,
    When the bird waketh and the shadows flee;
Fairer than morning, lovelier than the daylight,
    Dawns the sweet consciousness, *I am with Thee!*

Alone with Thee, amid the mystic shadows,
    The solemn hush of nature newly born;
Alone with Thee, in breathless adoration,
    In the calm dew and freshness of the morn.

Still, still with Thee, as to each new-born morning
    A fresh and solemn splendor still is given,
So doth this blessed consciousness, awaking,
    Breathe, each day, nearness unto Thee and heaven.

When sinks the soul, subdued by toil, to slumber,
    Its closing eye looks up to Thee in prayer;
Sweet the repose beneath Thy wings o'ershading,
    But sweeter still to wake and find Thee there.

So shall it be at last, in that bright morning
  When the soul waketh and life's shadows flee;
O, in that hour fairer than daylight dawning,
  Shall rise the glorious thought, *I am with Thee!*

Christopher Pearse Cranch

GNOSIS

THOUGHT is deeper than all speech,
    Feeling deeper than all thought;
Souls to souls can never teach
    What unto themselves was taught.

We are spirits clad in veils;
    Man by man was never seen;
All our deep communing fails
    To remove the shadowy screen.

Heart to heart was never known;
    Mind with mind did never meet;
We are columns, left alone,
    Of a temple once complete.

Like the stars that gem the sky,
    Far apart, though seeming near,
In our light we scattered lie;
    All is thus but starlight here.

What is social company
    But a babbling summer stream?
What our wise philosophy
    But the glancing of a dream?

Only when the sun of love
    Melts the scattered stars of thought;
Only when we live above
    What the dim-eyed world hath taught;

Only when our souls are fed
    By the Fount which gave them birth,
And by inspiration led
    Which they never drew from earth;

We, like parted drops of rain,
    Swelling till they melt and run,
Shall be all absorbed again,
    Melting, flowing into one.

COMPENSATION

TEARS wash away the atoms in the eye
    That smarted for a day;
Rain-clouds that spoiled the splendors of the sky
    The fields with flowers array.

No chamber of pain but has some hidden door
    That promises release;
No solitude so drear but yields its store
    Of thought and inward peace.

No night so wild but brings the constant sun
    With love and power untold;
No time so dark but through its woof there run
    Some blessed threads of gold.

And through the long and storm-tost centuries burn
    In changing calm and strife
The Pharos-lights of truth, where'er we turn,--
    The unquenched lamps of life.

O Love supreme! O Providence divine!
    What self-adjusting springs
Of law and life, what even scales, are Thine,
    What sure-returning wings

Of hopes and joys that flit like birds away,
    When chilling autumn blows,
But come again, long ere the buds of May
    Their rosy lips unclose!

What wondrous play of mood and accident
    Through shifting days and years;
What fresh returns of vigor overspent
    In feverish dreams and fears!

What wholesome air of conscience and of thought
        When doubts and forms oppress;
What vistas opening to the gates we sought
        Beyond the wilderness :

Beyond the narrow cells where self-involved,
        Like chrysalids, we wait
The unknown births, the mysteries unsolved
        Of death and change and fate !

O Light divine! we need no fuller test
        That all is ordered well ;
We know enough to trust that all is best
        Where love and wisdom dwell.

I IN THEE, AND THOU IN ME

I AM but clay in Thy hands, but Thou art the all-
        loving Artist.
Passive I lie in Thy sight, yet in my selfhood I strive
So to embody the life and the love Thou ever impartest,
        That in my sphere of the finite I may be truly alive.

Knowing Thou needest this form, as I Thy divine in-
        spiration,
        Knowing Thou shapest the clay with a vision and
            purpose divine,
So would I answer each touch of Thy hand in its
        loving creation,
        That in my conscious life Thy power and beauty may
            shine,

Reflecting the noble intent Thou hast in forming Thy
        creatures ;
        Waking from sense into life of the soul, and the image
            of Thee ;
Working with Thee in Thy work to model humanity's
        features
        Into the likeness of God, myself from myself I would
            free.

One with all human existence, no one above or below me ;
   Lit by Thy wisdom and love, as roses are steeped in
      the morn ;
Growing from clay to a statue, from statue to flesh, till
   Thou know me
   Wrought into manhood celestial, and in Thine image
      re-born.

So in Thy love will I trust, bringing me sooner or later
   Past the dark screen that divides these shows of the
      finite from Thee.
Thine, Thine only, this warm dear life, O loving Creator !
   Thine the invisible future, born of the present, must be.

LIFE AND DEATH

IF death be final, what is life, with all
   Its lavish promises, its thwarted aims,
   Its lost ideals, its dishonoured claims,
Its uncompleted growth ? A prison wall,
Whose heartless stones but echo back our call ;
   An epitaph recording but our names ;
   A puppet-stage where joys and griefs and shames
Furnish a demon jesters' carnival ;
A plan without a purpose or a form ;
   A roofless temple ; an unfinished tale.
And men like madrepores through calm and storm
   Toil, die to build a branch of fossil frail,
And add from all their dreams, thoughts, acts, belief,
A few more inches to a coral-reef.

Jones Very

NATURE

THE bubbling brook doth leap when I come by,
   Because my feet find measure with its call,
The birds know when the friend they love is nigh,
   For I am known to them both great and small ;

The flowers that on the lovely hill-side grow
  Expect me there when Spring their bloom has given;
And many a tree and bush my wanderings know,
  And e'en the clouds and silent stars of heaven;
For he who with his Maker walks aright,
  Shall be their lord, as Adam was before;
His ear shall catch each sound with new delight,
  Each object wear the dress which then it wore;
And he, as when erect in soul he stood,
Hear from his Father's lips, that all is good.

THE SABBATIA

THE sweet-briar rose has not a form more fair,
  Nor are its hues more beauteous than thine own,
Sabbatia, flower most beautiful and rare!
  In lonely spots blooming unseen, unknown.
So spiritual thy look, thy stem so light,
  Thou seemest not from the dark earth to grow;
But to belong to heavenly regions bright,
  Where night comes not, nor blasts of winter blow.
To me thou art a pure, ideal flower,
  So delicate that mortal touch might mar;
Not born, like other flowers, of sun and shower,
  But wandering from thy native home afar
To lead our thoughts to some serener clime
Beyond the shadows and the storms of time.

LIFE

IT is not life upon Thy gifts to live,
  But to grow fixed with deeper roots in Thee;
And when the sun and shower their bounties give,
  To send out thick-leaved limbs; a fruitful tree,
Whose green head meets the eye for many a mile,
  Whose spreading boughs a friendly shelter rear,
Where full-faced fruits their blushing welcome smile,
  As to its goodly shade our feet draw near;

Who tastes its gifts shall never hunger more,
   For 'tis the Father spreads the pure repast,
Who, while we eat, renews the ready store,
   Which at His bounteous board must ever last;
For none the Bridegroom's supper shall attend,
Who will not hear and make His Word their friend.

THE PRESENCE

I SIT within my room, and joy to find
   That Thou who always lov'st art with me here,
That I am never left by Thee behind,
   But by Thyself Thou keep'st me ever near;
The fire burns brighter when with Thee I look,
   And seems a kinder servant sent to me;
With gladder heart I read Thy holy book,
   Because Thou art the eyes by which I see;
This aged chair, that table, watch, and door
   Around in ready service ever wait;
Nor can I ask of Thee a menial more
   To fill the measure of my large estate,
For Thou Thyself, with all a Father's care
Where'er I turn, art ever with me there.

THE SPIRIT

I WOULD not breathe, when blows Thy mighty wind
   O'er desolate hill and winter-blasted plain,
But stand, in waiting hope, if I may find
   Each flower recalled to newer life again,
That now unsightly hides itself from Thee,
   Amid the leaves or rustling grasses dry,
With ice-cased rock and snowy-mantled tree,
   Ashamed lest Thou its nakedness should spy;
But Thou shalt breathe, and every rattling bough
   Shall gather leaves; each rock with rivers flow;
And they that hide them from Thy presence now,
   In new-found robes along Thy path shall glow,
And meadows at Thy coming fall and rise,
Their green waves sprinkled with a thousand eyes.

LABOR AND REST

THOU need'st not rest: the shining spheres are Thine
    That roll perpetual on their silent way,
And Thou dost breathe in me a voice divine,
    That tells more sure of Thine eternal sway;
Thine the first starting of the early leaf,
    The gathering green, the changing autumn hue;
To Thee the world's long years are but as brief
    As the fresh tints that Spring will soon renew.
Thou needest not man's little life of years,
    Save that he gather wisdom from them all;
That in Thy fear he lose all other fears,
    And in Thy calling heed no other call.
Then shall he be Thy child to know Thy care,
And in Thy glorious Self the eternal Sabbath share.

THE PRAYER

WILT Thou not visit me?
    The plant beside me feels Thy gentle dew;
    And every blade of grass I see,
From Thy deep earth its quickening moisture drew.

Wilt Thou not visit me?
Thy morning calls on me with cheering tone;
    And every hill and tree
Lend but one voice, the voice of Thee alone.

Come, for I need Thy love,
More than the flower the dew, or grass the rain;
    Come, gently as Thy holy Dove;
And let me in Thy sight rejoice to live again.

I will not hide from them
When Thy storms come, though fierce may be their
      wrath;
    But bow with leafy stem,
And strengthened follow on Thy chosen path.

Yes, Thou wilt visit me,
Nor plant nor tree Thine eye delights so well,
    As when, from sin set free
My spirit loves with Thine in peace to dwell.

THE LIGHT FROM WITHIN

I SAW on earth another light
   Than that which lit my eye
Come forth as from my soul within,
   And from a higher sky.

Its beams shone still unclouded on,
   When in the farthest west
The sun I once had known had sunk
   Forever to his rest.

And on I walked, though dark the night,
   Nor rose his orb by day;
As one who by a surer guide
   Was pointed out the way.

'Twas brighter far than noonday's beam;
   It shone from God within,
And lit, as by a lamp from heaven,
   The world's dark track of sin.

Cyrus Augustus Bartol

THE MOUNTAINS

OLD mountains! dim and gray ye rise
   As ceaseless prayer,—earth's sacrifice!
Sharing your breath, the soul adores,
And with your soaring summits soars.

Where Moses taught, where Jesus trod,
Your tops stand altars unto God.
O shapes of glory, sacred all,
From every height heaven's blessings fall.

The minaret-watchman's punctual cry
Summons loud worship to the sky;
Voiceless appeals, from you sent down,
A million silent throbbings own.

Charles Timothy Brooks

SUCH IS LIFE

LIFE is a sea; like ships we meet,—
  We speak each other and are gone.
Across that deep, Oh, what a fleet
  Of human souls is hurrying on!

We meet, we part, and hope some day
  To meet again on sea or shore,
Before we reach that peaceful bay,
  Where all shall meet to part no more.

O great Commander of the fleet!
  O Ruler of the tossing seas!
Thy signal to our eyes how sweet!
  How sweet Thy breath,—the heavenly breeze!

THE GREAT VOICES

A VOICE from the sea to the mountains,
  From the mountains again to the sea:
A call from the deep to the fountains,
  O spirit! be glad and be free!

A cry from the floods to the fountains,
  And the torrents repeat the glad song,
As they leap from the breast of the mountains,
  O spirit! be free and be strong!

The pine forests thrill with emotion
  Of praise, as the spirit sweeps by;
With a voice like the murmur of ocean,
  To the soul of the listener they cry.

O sing, human heart, like the fountains,
  With joy reverential and free;
Contented and calm as the mountains,
  And deep as the woods and the sea.

James Thomas Fields

DIRGE FOR A YOUNG GIRL

UNDERNEATH the sod, low lying,
    Dark and drear,
Sleepeth one who left, in dying,
    Sorrow here.

Yes, they're ever bending o'er her,
    Eyes that weep;
Forms that to the cold grave bore her,
    Vigils keep.

When the summer moon is shining
    Soft and fair,
Friends she loved in tears are twining
    Chaplets there.

Rest in peace, thou gentle spirit,
    Throned above ;
Souls like thine with God inherit
    Life and love !

Charles Gamage Eastman

DIRGE

SOFTLY !
    She is lying
With her lips apart.
    Softly !
She is dying
Of a broken heart.

    Whisper !
She is going
To her final rest.
    Whisper !
Life is growing
Dim within her breast.

> Gently.
> She is sleeping;
> She has breathed her last.
> Gently!
> While you're weeping,
> She to heaven has past.

Henry David Thoreau

INSPIRATION

IF with light head erect I sing,
   Though all the Muses lend their force,
From my poor love of anything,
   The verse is weak and shallow as its source.

But if with bended neck I grope,
   Listening behind me for my wit,
With faith superior to hope,
   More anxious to keep back than forward it;

Making my soul accomplice there
   Unto the flame my heart hath lit,
Then will the verse for ever wear,—
   Time cannot bend the line which God has writ.

I hearing get, who had but ears,
   And sight, who had but eyes before;
I moments live, who lived but years,
   And truth discern, who knew but learning's lore.

Now chiefly is my natal hour,
   And only now my prime of life;
Of manhood's strength it is the flower,
   'Tis peace's end, and war's beginning strife.

It comes in summer's broadest noon
   By a gray wall, or some chance place,
Unseasoning time, insulting June,
   And vexing day with its presuming face.

I will not doubt the love untold
   Which not my worth nor want hath bought,
Which woo'd me young, and wooes me old,
   And to this evening hath me brought.

Arthur Cleveland Coxe

THE DESIRE OF ALL NATIONS

SAVIOUR, sprinkle many nations,
  Fruitful let Thy sorrows be;
By Thy pains and consolations
  Draw the Gentiles unto Thee:
Of Thy Cross the wondrous story
  Be to all the nations told;
Let them see Thee in Thy glory,
  And Thy mercy manifold.

Far and wide, though all unknowing,
  Pants for Thee each mortal breast;
Human tears for Thee are flowing,
  Human hearts in Thee would rest:
Thirsting as for dews of even,
  As the new-mown grass for rain,
Thee they seek, as God of heaven,
  Thee as Man for sinners slain.

Saviour, lo, the isles are waiting,
  Stretched the hand, and strained the sight
For Thy Spirit, new-creating,
  Love's pure flame and wisdom's light;
Give the word, and of the preacher
  Speed the foot and touch the tongue,
Till on earth by every creature
  Glory to the Lamb be sung.

Thomas William Parsons

EPITAPH ON A CHILD

THIS little seed of life and love,
  Just lent us for a day,
Came like a blessing from above, —
  Passed like a dream away.

And when we garnered in the earth
   The foison that was ours,
We felt that burial was but birth
   To spirits, as to flowers.

And still that benediction stays
   Although its angel passed :
Dear God ! Thy ways, if bitter ways,
   We learn to love at last.

But for the dream,— it broke indeed,
   Yet still great comfort gives ;
What was a dream is now our creed,—
   We know our darling lives.

PARADISI GLORIA

O frate mio ! ciascuna e cittadina
D' una vera città. . . .

THERE is a city, builded by no hand,
   And unapproachable by sea or shore,
And unassailable by any band
   Of storming soldiery for evermore.

There we no longer shall divide our time
   By acts or pleasures,— doing petty things
Of work or warfare, merchandise or rhyme ;
   But we shall sit beside the silver springs

That flow from God's own footstool, and behold
   Sages and martyrs, and those blessed few
Who loved us once and were beloved of old,
   To dwell with them and walk with them anew,

In alternations of sublime repose,
   Musical motion, the perpetual play
Of every faculty that heaven bestows
   Through the bright, busy, and eternal day.

TO A YOUNG GIRL DYING

THIS is Palm Sunday. Mindful of the day,
I bring palm-branches, found upon my way;
But these will wither, thine shall never die,
The sacred palms thou bearest to the sky!
Dear little saint, though but a child in years,
Older in wisdom than thy gray compeers!
We doubt and tremble, *we* with bated breath,
Talk of this mystery of life and death:
Thou, strong in faith, and gifted to conceive
Beyond thy years, and teach us to believe!

Then take thy palms triumphal to thy home,
Gentle white palmer, never more to roam!
Only, sweet sister, give me, ere thou go'st,
Thy benediction, for my love thou know'st;
We, too, are pilgrims, travelling towards the shrine:
Pray that our pilgrimage may end like thine.

Julia Ward Howe

BATTLE-HYMN OF THE REPUBLIC

MINE eyes have seen the glory of the coming of the
Lord:
He is trampling out the vintage where the grapes of
wrath are stored;
He hath loosed the fatal lightning of His terrible swift
sword:
His truth is marching on.

I have seen Him in the watch-fires of a hundred cir-
cling camps;
They have builded Him an altar in the evening dews
and damps;
I can read His righteous sentence by the dim and
flaring lamps:
His day is marching on.

I have read a fiery gospel, writ in burnished rows of
    steel :
' As ye deal with My contemners, so with you My grace
    shall deal ;
Let the Hero, born of woman, crush the serpent with
    His heel !
    Since God is marching on.'

He has sounded forth the trumpet that shall never call
    retreat ;
He is sifting out the hearts of men before His judgment
    seat ;
Oh! be swift, my soul, to answer Him ! be jubilant, my
    feet !
    Our God is marching on.

In the beauty of the lilies Christ was born, across the
    sea,
With a glory in His bosom that transfigures you and
    me :
As He died to make men holy, let us die to make men
    free,
    While God is marching on.

Josiah Gilbert Holland

A SONG OF DOUBT

THE day is quenched, and the sun is fled ;
   God has forgotten the world !
The moon is gone, and the stars are dead ;
   God has forgotten the world !

Evil has won in the horrid feud
   Of ages with the throne ;
Evil stands on the neck of Good,
   And rules the world alone.

There is no good ; there is no God ;
   And faith is a heartless cheat,
Who bares the back for the Devil's rod,
   And scatters thorns for the feet.

What are prayers in the lips of death,
   Filling and chilling with hail?
What are prayers but wasted breath,
   Beaten back by the gale?

The day is quenched, and the sun is fled;
   God has forgotten the world!
The moon is gone, and the stars are dead;
   God has forgotten the world!

A SONG OF FAITH

DAY will return with a fresher boon;
   God will remember the world!
Night will come with a newer moon;
   God will remember the world!

Evil is only the slave of good;
   Sorrow the servant of joy;
And the soul is mad that refuses food
   Of the meanest in God's employ.

The fountain of joy is fed by tears,
   And love is lit by the breath of sighs;
The deepest griefs and the wildest fears
   Have holiest ministries;

Strong grows the oak in the sweeping storm;
   Safely the flower sleeps under the snow;
And the farmer's hearth is never warm
   Till the cold wind starts to blow.

Day will return with a fresher boon;
   God will remember the world!
Night will come with a newer moon;
   God will remember the world!

A CHRISTMAS CAROL

THERE'S a song in the air!
   There's a star in the sky!
There's a mother's deep prayer
   And a baby's low cry;
And the star rains its fire while the beautiful sing,
For the manger of Bethlehem cradles a king!

There's a tumult of joy
    O'er the wonderful birth,
For the Virgin's sweet boy
    Is the Lord of the earth.
Ay, the star rains its fire, and the beautiful sing,
For the manger of Bethlehem cradles a king!

In the light of that star
    Lie the ages impearled;
And that song from afar
    Has swept over the world;
Every hearth is aflame, and the beautiful sing,
In the homes of the nations, that Jesus is king!

James Russell Lowell

ELEGY ON THE DEATH OF DR. CHANNING

I DO not come to weep above thy pall,
    And mourn the dying-out of noble powers;
The poet's clearer eye should see, in all
    Earth's seeming woe, the seed of heaven's flowers.

Truth needs no champions: in the infinite deep
    Of everlasting Soul her strength abides,
From Nature's heart her mighty pulses leap,
    Through Nature's veins her strength, undying tides.

Peace is more strong than war, and gentleness,
    Where force were vain, makes conquest o'er the wave;
And love lives on and hath a power to bless,
    When they who loved are hidden in the grave.

The sculptured marble brags of death-strewn fields,
    And Glory's epitaph is writ in blood;
But Alexander now to Plato yields,
    Clarkson will stand where Wellington hath stood.

I watch the circle of the eternal years,
    And read for ever in the storied page
One lengthened roll of blood, and wrong, and tears,—
    One onward step of Truth from age to age.

The poor are crushed; the tyrants link their chain;
  The poet sings through narrow dungeon-grates;
Man's hope lies quenched;—and, lo! with steadfast gain
  Freedom doth forge her mail of adverse fates.

Men slay the prophets; fagot, rack, and cross
  Make up the groaning record of the past;
But Evil's triumphs are her endless loss,
  And sovereign Beauty wins the soul at last.

No power can die that ever wrought for Truth;
  Thereby a law of Nature it became,
And lives unwithered in its sinewy youth,
  When he who called it forth is but a name.

Therefore I cannot think thee wholly gone;
  The better part of thee is with us still;
Thy soul its hampering clay aside hath thrown,
  And only freer wrestles with the Ill.

Thou livest in the life of all good things;
  What words thou spak'st for Freedom shall not die;
Thou sleepest not, for now thy Love hath wings
  To soar where hence thy Hope could hardly fly.

And often, from that other world, on this
  Some gleams from great souls gone before may shine
To shed on struggling hearts a clearer bliss,
  And clothe the Right with lustre more divine.

Thou art not idle: in thy higher sphere
  Thy spirit bends itself to loving tasks,
And strength, to perfect what it dreamed of here,
  Is all the crown and glory that it asks.

For sure, in Heaven's wide chambers, there is room
  For love and pity, and for helpful deeds;
Else were our summons thither but a doom
  To life more vain than this in clayey weeds.

From off the starry mountain-peak of song,
  Thy spirit shows me, in the coming time,
An earth unwithered by the foot of wrong,
  A race revering its own soul sublime.

What wars, what martyrdoms, what crimes may come,
  Thou knowest not, nor I; but God will lead
The prodigal soul from want and sorrow home,
  And Eden ope her gates to Adam's seed.

Farewell! good man, good angel now! this hand
  Soon, like thine own, shall lose its cunning too;
Soon shall this soul, like thine, bewildered stand,
  Then leap to thread the free, unfathomed blue:

When that day comes, O, may this hand grow cold,
  Busy, like thine, for Freedom and the Right;
O, may this soul, like thine, be ever bold
  To face dark Slavery's encroaching blight!

This laurel-leaf I cast upon thy bier;
  Let worthier hands than these thy wreath intwine;
Upon thy hearse I shed no useless tear,—
  For us weep rather thou in calm divine!

THE PRESENT CRISIS

WHEN a deed is done for Freedom, through the
    broad earth's aching breast
Runs a thrill of joy prophetic, trembling on from east
    to west,
And the slave, where'er he cowers, feels the soul
    within him climb
To the awful verge of manhood, as the energy sublime
Of a century bursts full-blossomed on the thorny stem
    of Time.

Through the walls of hut and palace shoots the instan-
    taneous throe,
When the travail of the Ages wrings earth's systems
    to and fro;
At the birth of each new Era, with a recognising start,
Nation wildly looks at nation, standing with mute lips
    apart,
And glad Truth's yet mightier man-child leaps beneath
    the Future's heart.

So the Evil's triumph sendeth, with a terror and a chill,
Under continent to continent, the sense of coming ill,
And the slave, where'er he cowers, feels his sympathies
    with God
In hot tear-drops ebbing earthward, to be drunk up by
    the sod,
Till a corpse crawls round unburied, delving in the
    nobler clod.

For mankind are one in spirit, and an instinct bears
    along,
Round the earth's electric circle, the swift flash of right
    or wrong;
Whether conscious or unconscious, yet Humanity's vast
    frame
Through its ocean-sundered fibres feels the gush of joy
    or shame;—
In the gain or loss of one race all the rest have equal
    claim.

Once to every man and nation comes the moment to
    decide,
In the strife of Truth with Falsehood, for the good or
    evil side;
Some great cause, God's new Messiah, offering each
    the bloom or blight,
Parts the goats upon the left hand, and the sheep upon
    the right,
And the choice goes by for ever 'twixt that darkness
    and that light.

Hast thou chosen, O my people, on whose party thou
    shalt stand,
Ere the Doom from its worn sandals shakes the dust
    against our land?
Though the cause of Evil prosper, yet 'tis Truth alone
    is strong,
And, albeit she wander outcast now, I see around her
    throng
Troops of beautiful, tall angels, to enshield her from all
    wrong.

Backward look across the ages and the beacon-moments
    see,
That, like peaks of some sunk continent, jut through
    Oblivion's sea;
Not an ear in court or market for the low foreboding
    cry
Of those Crises, God's stern winnowers, from whose
    feet earth's chaff must fly;
Never shows the choice momentous till the judgment
    hath passed by.

Careless seems the great Avenger; history's pages but
    record
One death-grapple in the darkness 'twixt old systems
    and the Word;
Truth for ever on the scaffold, Wrong for ever on the
    throne,—
Yet that scaffold sways the future, and, behind the dim
    unknown,
Standeth God within the shadow, keeping watch above
    His own.

We see dimly in the Present what is small and what
    is great,
Slow of faith, how weak an arm may turn the iron helm
    of fate,
But the soul is still oracular; amid the market's din,
List the ominous stern whisper from the Delphic cave
    within,—
'They enslave their children's children who make com-
    promise with sin.'

Slavery, the earthborn Cyclops, fellest of the giant brood,
Sons of brutish Force and Darkness, who have drenched
    the earth with blood,
Famished in his self-made desert, blinded by our purer
    day,
Gropes in yet unblasted regions for his miserable
    prey;—
Shall we guide his gory fingers where our helpless
    children play?

Then to side with Truth is noble when we share her
    wretched crust,
Ere her cause bring fame and profit, and 'tis prosperous
    to be just;
Then it is the brave man chooses, while the coward
    stands aside,
Doubting in his abject spirit, till his Lord is crucified,
And the multitude make virtue of the faith they had
    denied.

Count me o'er earth's chosen heroes,—they were souls
    that stood alone,
While the men they agonized for hurled the contu-
    melious stone,
Stood serene, and down the future saw the golden
    beam incline
To the side of perfect justice, mastered by their faith
    divine,
By one man's plain truth to manhood and to God's
    supreme design.

By the light of burning heretics Christ's bleeding feet
    I track,
Toiling up new Calvaries ever with the cross that turns
    not back,
And these mounts of anguish number how each genera-
    tion learned
One new word of that grand *Credo* which in prophet-
    hearts hath burned,
Since the first man stood God-conquered with his face
    to heaven upturned.

For Humanity sweeps onward : where to-day the martyr
    stands,
On the morrow crouches Judas with the silver in his
    hands ;
Far in front the cross stands ready and the crackling
    fagots burn,
While the hooting mob of yesterday in silent awe return
To glean up the scattered ashes into History's golden
    urn.

'Tis as easy to be heroes as to sit the idle slaves
Of a legendary virtue carved upon our fathers' graves,
Worshippers of light ancestral make the present light
    a crime;—
Was the Mayflower launched by cowards, steered by
    men behind their time?
Turn those tracks toward Past or Future, that make
    Plymouth rock sublime?

They were men of present valour, stalwart old icono-
    clasts,
Unconvinced by axe or gibbet that all virtue was the
    Past's;
But we make their truth our falsehood, thinking that
    hath made us free,
Hoarding it in mouldy parchments, while our tender
    spirits flee
The rude grasp of that great Impulse which drove them
    across the sea.

They have rights who dare maintain them; we are
    traitors to our sires,
Smothering in their holy ashes Freedom's new-lit altar-
    fires;
Shall we make their creed our jailer?
Shall we, in our haste to slay,
From the tombs of the old prophets steal the funeral
    lamps away
To light up the martyr-fagots round the prophets of
    to-day?

New occasions teach new duties; Time makes ancient
    good uncouth;
They must upward still, and onward, who would keep
    abreast of Truth;
Lo, before us gleam her camp-fires! we ourselves must
    Pilgrims be,
Launch our Mayflower, and steer boldly through the
    desperate winter sea,
Nor attempt the Future's portal with the Past's blood-
    rusted key.

THE CHANGELING

I HAD a little daughter,
  And she was given to me
To lead me gently backward
  To the Heavenly Father's knee,
That I, by the force of nature,
  Might in some dim wise divine
The depth of His infinite patience
  To this wayward soul of mine.

I know not how others saw her,
  But to me she was wholly fair,
And the light of the heaven she came from
  Still lingered and gleamed in her hair ;
For it was as wavy and golden,
  And as many changes took,
As the shadows of sun-gilt ripples
  On the yellow bed of a brook.

To what can I liken her smiling,
  Upon me, her kneeling lover,
How it leaped from her lips to her eyelids,
  And dimpled her wholly over,
Till her outstretched hands smiled also,
  And I almost seemed to see
The very heart of her mother
  Sending sun through her veins to me !

She had been with us scarce a twelvemonth,
  And it hardly seemed a day,
When a troop of wandering angels
  Stole my little daughter away ;
Or perhaps those heavenly Zingari
  But loosed the hampering strings,
And when they had opened her cage-door,
  My little bird used her wings.

But they left in her stead a changeling,
  A little angel child,
That seems like her bud in full blossom,
  And smiles as she never smiled :

When I wake in the morning, I see it
Where she always used to lie,
And I feel as weak as a violet
Alone 'neath the awful sky.

As weak, yet as trustful also;
For the whole year long I see
All the wonders of faithful Nature
Still worked for the love of me;
Winds wander, and dews drip earthward,
Rain falls, suns rise and set,
Earth whirls, and all but to prosper
A poor little violet.

This child is not mine as the first was,
I cannot sing it to rest,
I cannot lift it up fatherly
And bliss it upon my breast;
Yet it lies in my little one's cradle
And sits in my little one's chair,
And the light of the heaven she's gone to
Transfigures its golden hair.

BIBLIOLATRES

BOWING thyself in dust before a Book,
And thinking the great God is thine alone,
O rash iconoclast, thou wilt not brook
What gods the heathen carves in wood and stone,
As if the Shepherd, who from outer cold
Leads all His shivering lambs to one sure fold,
Were careful for the fashion of His crook.

There is no broken reed so poor and base,
No rush, the bending tilt of swamp-fly blue,
But He therewith the ravening wolf can chase,
And guide His flock to springs and pastures new;
Through ways unlooked for, and through many lands,
Far from the rich folds built with human hands,
The gracious footprints of His love I trace.

And what art thou, own brother of the clod,
That from His hand the crook would snatch away,
And shake instead thy dry and sapless rod,
To scare the sheep out of the wholesome day?
Yea, what art thou, blind, unconverted Jew,
That with thy idol-volume's covers two
Wouldst make a jail to coop the living God?

Thou hear'st not well the mountain organ-tones
By prophet ears from Hor and Sinai caught,
Thinking the cisterns of those Hebrew brains
Drew dry the springs of the All-knower's thought,
Nor shall thy lips be touched with living fire,
Who blow'st old altar-coals with sole desire
To weld anew the spirit's broken chains.

God is not dumb, that He should speak no more;
If thou hast wanderings in the wilderness
And find'st not Sinai, 'tis thy soul is poor;
There towers the mountain of the Voice no less,
Which whoso seeks shall find, but he who bends,
Intent on manna still and mortal ends,
Sees it not, neither hears its thundered lore.

Slowly the Bible of the race is writ,
And not on paper leaves nor leaves of stone;
Each age, each kindred, adds a verse to it,
Texts of despair or hope, of joy or moan.
While swings the sea, while mists the mountains shroud,
While thunder's surges burst on cliffs of cloud,
Still at the prophets' feet the nations sit.

ALL-SAINTS

ONE feast, of holy days the crest,
   I, though no Churchman, love to keep,
All-Saints,—the unknown good that rest
   In God's still memory folded deep;
The bravely dumb that did their deed,
   And scorned to blot it with a name,
Men of the plain heroic breed,
   That loved Heaven's silence more than fame.

Such lived not in the past alone,
  But thread to-day the unheeding street,
And stairs to Sin and Famine known
  Sing with the welcome of their feet;
The den they enter grows a shrine,
  The grimy sash an oriel burns,
Their cup of water warms like wine,
  Their speech is filled from heavenly urns.

About their brows to me appears
  An aureole traced in tenderest light,
The rainbow-gleam of smiles through tears
  In dying eyes, by them made bright,
Of souls that shivered on the edge
  Of that chill ford repassed no more,
And in their mercy felt the pledge
  And sweetness of the farther shore.

A CHRISTMAS CAROL

'WHAT means this glory round our feet,'
  The Magi mused, 'more bright than morn?'
And voices chanted clear and sweet,
  'To-day the Prince of Peace is born.'

'What means that star,' the shepherds said,
  'That brightens through the rocky glen?'
And angels, answering overhead,
  Sang, 'Peace on earth, good-will to men.'

'Tis eighteen hundred years and more
  Since those sweet oracles were dumb;
We wait for Him, like them of yore;
  Alas! He seems so slow to come.

But it was said in words of gold,
  No time or sorrow e'er shall dim,
That little children might be bold,
  In perfect trust to come to Him.

All round about our feet shall shine
  A light like that the wise men saw,
If we our willing hearts incline
  To that sweet Life which is the Law.

So shall we learn to understand
  The simple faith of shepherds then,
And, kindly clasping hand in hand,
  Sing, 'Peace on earth, good-will to men.'

For they who to their childhood cling,
  And keep their natures fresh as morn,
Once more shall hear the angels sing,
  'To-day the Prince of Peace is born.'

Samuel Longfellow

HYMN OF WINTER

'TIS winter now; the fallen snow
    Has left the heavens all coldly clear;
Through leafless boughs the sharp winds blow,
  And all the earth lies dead and drear.

And yet God's love is not withdrawn;
  His life within the keen air breathes,
His beauty paints the crimson dawn,
  And clothes the boughs with glittering wreaths.

And though abroad the sharp winds blow,
  And skies are chill, and frosts are keen,
Home closer draws her circle now,
  And warmer glows her light within.

O God! who giv'st the winter's cold,
  As well as summer's joyous rays,
Us warmly in Thy love enfold,
  And keep us through life's wintry days.

VESPER HYMN

NOW on land and sea descending,
    Brings the night its peace profound;
Let our vesper-hymn be blending
  With the holy calm around.
Soon as dies the sunset glory,
  Stars of heaven shine out above,
Telling still the ancient story,—
  Their Creator's changeless love.

Now our wants and burdens leaving
  To His care, who cares for all,
Cease we fearing, cease we grieving,
  At His touch our burdens fall.
As the darkness deepens o'er us,
  Lo! eternal stars arise;
Hope and Faith and Love rise glorious
  Shining in the spirit's skies.

THE CHURCH UNIVERSAL

ONE holy church of God appears
    Through every age and race,
Unwasted by the lapse of years,
  Unchanged by changing place.

From oldest time, on farthest shores,
  Beneath the pine or palm,
One Unseen Presence she adores,
  With silence, or with psalm.

Her priests are all God's faithful sons,
  To serve the world raised up;
The pure in heart her baptized ones,
  Love her communion-cup.

The truth is her prophetic gift,
  The soul her sacred page;
And feet on mercy's errand swift,
  Do make her pilgrimage.

O living church, thine errand speed,
  Fulfil thy task sublime;
With bread of life earth's hunger feed;
  Redeem the evil time!

LOOKING UNTO GOD

I LOOK to Thee in every need,
    And never look in vain;
I feel Thy strong and tender love,
  And all is well again:
The thought of Thee is mightier far
Than sin and pain and sorrow are.

Discouraged in the work of life;
   Disheartened by its load,
Shamed by its failures or its fears
   I sink beside the road ;
But let me only think of Thee,
And then new heart springs up in me.

Thy calmness bends serene above,
   My restlessness to still ;
Around me flows Thy quickening life,
   To nerve my faltering will ;
Thy presence fills my solitude ;
Thy providence turns all to good.

Embosomed deep in Thy dear love,
   Held in Thy law, I stand ;
Thy hand in all things I behold,
   And all things in Thy hand ;
Thou leadest me by unsought ways,
And turn'st my mourning into praise.

THE GOLDEN SUNSET

THE golden sea its mirror spreads
   Beneath the golden skies,
And but a narrow strip between
   Our earth and shadow lies.

The cloud-like cliffs, the cliff-like clouds,
   Dissolved in glory float,
And mid-way of the radiant floods
   Hangs silently the boat.

The sea is but another sky,
   The sky a sea as well ;
And which is earth, and which the heavens,
   The eye can scarcely tell.

So when for me life's latest hour
   Soft passes to its end,
May glory born of earth and heaven
   The earth and heaven blend ;

Flooded with light the spirit float,
　With silent rapture glow,
Till where earth ends and heaven begins,
　The soul can scarcely know.

LOVE

TO love and seek return,
　To ask but only this,
To feel where we have poured our heart
　The spirit's answering kiss;
　To dream that now our eyes
　The brightening eyes shall meet,
And that the word we've listened for
　Our hungering ears shall greet—
　How human and how sweet!

To love nor find return,—
　Our hearts poured out in vain;
No brightening look, no answering tone,
　Left lonely with our pain;
　The open heavens closed,
　Night when we looked for morn,
The unfolding blossom harshly chilled,
　Hope slain as soon as born,—
　How bitter, how forlorn!

To love nor ask return,
　To accept our solitude,
Not now for others' love to yearn
　But only for their good;
　To joy if they are crowned,
　Though thorns our head entwine,
And in the thought of blessing them
　All thought of self resign,—
　How god-like, how divine!

Walt Whitman

THE SEA OF FAITH

PASSAGE, immediate passage! the blood burns in
    my veins!
Away, O soul! hoist instantly the anchor!
Cut the hawsers—haul out—shake out every sail!
Have we not stood here like trees in the ground long
    enough?
Have we not grovell'd here long enough eating and
    drinking like mere brutes?
Have we not darken'd and dazed ourselves with books
    long enough?

Sail forth—steer for the deep waters only,
Reckless, O soul, exploring, I with thee, and thou
    with me,
For we are bound where mariner has not yet dared to go,
And we will risk the ship, ourselves and all.

O my brave soul!
O farther, farther sail!
O daring joy, but safe! are they not all the seas of God?
O farther, farther, farther sail!

THE PRAYER OF COLUMBUS

ONE effort more, my altar this bleak sand;
    That Thou, O God, my life hast lighted,
With ray of light, steady, ineffable, vouchsafed of Thee,
Light rare untellable, lighting the very light,
Beyond all signs, descriptions, languages;
For that, O God, be it my latest word, here on my
    knees,
Old, poor, and paralyzed, I thank Thee.

My terminus near,
The clouds already closing in upon me,
The voyage balk'd, the course disputed, lost,
I yield my ships to Thee.

My hands, my limbs grow nerveless,
My brain feels rack'd, bewilder'd,
Let the old timbers part, I will not part,
I will cling fast to Thee, O God, though the waves
　　buffet me,
Thee, Thee at least I know.

WHISPERS OF HEAVENLY DEATH

WHISPERS of heavenly death murmur'd I hear,
　　Labial gossip of night, sibilant chorals,
Footsteps gently ascending, mystical breezes wafted soft
　　and low,
Ripples of unseen rivers, tides of a current flowing,
　　forever flowing,
(Or is it the splashing of tears? the measureless waters
　　of human tears?)
I see, just see skyward, great cloud-masses,
Mournfully slowly they roll, silently swelling and
　　mixing,
With at times a half-dimm'd sadden'd far-off star,
Appearing and disappearing.
(Some parturition rather, some solemn immortal birth;
On the frontiers to eyes impenetrable,
Some soul is passing over.)

PENSIVE AND FALTERING

PENSIVE and faltering,
　　The words *the Dead* I write,
For living are the Dead,
(Haply the only living, only real,
And I the apparition, I the spectre).

THE LAST INVOCATION

AT the last, tenderly,
　　From the walls of the powerful fortress'd house,
From the clasp of the knitted locks, from the keep of
　　the well-closed doors,
Let me be wafted.

Let me glide noiselessly forth;
With the key of softness unlock the locks—with a
    whisper,
Set ope the doors, O soul.

Tenderly, be not impatient,
(Strong is your hold, O mortal flesh;
    Strong is your hold, O love.)

'THE MYSTIC TRUMPETER'

NOW, trumpeter! for thy close,
    Vouchsafe a higher strain than any yet,
Sing to my soul, renew its languishing faith and hope,
Rouse up my slow belief, give me some vision of the
    future,
Give me for once its prophecy and joy.

O glad, exulting, culminating song!
A vigor more than earth's is in thy notes!
Marches of victory—man disenthral'd—the conqueror at
    last,
Hymns to the universal God from universal man—all joy!
A reborn race appears—a perfect world, all joy!
Women and men in wisdom innocence and health—all
    joy!
Riotous, laughing bacchanals, fill'd with joy!
War, sorrow, suffering gone—the rank earth purged—
    nothing but joy left!
The ocean fill'd with joy—the atmosphere all joy!
Joy! joy! in freedom, worship, love! Joy in the ecstasy
    of life!
Enough to merely be! Enough to breathe!
Joy! joy! all over joy!

Alice Cary

LIGHT

BE not much troubled about many things,
    Fear often hath no whit of substance in it,
        And lives but just a minute;

While from the very snow the wheat-blade springs.
    And light is like a flower,
That bursts in full leaf from the darkest hour.
    And He who made the night,
Made, too, the flowery sweetness of the light.
Be it thy task, through His good grace, to win it.

SERMONS IN STONES

FLOWER of the deep red zone,
    Rain the fine light about thee, near and far,
Hold the wide earth, so as the evening star
    Holdeth all heaven, alone,
And with thy wondrous glory make men see
His greater glory who did fashion thee!

    Sing, little goldfinch, sing
Make the rough billows lift their curly ears
And listen, fill the violet's eyes with tears,
    Make the green leaves to swing
As in a dance, when thou dost hie along,
Showing the sweetness whence thou get'st thy song.

    O daisies of the hills,
When winds do pipe to charm ye, be not slow.
Crowd up, crowd up, and make your shoulders show
    White o'er the daffodils!
Yea, shadow forth through your excelling grace
With whom ye have held counsel face to face.

    Fill full our desire,
Gray grasses; trick your lowly stems with green,
And wear your splendors even as a queen
    Weareth her soft attire.
Unfold the cunning mystery of design
That combs out all your skirts to ribbons fine.

    And O, my heart, my heart,
Be careful to go strewing in and out
Thy way with good deeds, lest it come about
    That when thou shalt depart,
No low lamenting tongue be found to say,
The world is poorer since thou went'st away!

Thou shouldst not idly beat,
While beauty draweth good men's thoughts to prayer,
Even as the bird's wing draweth out the air,
    But make so fair and sweet
Thy house of clay, some dusk shall spread about,
When death unlocks the door and lets thee out.

TIME

WHAT is time, O glorious Giver,
        With its restlessness and might,
But a lost and wandering river
    Working back into the light?

Every gloomy rock that troubles
    Its smooth passage, strikes to life
Beautiful and joyous bubbles,
    That are only born through strife.

Overhung with mist-like shadows,
    Stretch its shores away, away,
To the long, delightful meadows
    Shining with immortal May:

Where its moaning reaches never,
    Passion, pain, or fear to move,
And the changes bring us ever
    Sabbaths and new moons of love.

THE SURE WITNESS

THE solemn wood had spread
    Shadows around my head;
'Curtains they are,' I said,
'Hung dim and still about the house of prayer;'
Softly among the limbs,
I heard the winds, and asked if God were there.
No voice replied, but while I listening stood,
Sweet peace made holy hushes through the wood.

With ruddy, open hand,
I saw the wild rose stand
Beside the green gate of the summer hills;
And pulling at her dress,
I cried, 'Sweet hermitess,
Hast thou beheld Him who the dew distils?'
No voice replied, but while I listening bent,
Her gracious beauty made my heart content.

The moon in splendor shone;
'She walketh heaven alone,
And seeth all things,' to myself I mused:
'Hast thou beheld Him, then,
Who hides himself from men
In that great power through nature interfused?'
No speech made answer, and no sign appeared,
But in the silence I was soothed and cheered.

Waking one time, strange awe
Thrilling my soul, I saw
A kingly splendor round about the night;
Such cunning work the hand
Of spinner never planned,—
The finest wool may not be washed so white.
'Hast thou come out of heaven?'
I asked; and lo!
The snow was all the answer of the snow.

Then my heart said, 'Give o'er;
Question no more, no more!
The wind, the snow-storm, the wild hermit flower,
The illuminated air,
The pleasure after prayer,
Proclaim the unoriginated Power!
The mystery that hides Him here and there
Bears the sure witness He is everywhere.'

A DREAM OF HOME

SUNSET! a hush is on the air,
      Their gray old heads the mountains bare,
As if the winds were saying prayer.

The woodland, with its broad, green wing,
Shuts close the insect whispering,
And lo! the sea gets up to sing.

The day's last splendor fades and dies,
And shadows one by one arise,
To light the candles of the skies.

O wild flowers, wet with tearful dew,
O woods, with starlight shining through!
My heart is back to-night with you!

I know each beech and maple tree,
Each climbing brier and shrub I see,—
Like friends they stand to welcome me.

Musing, I go along the streams,
Sweetly believing in my dreams;
For Fancy like a prophet seems.

Footsteps beside me tread the sod,
As in the twilights gone they trod;
And I unlearn my doubts, thank God!

Unlearn my doubts, forget my fears,
And that bad carelessness that sears,
And makes me older than my years.

I hear a dear, familiar tone,
A loving hand is in my own,
And earth seems made for me alone.

If I my fortunes could have planned,
I would not have let go that hand;
But they must fall who learn to stand.

And how to blend life's varied hues,
What ill to find, what good to lose,
My Father knoweth best to choose.

PLEA FOR CHARITY

IF one had never seen the full completeness
   Of the round year, but tarried half the way,
How should he guess the fair and flowery sweetness
   That cometh with the May—
Guess of the bloom, and of the rainy sweetness
   That come in with the May!

Suppose he had but heard the winds a-blowing,
   And seen the brooks in icy chains fast bound,
How should he guess that waters in their flowing
   Could make so glad a sound—
Guess how their silver tongues should be set going
   To such a tuneful sound!

Suppose he had not seen the bluebirds winging,
   Nor seen the day set, nor the morning rise,
Nor seen the golden balancing and swinging
   Of the gay butterflies—
Who could paint April pictures, worth the bringing
   To notice of his eyes?

Suppose he had not seen the living daisies,
   Nor seen the rose, so glorious and bright,
Were it not better than your far-off praises
   Of all their lovely light,
To give his hands the holding of the daisies,
   And of the roses bright?

O Christian man, deal gently with the sinner—
   Think what an utter wintry waste is his
Whose heart of love has never been the winner,
   To know how sweet it is—
Be pitiful, O Christian, to the sinner,
   Think what a world is his!

He never heard the lisping and the trembling
   Of Eden's gracious leaves about his head—
His mirth is nothing but the poor dissembling
   Of a great soul unfed—
Oh, bring him where the Eden-leaves are trembling,
   And give him heavenly bread.

As Winter doth her shriveled branches cover
  With greenness, knowing spring-time's soft desire,
Even so the soul, knowing Jesus for a lover,
  Puts on a new attire—
A garment fair as snow, to meet the Lover
  Who bids her come up higher.

KNOWN BY HIS WORKS

THY works, O Lord, interpret Thee,
    And through·them all Thy love is shown;
Flowing about us like a sea,
    Yet steadfast as the eternal throne.

Out of the light that runneth through
    Thy hand, the lily's dress is spun:
Thine is the brightness of the dew,
    And Thine the glory of the sun.

MY DARLINGS

WHEN steps are hurrying homeward,
    And night the world o'erspreads,
And I see at the open windows
    The shining of little heads,
I think of you, my darlings,
    In your low and lonesome beds.

And when the latch is lifted,
    And I hear the voices glad,
I feel my arms more empty,
    My heart more widely sad;
For we measure dearth of blessings
    By the blessings we have had.

But sometimes in sweet visions
    My faith to sight expands,
And with my babes in His bosom,
    My Lord before me stands,
And I feel on my head bowed lowly
    The touches of little hands.

Then pain is lost in patience,
  And tears no longer flow:
They are only dead to the sorrow
  And sin of life, I know:
For if they were not immortal
  My love would make them so.

LAST AND BEST

SOMETIMES, when rude, cold shadows run
  Across whatever light I see;
When all the work that I have done,
  Or can do, seems but vanity;

I strive, nor vainly strive, to get
  Some little heart's ease from the day
When all the weariness and fret
  Shall vanish from my life away;

For I, with grandeur clothed upon,
  Shall lie in state and take my rest,
And all my household, strangers grown,
  Shall hold me for an honored guest.

But ere that day when all is set
  In order, very still and grand,
And while my feet are lingering yet
  Along this troubled border-land,

What things will be the first to fade,
  And down to utter darkness sink?
The treasures that my hands have laid
  Where moth and rust corrupt, I think.

And Love will be the last to wait
  And light my gloom with gracious gleams;
For Love lies nearer heaven's glad gate,
  Than all imagination dreams.

Aye, when my soul its mask shall drop,
  The twain to be no more at one,
Love, with its prayers, shall bear me up
  Beyond the lark's wings, and the sun.

DREAMS

OFTEN I sit and spend my hour,
   Linking my dreams from heart to brain,
And as the child joins flower to flower,
   Then breaks and joins them on again,

Casting the bright ones in disgrace,
   And weaving pale ones in their stead,
Changing the honors and the place
   Of white and scarlet, blue and red;

And finding after all his pains
   Of sorting and selecting dyes,
No single chain of all the chains
   The fond caprice that satisfies;

So I from all things bright and brave,
   Select what brightest, bravest seems,
And, with the utmost skill I have,
   Contrive the fashion of my dreams.

Sometimes ambitious thoughts abound,
   And then I draw my pattern bold,
And have my shuttle only wound
   With silken threads or threads of gold.

Sometimes my heart reproaches me,
   And mesh from cunning mesh I pull,
And weave in sad humility
   With flaxen threads or threads of wool.

For here the hue too brightly gleams,
   And there the grain too dark is cast,
And so no dream of all my dreams
   Is ever finished, first or last.

And looking back upon my past
   Thronged with so many a wasted hour,
I think that I should fear to cast
   My fortunes if I had the power.

And think that he is mainly wise,
    Who takes what comes of good or ill,
Trusting that wisdom underlies
And worketh in the end—His will.

HERE AND THERE

DOWN in the darkness, deep in the darkness,
    All in the blind, black night;
Near to the morning, clear to the morning,
    All in the glad, gold light!

Down in the daisies, deep in the daisies,
    Under the daisies to lie;
Over the stork's wing, over the lark's wing,
    Over the moon and the sky!

Tears in the daisies, drowning the daisies,
    Blight that no moon can remove;
Praises, and praises, and evermore praises,
    Gladness, and glory, and love!

Broken and bruisèd, and heart-sick and sin-sick,
    Crying for mercy and grace;
Rising and risen and out of our prison,
    Spirits with face unto face!

Longing and looking, and thirsting and fainting,
    Deserts to left, and to right;
Coolness of shadows, and greenness of meadows,
    And fountains of living delight.

Hearts that are aching, and hearts that are breaking,
    Like waves on a rocky-bound shore;
Footsteps of lightness, and faces of brightness,
    And sickness and sighing no more.

Wanderers, wayfarers, desolate orphans,
    Deaf to the Shepherd's soft call;
Gathered together by God, our good Father,
    Blessèd forever, o'er all!

DYING HYMN

EARTH, with its dark and dreadful ills,
　　Recedes, and fades away;
Lift up your heads, ye heavenly hills;
　　Ye gates of death, give way!

My soul is full of whispered song;
　　My blindness is my sight;
The shadows that I feared so long
　　Are all alive with light.

The while my pulses faintly beat,
　　My faith doth so abound,
I feel grow firm beneath my feet
　　The green immortal ground.

That faith to me a courage gives,
　　Low as the grave, to go;
I know that my Redeemer lives:
　　That I shall live, I know.

The palace walls I almost see,
　　Where dwells my Lord and King;
O grave, where is thy victory!
　　O death, where is thy sting!

Anne Charlotte Lynch Botta

FAITH

SECURELY cabined in the ship below,
　　Through darkness and through storm I cross the sea,
A pathless wilderness of waves to me:
But yet I do not fear, because I know
That he who guides the good ship o'er that waste
Sees in the stars her shining pathway traced.
Blindfold I walk this life's bewildering maze;
Up flinty steep, through frozen mountain pass,
Through thorn-set barren and through deep morass;
But strong in faith I tread the uneven ways,
And bare my head unshrinking to the blast,
Because my Father's arm is round me cast;
And if the way seems rough, I only clasp
The hand that leads me with a firmer grasp.

Sarah Knowles Bolton

EARLY WORK

BESIDE my window, in the early spring,
　　A robin built her nest and reared her young;
And every day the same sweet song she sung
Until her little ones had taken wing
To try their own bird-living; everything
Was done before the summer roses hung
About our home, or purple clusters swung
Upon our vines at Autumn's opening.
Do your work early in the day or year,
Be it a song to sing, or word to cheer,
Or house to build, or gift to cheer the race;
Life may not reach its noon, or setting sun;
No one can do the work you leave undone,
For no one ever fills another's place.

HER CREED

SHE stood before a chosen few.
　　With modest air and eyes of blue;
A gentle creature, in whose face
Were mingled tenderness and grace.

'You wish to join our fold,' they said;
'Do you believe in all that's read
From ritual and written creed,
Essential to our human need?'

A troubled look was in her eyes;
She answered, as in vague surprise,
As though the sense to her were dim;
'I only strive to follow Him.'

They knew her life; how, oft she stood,
Sweet in her guileless maidenhood,
By dying bed, in hovel lone,
Whose sorrow she had made her own.

Oft had her voice in prayer been heard,
  Sweet as the voice of singing bird;
Her hand been open in distress;
  Her joy to brighten and to bless.

Yet still she answered when they sought
To know her inmost earnest thought,
  With look as of the seraphim,
'I only strive to follow Him.'

Creeds change as ages come and go;
  We see by faith, but little know:
Perchance the sense was not so dim,
  To her who 'strove to follow Him.'

Maria White Lowell

THE ALPINE SHEEP

WHEN on my ear your loss was knelled,
    And tender sympathy upburst,
A little spring from memory welled,
    Which once had quenched my bitter thirst.

And I was fain to bear to you
  A portion of its mild relief,
That it might be as healing dew,
  To steal some fever from your grief.

After our child's untroubled breath
  Up to the Father took its way,
And on our home the shade of Death
  Like a long twilight haunting lay,

And friends came round, with us to weep
  Her little spirit's swift remove,
The story of the Alpine sheep
  Was told to us by one we love.

They, in the valley's sheltering care,
  Soon crop the meadow's tender prime,
And when the sod grows brown and bare,
  The shepherd strives to make them climb

To airy shelves of pasture green,
    That hang along the mountain's side,
Where grass and flowers together lean,
    And down through mist the sunbeams slide.

But naught can tempt the timid things
    The steep and rugged path to try,
Though sweet the shepherd calls and sings,
    And seared below the pastures lie,

Till in his arms their lambs he takes,
    Along the dizzy verge to go ;
Then, heedless of the rifts and breaks,
    They follow on, o'er rock and snow.

And in those pastures, lifted fair,
    More dewy-soft than lowland mead,
The shepherd drops his tender care,
    And sheep and lambs together feed.

This parable by Nature breathed,
    Blew on me as the south-wind free
O'er frozen brooks, that flow unsheathed
    From icy thraldom to the sea.

A blissful vision through the night
    Would all my stony senses sway,
Of the Good Shepherd on the height,
    Or climbing up the happy way,

Holding our little lamb asleep,—
    While, like the murmur of the sea,
Sounded that voice along the deep,
    Saying, ' Arise and follow Me ! '

Eliza Scudder

THE LOVE OF GOD

THOU Grace Divine, encircling all,
    A shoreless, boundless sea,
Wherein at last our souls must fall,
    O Love of God most free !

When over dizzy heights we go,
   One soft hand blinds our eyes;
The other leads us safe and slow,
   O Love of God most wise!

And though we turn us from Thy face,
   And wander wide and long,
Thou hold'st us still in Thine embrace,
   O Love of God most strong!

The saddened heart, the restless soul,
   The toil-worn frame and mind,
Alike confess Thy sweet control,
   O Love of God most kind!

But not alone Thy care we claim,
   Our wayward steps to win;
We know Thee by a dearer name;
   O Love of God within!

And filled and quickened by Thy breath,
   Our souls are strong and free,
To rise o'er sin and fear and death;
   O Love of God to Thee!

TRUTH

THOU long disowned, reviled, opprest,
   Strange friend of human kind,
Seeking through weary years a rest
   Within our hearts to find.

How late thy bright and awful brow
   Breaks through these clouds of sin!
Hail, Truth divine! we know thee now,
   Angel of God, come in!

Come, though with purifying fire
   And desolating sword,
Thou of all nations the desire,
   Earth waits thy cleansing word.

Struck by the lightning of thy glance,
  Let old oppressions die!
Before thy cloudless countenance
  Let fear and falsehood fly!

Anoint our eyes with healing grace,
  To see, as ne'er before,
Our Father, in our brother's face,
  Our Master, in His poor.

Flood our dark life with golden day,
  Convince, subdue, enthrall!
Then to a mightier yield thy sway,
  And Love be all in all.

THE QUEST

I CANNOT find Thee! Still on restless pinion
  My spirit beats the void where Thou dost dwell;
I wander lost through all Thy vast dominion,
  And shrink beneath Thy light ineffable.

I cannot find Thee! E'en when most adoring,
  Before Thy throne, I bend in lowliest prayer;
Beyond these bounds of thought, my thought upsoaring,
  From farthest quest comes back: Thou art not there.

Yet high above the limits of my seeing,
  And folded far within the inmost heart,
And deep below the deeps of conscious being,
  Thy splendor shineth; there, O God! Thou art.

I cannot lose Thee! Still in Thee abiding,
  The end is clear, how wide soe'er I roam;
The Hand that holds the worlds my steps is guiding,
  And I must rest at last, in Thee, my home.

THE NEW HEAVEN

LET whosoever will, inquire
  Of spirit or of seer,
To shape unto the heart's desire
  The new life's vision clear.

My God, I rather look to Thee
  Than to these fancies fond,
And wait till Thou reveal to me
  That fair and far Beyond.

I seek not of Thine Eden-land
  The forms and hues to know,—
What trees in mystic order stand,
  What strange, sweet waters flow;

What duties fill the heavenly day,
  Or converse glad and kind;
Or how along each shining way
  The bright processions wind.

Oh joy! to hear with sense new born
  The angels' greeting strains,
And sweet to see the first fair morn
  Gild the celestial plains.

But sweeter far to trust in Thee
  While all is yet unknown,
And through the death-dark cheerily
  To walk with Thee alone!

In Thee my powers, my treasures live;
  To Thee my life shall tend;
Giving Thyself, Thou all dost give,
  O soul-sufficing Friend.

And wherefore should I seek above
  Thy city in the sky?
Since firm in faith and deep in love
  Its broad foundations lie;

Since in a life of peace and prayer,
  Not known on earth, nor praised,
By humblest toil, by ceaseless care,
  Its holy towers are raised.

Where pain the soul hath purified,
  And penitence hath shriven,
And truth is crowned and glorified,
  There—only there—is Heaven.

WHOM BUT THEE

FROM past regret and present faithlessness,
   From the deep shadow of foreseen distress,
And from the nameless weariness that grows
As life's long day seems wearing to its close;

Thou Life within my life, than self more near!
Thou veilèd Presence infinitely clear!
From all illusive shows of sense I flee,
To find my centre and my rest in Thee.

Below all depths Thy saving mercy lies,
Through thickest glooms I see Thy light arise,
Above the highest heaven Thou art not found
More surely than within this earthly round.

Take part with me against those doubts that rise
And seek to throne Thee far in distant skies!
Take part with me against this self that dares
Assume the burden of these sins and cares!

How shall I call Thee who art always here,
How shall I praise Thee who art still most dear,
What may I give Thee save what Thou hast given,
And whom but Thee have I in earth or heaven?

VESPER HYMN

THE day is done; the weary day of thought and toil
   is past,
Soft falls the twilight cool and gray, on the tired earth
   at last;
By wisest teachers wearièd, by gentlest friends opprest,
In Thee alone, the soul, out-worn, refreshment finds
   and rest.

Bend, gracious Spirit, from above, like these o'erarch-
   ing skies,
And to Thy firmament of love lift up these longing
   eyes;
And folded by Thy sheltering Hand, in refuge still
   and deep,
Let blessed thoughts from Thee descend, as drop the
   dews of sleep.

And when, refreshed, the soul once more puts on new
    life and power,
Oh, let Thine image, Lord, alone, gild the first waking
    hour!
Let that dear Presence rise and glow fairer than
    morn's first ray,
And Thy pure radiance overflow the splendor of the
    day.

So in the hastening evening, so in the coming morn,
When deeper slumber shall be given, and fresher life
    be born,
Shine out, true Light! to guide my way amid that
    deepening gloom,
And rise, O Morning Star, the first that dayspring to
    illume.

I cannot dread the darkness, where Thou wilt watch
    o'er me,
Nor smile to greet the sunrise, unless Thy smile I see;
Creator, Saviour, Comforter! on Thee my soul is cast;
At morn, at night, in earth, in heaven, be Thou my
    First and Last.

Samuel Johnson

MADE PERFECT THROUGH SUFFERING

I BLESS Thee, Lord, for sorrows sent
    To break my dream of human power;
For now, my shallow cistern spent,
    I find Thy founts, and thirst no more.

I take Thy hand, and fears grow still;
    Behold Thy face, and doubts remove;
Who would not yield his wavering will
    To perfect Truth and boundless Love?

That Love this restless soul doth teach
    The strength of Thine eternal calm;
And tune its sad and broken speech,
    To join, on earth, the angels' psalm.

O be it patient in Thy hands,
    And drawn, through each mysterious hour,
To service of Thy pure commands,
    The narrow way to Love and Power!

THE CITY OF GOD

CITY of God, how broad and far
    Outspread thy walls sublime!
The true thy chartered freemen are
    Of every age and clime.

One holy Church, one army strong,
    One steadfast high intent,
One working hand, one harvest song,
    One King Omnipotent!

How purely hath thy speech come down
    From man's primeval youth!
How grandly hath thine empire grown
    Of freedom, love, and truth!

How gleam thy watchfires through the night
    With never-fainting ray!
How rise thy towers, serene and bright,
    To meet the dawning day!

In vain the surge's angry shock,
    In vain the drifting sands;
Unharmed upon the Eternal Rock,
    The Eternal City stands.

Caroline Atherton Mason

CAGED

POOR prisoned bird, that sings and sings,
    Unconscious of the gift of wings;
Or, knowing it, content to be
Shorn of its birthright liberty!

Like souls—a sadder thrall who bear,
Or wittingly or unaware—
Consenting to their prison bars,
When, haply, they might pierce the stars.

Oh, I would rather be the clod
That knows not, cannot know, of God,
Than thus, in sluggish wise, deny
My title to His open sky!

He gave us wings; He must have meant,
Thereby, a noble discontent
To teach us, that we might essay
To break each bond and soar away.

What is the cage that shuts us in,
But our own sloth? but our own sin?
All outward limitations are
But cobwebs to such bolt and bar.

For me, no idle lance I tilt
Against my lot: mine all the guilt;
I am mine own most bitter foe—
Ah, this it is which irks me so!

If from myself I could set free
Myself! At odds I still must be,
Till my victorious wings shall rise,
Unclogged, and sweep the farthest skies.

EVENTIDE

AT cool of day, with God I walk
   My garden's grateful shade;
I hear His voice among the trees,
   And I am not afraid.

I see His presence in the night,—
   And, though my heart is awed,
I do not quail beneath the sight
   Or nearness of my God.

K 2

He speaks to me in every wind,
　　He smiles from every star;
He is not deaf to me, nor blind,
　　Nor absent, nor afar.

His hand, that shuts the flowers to sleep,
　　Each in its dewy fold,
Is strong my feeble life to keep,
　　And competent to hold.

I cannot walk in darkness long,—
　　My light is by my side;
I cannot stumble or go wrong,
　　While following such a guide.

He is my stay and my defence;—
　　How shall I fail or fall?
My helper is Omnipotence!
　　My ruler ruleth all.

The powers below and powers above
　　Are subject to His care:—
I cannot wander from His love
　　Who loves me everywhere.

Thus dowered, and guarded thus, with Him
　　I walk this peaceful shade;
I hear His voice among the trees,
　　And I am not afraid!

EN VOYAGE

WHICHEVER way the wind doth blow
　　Some heart is glad to have it so;
Then blow it east or blow it west,
The wind that blows, that wind is best.

My little craft sails not alone;
A thousand fleets from every zone
Are out upon a thousand seas;
And what for me were favoring breeze
Might dash another, with the shock
Of doom, upon some hidden rock.

And so I do not dare to pray
For winds to waft me on my way,
But leave it to a Higher Will
To stay or speed me; trusting still
That all is well, and sure that He
Who launched my bark will sail with me
Through storm and calm, and will not fail,
Whatever breezes may prevail,
To land me, every peril past,
Within His sheltering heaven at last.

Then, whatsoever wind doth blow,
My heart is glad to have it so;
And blow it east or blow it west,
The wind that blows, that wind is best.

NOT YET

NOT yet! Along the purpling sky
    We see the dawning ray;
But leagues of cloudy distance lie
    Between us and the day.

Not yet! The aloe waits serene
    Its promised advent hour,—
A patient century of green
    To one full, perfect flower.

Not yet! No harvest song is sung
    In the sweet ear of spring,
Nor hear we while the blade is young
    The reaper's sickle swing.

Not yet! Before the crown, the cross;
    The struggle, ere the prize;
Before the gain the fearful loss,
    And death ere Paradise!

LOST AND FOUND

I HAD a treasure in my house,
    And woke one day to find it gone;
I mourned for it from dawn till night,
    From night till dawn.

I said, 'Behold, I will arise
  And sweep my house,' and so I found
What I had lost, and told my joy
    To all around.

I had a treasure in my heart,
  And scarcely knew that it had fled,
Until communion with my Lord
    Grew cold and dead.

'Behold,' I said, 'I will arise
  And sweep my heart of self and sin;
And so the peace that I have lost
    May enter in.'

O friends, rejoice with me! Each day
  Helps my lost treasure to restore;
And sweet communion with my Lord
    Is mine once more.

MARTHA OR MARY?

I CANNOT choose; I should have liked so much
    To sit at Jesus' feet,—to feel the touch
Of His kind, gentle hand upon my head
While drinking in the gracious words He said.

And yet to serve Him!—Oh, divine employ,—
To minister and give the Master joy,
To bathe in coolest springs His weary feet,
And wait upon Him while He sat at meat!

Worship or service,—which? Ah, that is best
To which He calls us, be it toil or rest,—
To labor for Him in life's busy stir,
Or seek His feet, a silent worshipper.

David Atwood Wasson

SEEN AND UNSEEN

THE wind ahead, the billows high,
    A whited wave, but sable sky,
And many a league of tossing sea
Between the hearts I love and me.

The wind ahead : day after day
These weary words the sailors say;
To weeks the days are lengthened now,—
Still mounts the surge to meet our prow.

Through longing day and lingering night,
I still accuse Time's lagging flight,
Or gaze out o'er the envious sea,
That keeps the hearts I love from me.

Yet, ah! how shallow is all grief!
How instant is the deep relief!
And what a hypocrite am I,
To feign forlorn, to 'plain and sigh!

The wind ahead? The wind is free!
For evermore it favoreth me,—
To shores of God still blowing fair,
O'er seas of God my bark doth bear.

This surging brine *I* do not sail;
This blast adverse is not my gale;
'Tis here I only seem to be,
But really sail another sea,—

Another sea, pure sky its waves,
Whose beauty hides no heaving graves,—
A sea all haven, whereupon
No helpless bark to wreck hath gone.

The winds that o'er my ocean run
Reach through all heavens beyond the sun;
Through life and death, through fate, through time,
Grand breaths of God, they sweep sublime.

Eternal 'trades,' they cannot veer,
And, blowing, teach us how to steer;
And well for him whose joy, whose care,
Is but to keep before them fair.

O thou, God's mariner, heart of mine,
Spread canvas to the airs divine!
Spread sail! and let thy Fortune be
Forgotten in thy Destiny!

For Destiny pursues us well,
By sea, by land, through heaven or hell;
It suffers Death alone to die,
Bids Life all change and chance defy.

Would earth's dark ocean suck thee down?
Earth's ocean thou, O Life! shalt drown,
Shalt flood it with thy finer wave,
And, sepulchred, entomb thy grave!

Life loveth life and good; then trust
What most the spirit would, it must;
Deep wishes, in the heart that be,
Are blossoms of Necessity.

A thread of Law runs through thy prayer,
Stronger than iron cables are;
And Love and Longing toward her goal
Are pilots sweet to guide the Soul.

So Life must live, and Soul must sail,
And Unseen over Seen prevail,
And all God's argosies come to shore,
Let ocean smile, or rage and roar.

And so, 'mid storm or calm, my bark
With snowy wake still nears her mark;
Cheerly the 'trades' of being blow,
And sweeping down the wind I go.

ALL'S WELL

SWEET-VOICÈD Hope, thy fine discourse
    Foretold not half life's good to me;
Thy painter, Fancy, hath not force
    To show how sweet it is to be!
        Thy witching dream
        And pictured scheme
To match the fact still want the power;
        Thy promise brave
        From birth to grave
Life's boon may beggar in an hour.

Ask and receive,—'tis sweetly said;
  Yet what to plead for, know I not;
For Wish is worsted, Hope o'ersped,
  And aye to thanks returns my thought.
      If I would pray,
      I've naught to say
But this, that God may be God still,
      For Him to live
      Is still to give,
And sweeter than my wish His will.

O wealth of life beyond all bound!
  Eternity each moment given!
What plummet may the Present sound?
  Who promises a *future* heaven?
      Or glad, or grieved,
      Oppressed, relieved,
In blackest night, or brightest day
      Still pours the flood
      Of golden good,
And more than heartfull fills me aye.

My wealth is common; I possess
  No petty province, but the whole;
What's mine alone is mine far less
  Than treasure shared by every soul.
      Talk not of store,
      Millions or more,—
Of values which the purse may hold,—
      But this divine!
      I own the mine
Whose grains outweigh a planet's gold.

I have a stake in every star,
  In every beam that fills the day;
All hearts of men my coffers are,
  My ores arterial tides convey;
      The fields, the skies,
      The sweet replies
Of thought to thought are my gold-dust;
      The oaks, the brooks,
      And speaking looks
Of lovers, faith and friendship's trust.

Life's youngest tides joy-brimming flow
  For him who lives above all years,
Who all-immortal makes the Now,
  And is not ta'en in Time's arrears:
        His life's a hymn
        The seraphim
Might hark to hear or help to sing,
        And to his soul
        The boundless whole
Its bounty all doth daily bring.

'All Mine is thine,' the Sky-Soul saith:
  'The wealth I Am must thou become;
Richer and richer, breath by breath,—
  Immortal gain, immortal room!'
        And since all His
        Mine also is,
Life's gift outruns my fancies far,
        And drowns the dream
        In larger stream,
As morning drinks the morning-star.

IDEALS

ANGELS of Growth, of old in that surprise
    Of your first vision, wild and sweet,
  I poured in passionate sighs
      My wish unwise
  That ye descend my heart to meet,—
      My heart so slow to rise!

Now thus I pray: Angelic be to hold
  In heaven your shining poise afar,
      And to my wishes bold
      Reply with cold,
  Sweet invitation, like a star
      Fixed in the heavens old.

Did ye descend: what were ye more than I?
  Is't not by this ye are divine,—
      That, native to the sky,
      Ye cannot hie
  Downward, and give low hearts the wine
      That should reward the high?

Weak, yet in weakness I no more complain
  Of your abiding in your places:
      Oh! still, howe'er my pain
      Wild prayers may rain,
  Keep pure on high the perfect graces
      That stooping could but stain.

Not to content our lowness, but to lure
  And lift us to your angelhood,
      Do your surprises pure,
      Dawn far and sure
  Above the tumult of young blood,
      And, star-like, there endure.

Wait there! wait and invite me while I climb;
  For see, I come! but slow, but slow!
      Yet ever as your chime
      Soft and sublime,
  Lifts at my feet, they move, they go
      Up the great stair of time.

Thomas Wentworth Higginson

I WILL ARISE AND GO UNTO MY FATHER

TO Thine eternal arms, O God,
    Take us, Thine erring children, in;
From dangerous paths too boldly trod,
    From wandering thoughts and dreams of sin.

Those arms were round our childish ways,
    A guard through helpless years to be;
O, leave not our maturer days,
    We still are helpless without Thee!

We trusted hope and pride and strength:
    Our strength proved false, our pride was vain,
Our dreams have faded all at length,—
    We come to Thee, O Lord, again!

A guide to trembling steps yet be!
    Give us of Thine eternal powers!
So shall our paths all lead to Thee,
    And life smile on, like childhood's hours.

PANTHEISM AND THEISM

NO human eyes Thy face may see;
　　No human thought Thy form may know;
But all creation dwells in Thee,
　　And Thy great life through all doth flow!

And yet, O, strange and wondrous thought!
　　Thou art a God who hearest prayer,
And every heart with sorrow fraught
　　To seek Thy present aid may dare.

And though most weak our efforts seem
　　Into one creed these thoughts to bind,
And vain the intellectual dream
　　To see and know the Eternal Mind,—

Yet Thou wilt turn them not aside,
　　Who cannot solve Thy life divine,
But would give up all reason's pride
　　To know their hearts approved by Thine.

So, though we faint on life's dark hill,
　　And thought grow weak, and knowledge flee,
Yet faith shall teach us courage still,
　　And love shall guide us on to Thee!

THE THINGS I MISS

AN easy thing, O Power Divine,
　　To thank Thee for these gifts of Thine!
For summer's sunshine, winter's snow,
For hearts that kindle, thoughts that glow.
But when shall I attain to this,—
To thank Thee for the things I miss?

For all young Fancy's early gleams,
The dreamed-of joys that still are dreams,
Hopes unfulfilled, and pleasures known
Through others' fortunes, not my own,
And blessings seen that are not given,
And never will be, this side heaven.

Had I too shared the joys I see,
Would there have been a heaven for me?
Could I have felt Thy presence near,
Had I possessed what I held dear?
My deepest fortune, highest bliss,
Have grown perchance from things I miss.

Sometimes there comes an hour of calm;
Grief turns to blessing, pain to balm;
A Power that works above my will
Still leads me onward, upward still:
And then my heart attains to this,—
To thank Thee for the things I miss.

TO MY SHADOW*

A MUTE companion at my side
    Paces and plods, the whole day long,
Accepts the measure of my stride,
    Yet gives no cheer by word or song.

More close than any doggish friend,
    Not ranging far and wide, like him,
He goes where'er my footsteps tend,
    Nor shrinks for fear of life or limb.

I do not know when first we met,
    But till each day's bright hours are done
This grave and speechless silhouette
    Keeps me betwixt him and the sun.

They say he knew me when a child;
    Born with my birth, he dies with me;
Not once from his long task beguiled,
    Though sin or shame bid others flee.

What if, when all this world of men
    Shall melt and fade and pass away,
This deathless sprite should rise again
    And be himself my Judgment Day?

* See Note.

VESTIS ANGELICA *

O GATHER, gather! Stand
    Round her on either hand!
O shining angel-band
  More pure than priest!
A garment white and whole
Weave for this passing soul,
Whose earthly joy and dole
  Have almost ceased.

Weave it of mothers' prayers,
Of sacred thoughts and cares,
Of peace beneath grey hairs,
  Of hallowed pain ;
Weave it of vanished tears,
Of childlike hopes and fears,
Of joys, by saintly years
  Washed free from stain.

Weave it of happy hours,
Of smiles and summer flowers,
Of passing sunlit showers,
  Of acts of love ;
Of footsteps that did go
Amid life's work and woe,—
Her eyes still fixed below,
  Her thoughts above.

Then as those eyes grow dim
Chant we her best-loved hymn,
While from yon church-tower's brim
  A soft chime swells.
Her freed soul floats in bliss
To unseen worlds from this,
Nor knows in which it is
  She hears the bells.

* See Note.

BENEATH THE VIOLETS

SAFE 'neath the violets
   Rests the baby form;
Every leaf that springtime sets
   Shields it from the storm.
Peace to all vain regrets
   Mid this sunshine warm!

Shadows come and shadows go
   O'er the meadows wide;
Twice each day, to and fro,
   Steals the river-tide;
Each morn with sunrise-glow
   Gilds the green hillside.

Peace that no sorrow frets
   In our souls arise!
Over all our wild regrets
   Arching, like the skies;
While safe 'neath the violets
   Sleep the violet eyes.

TWO VOYAGERS

WHEN first I mark upon my child's clear brow
   Thought's wrestling shadows their new struggle
      keep,
Read my own conflicts in her questions deep,
My own remorse in her repentant vow,
My own vast ignorance in her 'Why?' and 'How?'
When my precautions only serve to heap
New burdens, and my cares her needs o'erleap,
Then to her separate destiny I bow.
So seem we like two ships, that side by side,
Older and younger, breast the same rough main
Bound for one port, whatever winds betide,
In solemn interchange of joy or pain.
I may not hold thee back. Though skies be dark,
Put forth upon the seas, O priceless bark!

Sarah Hammond Palfrey

THE EXCHANGE

SAD souls, that harbor fears and woes
  In many a haunted breast,
Turn but to meet your lowly Lord,
  And He will give you rest.

Into His commonwealth alike
  Are ills and blessings thrown;
Bear ye your neighbors' burdens; lo!
  Their ease shall be your own.

Yield only up His price, your heart,
  Into God's loving hold;
He turns, with heavenly alchemy,
  Your lead of life to gold.

Some needful pangs endure in peace,
  Nor yet for freedom pant;
He cuts the bane you cleave to off,
  Then gives the boon you want.

THE CHILD'S PLEA

BECAUSE I wear the swaddling-bands of Time,
  Still mark and watch me,
Eternal Father on Thy throne sublime,
  Lest Satan snatch me.

Because to seek Thee I have yet to learn,
  Come down and lead me;
Because I am too weak my bread to earn,
  My Father, feed me.

Because I grasp at things that are not mine
  And might undo me,
Give, from thy treasure-house of goods divine,
  Good gifts untó me.

Because too near the pit I creeping go,
   Do not forsake me;
To climb into Thine arms I am too low,
   O Father, take me!

George Henry Boker

THE YEARLY MIRACLE OF SPRING

THE yearly miracle of spring,
   Of budding tree and blooming flower,
Which Nature's feathered laureates sing
   In my cold ear from hour to hour,

Spreads all its wonders round my feet;
   And every wakeful sense is fed
On thoughts that o'er and o'er repeat,
   ' *The Resurrection of the Dead!* '

If these half vital things have force
   To break the spell which winter weaves,
To wake, and clothe the wrinkled corse
   In the full life of shining leaves;

Shall I sit down in vague despair,
   And marvel if the nobler soul
We laid in earth shall ever dare
   To wake to life, and backward roll

The sealing stone, and striding out,
   Claim its eternity, and head
Creation once again, and shout,
   ' *The Resurrection of the Dead*'?

SUMMER MORNING

WITH song of birds and hum of bees,
   And odorous breath of swinging flowers,
With fluttering herbs and swaying trees,
   Begin the early morning hours.

The warm tide of the southern air
  Swims round, with gentle rise and fall,
And, burning through a golden glare,
  The sun looks broadly over all.

So fair and fresh the landscape stands,
  So vital, so beyond decay,
It looks as though God's shaping hands
  Had just been raised and drawn away.

The holy baptism of the rain
  Yet lingers, like a special grace ;
For I can see an aureole plain
  Above the world's transfigured face.

The moments come in dreamy bliss,
  In dreamy bliss they pause and pass :
It seems not hard on days like this,
  Dear Lord, to lie beneath the grass.

Phœbe Cary

UNBELIEF

FAITHLESS, perverse, and blind,
    We sit in our house of fear,
When the winter of sorrow comes to our souls,
    And the days of our life are drear.

For when in darkness and clouds
    The way of God is concealed,
We doubt the words of His promises,
    And the glory to be revealed.

We do but trust in part ;
    We grope in the dark alone ;
Lord, when shall we see Thee as Thou art,
    And know as we are known ?

When shall we live to Thee,
    And die to Thee, resigned,
Nor fear to hide what we would keep,
    And lose what we would find ?

For we doubt our Father's care,
  We cover our faces and cry,
If a little cloud, like the hand of a man,
  Darkens the face of our sky.

We judge of His perfect day
  By our life's poor glimmering spark,
And measure eternity's circle
  By the segment of an arc.

We say, they have taken our Lord,
  And we know not where He lies,
When the light of His resurrection morn
  Is breaking out of the skies.

And we stumble at last when we come
  On the brink of the grave to stand ;
As if the souls that are born of His love
  Could slip from their Father's hand !

ANSWERED

I THOUGHT to find some healing clime
  For her I loved ; she found that shore,
That city, whose inhabitants
  Are sick and sorrowful no more.

I asked for human love for her ;
  The Loving knew how best to still
The infinite yearning of a heart,
  Which but infinity could fill.

Such sweet communion had been ours,
  I prayed that it might never end ;
My prayer is more than answered ; now
  I have an angel for my friend.

I wished for perfect peace, to soothe
  The troubled anguish of her breast ;
And, numbered with the loved and called,
  She entered on untroubled rest.

L 2

Life was so fair a thing to her,
    I wept and pleaded for its stay;
My wish was granted me, for lo!
    She hath eternal life to-day.

SUNSET

AWAY in the dim and distant past
    That little valley lies,
Where the clouds that dimmed life's morning hours
    Were tinged with hope's sweet dyes;

That peaceful spot from which I looked
    To the future,—unaware
That the heat and burden of the day
    Were meant for me to bear.

Alas, alas! I have borne the heat,
    To the burden learned to bow;
For I stand on the top of the hill of life,
    And I see the sunset now!

I stand on the top, but I look not back
    To the way behind me spread;
Not to the path my feet have trod,
    But the path they still must tread.

And straight and plain before my gaze
    The certain future lies;
But my sun grows larger all the while,
    As he travels down the skies.

Yea, the sun of my hope grows large and grand;
    For, with my childish years,
I have left the mist that dimmed my sight,
    I have left my doubts and fears.

And I have gained in hope and trust,
    Till the future looks so bright,
That, letting go of the hand of Faith,
    I walk, at times, by sight.

For we only feel that faith is life,
  And death is the fear of death,
When we suffer up to the solemn heights
  Of a true and living faith;

When we do not say, the dead shall rise
  At the resurrection's call;
But when we trust in the Lord, and know
  That we cannot die at all!

'FIELD PREACHING'

I HAVE been out to-day in field and wood,
  Listening to praises sweet and counsel good,
Such as a little child had understood,
    That, in its tender youth,
Discerns the simple eloquence of truth.

The modest blossoms, crowding round my way,
Though they had nothing great or grand to say,
Gave out their fragrance to the wind all day;
    Because his loving breath,
With soft persistence, won them back from death.

And the right royal lily, putting on
Her robes, more rich than those of Solomon,
Opened her gorgeous missal in the sun,
    And thanked Him, soft and low,
Whose gracious, liberal hand had clothed her so.

When wearied, on the meadow-grass I sank;
So narrow was the rill from which I drank,
An infant might have stepped from bank to bank;
    And the tall rushes near,
Lapping together, hid its waters clear.

Yet to the ocean joyously it went;
And, rippling in the fulness of content,
Watered the pretty flowers that o'er it leant;
    For all the banks were spread
With delicate flowers that on its bounty fed.

The stately maize, a fair and goodly sight,
With serried spear-points bristling sharp and bright,
Shook out his yellow tresses, for delight,
    To all their tawny length,
Like Samson, glorying in his lusty strength.

And every little bird upon the tree,
Ruffling his plumage bright, for ecstasy,
Sang in the wild insanity of glee;
    And seemed, in the same lays,
Calling his mate and uttering songs of praise.

The golden grasshopper did chirp and sing;
The plain bee, busy with her housekeeping,
Kept humming cheerfully upon the wing,
    As if she understood
That, with contentment, labor was a good.

I saw eacn creature, in his own best place,
To the Creator lift a smiling face,
Praising continually His wondrous grace;
    As if the best of all
Life's countless blessings was to live at all!

So with a book of sermons, plain and true,
Hid in my heart, where I might turn them through,
I went home softly, through the falling dew,
    Still listening, rapt and calm,
To Nature giving out her evening psalm.

While, far along the west, mine eyes discerned,
Where, lit by God, the fires of sunset burned,
The tree-tops, unconsumed, to flame were turned,
    And I, in that great hush,
Talked with His angels in each burning bush!

NEARER HOME

ONE sweetly solemn thought
    Comes to me o'er and o'er:
I am nearer home to-day
    Than I ever have been before;

Nearer my Father's house,
  Where the many mansions be;
Nearer the great white throne,
  Nearer the crystal sea;

Nearer the bound of life,
  Where we lay our burdens down;
Nearer leaving the cross,
  Nearer gaining the crown!

But lying darkly between,
  Winding down through the night,
Is the silent, unknown stream,
  That leads at last to the light.

Closer and closer my steps
  Come to the dread abysm:
Closer Death to my lips
  Presses the awful chrism.

Oh, if my mortal feet
  Have almost gained the brink;
If it be I am nearer home
  Even to-day than I think;

Father, perfect my trust;
  Let my spirit feel in death,
That her feet are firmly set
  On the rock of a living faith!

Adeline D. Train Whitney

BEHIND THE MASK

IT was an old distorted face,
  An uncouth visage rough and wild,
Yet from behind with laughing grace
  Peep'd the fresh beauty of a child.

And so, contrasting strange to-day,
  My heart of youth doth inly ask
If half earth's wrinkled grimness may
  Be but the baby in the mask.

Behind gray hairs and furrow'd brow
  And wither'd look that life puts on,
Each, as he wears it, comes to know
  How the child hides, and is not gone.

For while the inexorable years
  To sadden'd features fix their mold,
Beneath the work of time and tears
  Waits something that will not grow old.

The rifted pine upon the hill,
  Scarr'd by the lightning and the wind,
Through bolt and blight doth nurture still
  Young fibres underneath the rind.

And many a storm-blast, fiercely sent,
  And wasted hope, and sinful stain,
Roughen the strange integument
  The struggling soul must wear in pain.

Yet, when she comes to claim her own,
  Heaven's angels haply shall not ask
For that last look the world hath known,—
  But for the face behind the mask.

KYRIE ELEISON

IN His glory! When the spheres
  Lighten with that wondrous blaze,
How shall all my sins and fears
  Meet thy dawning, Day of days?

'Nothing hid!' No thought so mean
  That to darkness it may creep;
Very darkness shall be seen,
  Very death to life shall leap.

Nothing deep, or far, or old;
  Nothing left in years behind;
All the secret self unrolled:
  Light of God! I would be blind!

Only I shall see a Face
　In the glory lifted up ;
And a Hand,—the Hand of grace,
　Whose sweet mercy held the Cup.

And a Voice, I think, will speak,
　Asking of each sin-defiled
Whom His saving came to seek,
　As a mother asks her child :

' Wert thou sorry ? ' ' Yea, dear Christ,
　Sick and sorry I have been,
Wearily Thy ways have missed :
　Wash my feet, and lead me in !

' Though in this clear light of Thine
　Sin and sore must stand revealed,
Though no stainless health be mine,
　Count me, Lord, among the healed.

' Not with Scribe and Pharisee
　Dare I crave an upmost seat ;
Only, Saviour, suffer me
　With the sinners at Thy feet ! '

SUNLIGHT AND STARLIGHT

GOD sets some souls in shade, alone ;
　They have no daylight of their own :
Only in lives of happier ones
They see the shine of distant suns.

God knows. Content thee with thy night ;
The greater heaven hath grander light.
To-day is close ; the hours are small ;
Thou sitt'st afar, and hast them all.

Lose the less joy that doth but blind ;
Reach forth a larger bliss to find.
To-day is brief : the inclusive spheres
Rain raptures of a thousand years.

RELEASED

A LITTLE, low-ceiled room. Four walls
    Whose blank shut out all else of life,
And crowded close within their bound
    A world of pain, and toil, and strife.

Her world. Scarce furthermore she knew
    Of God's great globe that wondrously
Outrolls a glory of green earth,
    And frames it with the restless sea.

Four closer walls of common pine;
    And therein lying, cold and still,
The weary flesh that long hath borne
    Its patient mystery of ill.

Regardless now of work to do,
    No queen more careless in her state,
Hands crossed in an unbroken calm;
    For other hands the work may wait.

Put by her implements of toil;
    Put by each coarse, intrusive sign;
She made a sabbath when she died,
    And round her breathes a rest divine.

Put by, at last, beneath the lid,
    The exempted hands, the tranquil face;
Uplift her in her dreamless sleep,
    And bear her gently from the place.

Oft she hath gazed, with wistful eyes,
    Out from that threshold on the night;
The narrow bourn she crosseth now;
    She standeth in the eternal light.

Oft she hath pressed, with aching feet,
    Those broken steps that reach the door;
Henceforth, with angels, she shall tread
    Heaven's golden stair, for evermore!

Lucy Larcom

OUR CHRIST

IN Christ I feel the heart of God
　　Throbbing from heaven through earth;
Life stirs again within the clod,
　　Renewed in beauteous birth;
The soul springs up, a flower of prayer,
Breathing His breath out on the air.

In Christ I touch the hand of God,
　　From His pure height reached down,
By blessed ways before untrod,
　　To lift us to our crown;
Victory that only perfect is
Through loving sacrifice, like His.

Holding His hand, my steadied feet
　　May walk the air, the seas;
On life and death His smile falls sweet,
　　Lights up all mysteries:
Stranger nor exile can I be
In new worlds where He leadeth me.

Not my Christ only; He is ours;
　　Humanity's close bond;
Key to its vast, unopened powers,
　　Dream of our dreams beyond.
What yet we shall be none can tell:
Now are we His, and all is well.

HINTS

THEY whose hearts are whole and strong,
　　Loving holiness,
Living clean from soil of wrong,
　　Wearing truth's white dress,—
They unto no far-off height
　　Wearily need climb;
Heaven to them is close in sight
　　From these shores of time.

Only the anointed eye
      Sees in common things,—
Gleam of wave, and tint of sky,—
      Heavenly blossomings.
To the hearts where light has birth
      Nothing can be drear;
Budding through the bloom of earth,
      Heaven is always near.

THE PROOF

IMPOSSIBLE,—the eagle's flight!
      A body lift itself in air?
Yet see, he soars away from sight!—
      Can mortals with the immortal share?
To argue it were wordy strife;
Life only is the proof of life.

Duration, circumstances, things,—
      These measure not the eternal state:
Ah, cease from thy vain questionings
      Whether an after-life await!
Rise thou from self to God, and see
That immortality must be!

IMMORTAL

INTO the heaven of Thy heart, O God,
      I lift up my life, like a flower;
Thy light is deep, and Thy love is broad,
      And I am not the child of an hour.

As a little blossom is fed from the whole
      Vast depth of unfathomed air,
Through every fibre of thought my soul
      Reaches forth, in Thyself to share.

I dare to say unto Thee, my God,
      Who hast made me to climb so high,
That I shall not crumble away with the clod:
      I am Thine, and I cannot die!

The throb of Thy infinite life I feel
  In every beat of my heart ;
Upon me hast Thou set eternity's seal ;
  Forever alive, as Thou art.

I know not Thy mystery, O my God,
  Nor yet what my own life means,
That feels after Thee, through the mould and the sod,
  And the darkness that intervenes.

But I know that I live, since I hate the wrong,
  The glory of truth can see ;
Can cling to the right with a purpose strong,
  Can love and can will with Thee.

GROWING OLD

OLD,—we are growing old :
    Going on through a beautiful road,
Finding earth a more blessed abode ;
Nobler work by our hearts to be wrought,
Freer paths for our hope and our thought :
Because of the beauty the years unfold,
  We are cheerfully growing old !

  Old,—we are growing old :
Going up where the sunshine is clear ;
Watching grander horizons appear
Out of clouds that enveloped our youth ;
Standing firm on the mountains of truth :
Because of the glory the years unfold,
  We are joyfully growing old.

  Old,—we are growing old :
Going in to the gardens of rest
That glow through the gold of the west,
Where the rose and the amaranth blend,
And each path is the way to a friend :
Because of the peace that the years unfold,
  We are thankfully growing old.

Old,—are we growing old?
Life blooms as we travel on
Up the hills, into fresh, lovely dawn:
We are children, who do but begin
The sweetness of living to win:
Because heaven is in us, to bud and unfold,
     We are younger, for growing old!

EASTER DAWN

BREAKS the joyful Easter dawn,
     Clearer yet, and stronger;
Winter from the world has gone,
     Death shall be no longer!
Far away good angels drive
     Night and sin and sadness;
Earth awakes in smiles, alive
     With her dear Lord's gladness.

Roused by Him from dreary hours
     Under snowdrifts chilly,—
In His hand He brings the flowers,
     Brings the rose and lily.
Every little buried bud
     Into life He raises;
Every wild-flower of the wood
     Chants the dear Lord's praises.

Open, happy flowers of spring,
     For the Sun has risen!
Through the sky glad voices ring,
     Calling you from prison.
Little children dear, look up!
     Toward His brightness pressing,
Lift up every heart, a cup
     For the dear Lord's blessing.

ACROSS THE RIVER

WHEN for me the silent oar
     Parts the Silent River,
And I stand upon the shore
     Of the strange Forever,
Shall I miss the loved and known?
Shall I vainly seek mine own?

Mid the crowd that come to meet
    Spirits sin-forgiven,—
Listening to their echoing feet
    Down the streets of heaven,—
Shall I know a footstep near
That I listen, wait for here?

Then will one approach the brink
    With a hand extended,
One whose thoughts I loved to think
    Ere the veil was rended;
Saying, 'Welcome! we have died,
And again are side by side'?

Saying, 'I will go with thee,
    That thou be not lonely,
To yon hills of mystery:
    I have waited only
Until now, to climb with thee
Yonder hills of mystery.'

Can the bonds that make us here
    Know ourselves immortal,
Drop away, like foliage sear,
    At life's inner portal?
What is holiest below
Must forever live and grow.

I shall love the angels well,
    After I have found them
In the mansions where they dwell,
    With the glory round them:
But at first, without surprise,
Let me look in human eyes.

Step by step our feet must go
    Up the holy mountain;
Drop by drop within us flow
    Life's unfailing fountain.
Angels sing with crowns that burn:
We shall have our song to learn.

He who on our earthly path
 Bids us help each other---
Who His Well-beloved hath
 Made our Elder Brother—
Will but clasp the chain of love
Closer, when we meet above.

Therefore dread I not to go
 O'er the Silent River.
Death, thy hastening oar I know;
 Bear me, thou Life-giver,
Through the waters, to the shore,
Where mine own have gone before!

Richard Henry Stoddard

OUT OF THE DEEPS OF HEAVEN

OUT of the deeps of heaven
 A bird has flown to my door,
As twice in the ripening summers
 Its mates have flown before.

Why it has flown to my dwelling
 Nor it nor I may know,
And only the silent angels
 Can tell when it shall go.

That it will not straightway vanish,
 But fold its wings with me,
And sing in the greenest branches
 Till the axe is laid to the tree,

Is the prayer of my love and terror,
 For my soul is sore distrest,
Lest I wake some dreadful morning,
 And find but its empty nest!

ADSUM *

I

THE Angel came by night,
   (Such angels still come down,)
And like a winter cloud
   Passed over London town ;
Along its lonesome streets,
   Where want had ceased to weep,
Until it reached a house
   Where a great man lay asleep ;
The man of all his time
   Who knew the most of men,
The soundest head and heart,
   The sharpest, kindest pen.
It paused beside his bed,
   And whispered in his ear ;
He never turned his head,
   But answered, 'I am here.'

II

Into the night they went ;
   At morning, side by side,
They gained the sacred Place
   Where the greatest Dead abide.
Where grand old Homer sits
   In godlike state benign ;
Where broods in endless thought
   The awful Florentine ;
Where sweet Cervantes walks,
   A smile on his grave face ;
Where gossips quaint Montaigne,
   The wisest of his race ;
Where Goethe looks through all
   With that calm eye of his,
Where—little seen but Light—
   The only Shakespeare is !
When that new Spirit came,
   They asked him, drawing near,
'Art thou become like us?'
   He answered, 'I am here.'

* See note.

Bayard Taylor

PRAISE

THOU who sendest sun and rain,
   Thou who spendest bliss and pain,
Good with bounteous hand bestowing,
Evil, for Thy will allowing,—
Though Thy ways we cannot see,
All is just that comes from Thee.

In the peace of hearts at rest,
In the child at mother's breast,
In the lives that now surround us,
In the deaths that sorely wound us,
Though we may not understand,
Father, we behold Thy hand!

Hear the happy hymn we raise;
Take the love which is Thy praise;
Give content in each condition;
Bend our hearts in sweet submission,
And Thy trusting children prove
Worthy of the Father's love.

A PRAYER

GOD, to whom we look up blindly,
   Look Thou down upon us kindly:
We have sinned, but not designedly.

If our faith in Thee was shaken,
Pardon Thou our hearts mistaken,
Our obedience re-awaken.

We are sinful, Thou art holy:
Thou art mighty, we are lowly:
Let us reach Thee, climbing slowly.

Our ingratitude confessing,
On Thy mercy still transgressing,
Thou dost punish us with blessing.

WAIT*

NOT so in haste, my heart!
   Have faith in God and wait;
Although He linger long,
   He never comes too late.

He never comes too late,
   He knoweth what is best;
Vex not thyself in vain:
   Until He cometh, rest.

Until He cometh, rest,
   Nor grudge the hours that roll;
The feet that wait for God
   Are soonest at the goal;

Are soonest at the goal
   That is not gained by speed;
Then hold thee still, my heart,
   For I shall wait His lead.

Julia C. R. Dorr

SOMEWHERE

HOW can I cease to pray for thee? Somewhere
   In God's great universe thou art to-day;
Can He not reach thee with His tender care?
   Can He not hear me when for thee I pray?

What matters it to Him who holds within
   The hollow of His hand all worlds, all space,
That thou art done with earthly pain and sin?
   Somewhere within His ken thou hast a place.

Somewhere thou livest and hast need of Him:
   Somewhere thy soul sees higher heights to climb;
And somewhere still there may be valleys dim,
   That thou must pass to reach the hills sublime.

* See note.

M 2

Then all the more, because thou canst not hear
　　Poor human words of blessing, will I pray,
O true, brave heart! God bless thee, wheresoe'er
　　In His great universe thou art to-day!

THE BLIND BIRD'S NEST

The nest of the blind bird is built by God.—Turkish Proverb.

THOU who dost build the blind bird's nest,
　　Am I not blind?
Each bird that flieth east or west
　　The track can find.

Each bird that flies from north to south
　　Knows the far way;
From mountain's crest to river's mouth
　　It does not stray.

Not one in all the lengthening land,
　　In all the sky,
Or by the ocean's silver strand,
　　Is blind as I!

And dost Thou build the blind bird's nest?
　　Build Thou for me
Some shelter where my soul may rest
　　Secure in Thee.

Close clinging to the bending bough,
　　Bind it so fast
It shall not loose, if high or low
　　Blows the loud blast.

If fierce storms break, and the wild rain
　　Comes pelting in,
Cover the shrinking nest, restrain
　　The furious din.

At sultry noontide, when the air
　　Trembles with heat,
Draw close the leafy covert where
　　Cool shadows meet.

And when night falleth, dark and chill,
    Let one fair star,
Love's star all luminous and still,
    Shine from afar.

Thou who dost build the blind bird's nest,
    Build Thou for me;
So shall my being find its rest
    For evermore in Thee.

MARTHA

YEA, Lord!—Yet some must serve.
    Not all with tranquil heart,
Even at Thy dear feet,
Wrapped in devotion sweet,
    May sit apart!

Yea, Lord!—Yet some must bear
    The burden of the day,
Its labor and its heat,
While others at Thy feet
    May muse and pray!

Yea, Lord!—Yet some must do
    Life's daily task-work; some
Who fain would sing must toil
Amid earth's dust and moil,
    While lips are dumb!

Yea, Lord!—Yet man must earn;
    And woman bake the bread!
And some must watch and wake
Early, for others' sake,
    Who pray instead!

Yea, Lord!—Yet even Thou
    Hast need of earthly care,
I bring the bread and wine
To Thee, O Guest Divine!
    Be this my prayer!

QUIETNESS

I WOULD be quiet, Lord,
  Nor tease, nor fret;
Not one small need of mine
  Wilt Thou forget.

I am not wise to know
  What most I need;
I dare not cry too loud,
  Lest Thou shouldst heed;

Lest Thou at length shouldst say,
  'Child, have thy will;
As thou hast chosen, lo!
  Thy cup I fill!'

What I most crave, perchance
  Thou wilt withhold;
As we from hands unmeet
  Keep pearls, or gold;

As we, wnen childish hands
  Would play with fire,
Withhold the burning goal
  Of their desire.

Yet choose Thou for me—Thou
  Who knowest best;
This one short prayer of mine
  Holds all the rest!

Horatio Nelson Powers

FIREFLIES

ON the warm and perfumed dark
  Glows the firefly's tender spark.
Copse, and dell, and lonesome plain
Catch the drops of lambent rain.
Scattered swarms are snarled among
Boughs where thrushes brood their young.
Little cups of daisies hold
Tapers that illume their gold.

See! they light their floating lamps
Where the katydid encamps,
Glint the ripples, soft and cool,
On the grassy-cinctured pool,
Poise where blood-red roses burn
And rills creep under drooping fern,
Weave inconstant spangles through
Vines that drip with fragrant dew,
And mid clumps of dusky pine
In the mournful silence shine.
They cling to tufts of the morass:
The meadow lilies feel them pass;
They deck the turf about the feet
Of lovers hid in shadows sweet,
And round the musing poet gleam
Like scintillations of his dream.

O wingèd spark! effulgent mite!
Live atom of the Infinite!
Thou doest what for thee is done,
In thy place faithful as the sun;
Love's highest law compels thy heart;
All that thou hast thou dost impart;
Thy life is lighted at its core —
Sages and saints achieve no more.

MY WALK TO CHURCH

(From HARPER'S MAGAZINE. *Copyright* 1888 *by* HARPER & BROTHERS)

BREATHING the summer-scented air
    Along the bowery mountain way,
Each Lord's day morning I repair
    To serve my church, a mile away.

Below, the glorious river lies —
    A bright, broad-breasted, sylvan sea—
And round the sumptuous highlands rise,
    Fair as the hills of Galilee.

Young flowers are in my path. I hear
    Music of unrecorded tone:
The heart of Beauty beats so near,
    Its pulses modulate my own.

†

The shadow on the meadow's breast
  Is not more calm than my repose
As, step by step, I am the guest
  Of every living thing that grows.

Ah, something melts along the sky,
  And something rises from the ground,
And fills the inner ear and eye
  Beyond the sense of sight and sound.

It is not that I strive to see
  What Love in lovely shapes has wrought,—
Its gracious messages to me
  Come, like the gentle dews, unsought.

I merely walk with open heart
  Which feels the secret in the sign:
But, oh, how large and rich my part
  In all that makes the feast divine!

Sometimes I hear the happy birds
  That sang to Christ beyond the sea,
And softly His consoling words
  Blend with their joyous minstrelsy.

Sometimes in royal vesture glow
  The lilies that He called so fair,
Which never toil nor spin, yet show
  The loving Father's tender care.

And then along the fragrant hills
  A radiant presence seems to move,
And earth grows fairer, as it fills
  The very air I breathe with love.

And now I see one perfect Face,
  And hastening to my church's door,
Find Him within the holy place
  Who, all my way, went on before.

John Townsend Trowbridge

BEYOND

FROM her own fair dominions
    Long since, with shorn pinions,
      My spirit was banished:
But above her still hover, in vigils and dreams,
Ethereal visitants, voices, and gleams,
      That for ever remind her
      Of something behind her
        Long vanished.

Through the listening night,
    With mysterious flight,
      Pass those winged intimations;
Like stars shot from heaven, their still voices fall to me;
Far and departing, they signal and call to me,
      Strangely beseeching me,
      Chiding, yet teaching me
        Patience.

Then at times, oh! at times,
    To their luminous climes
      I pursue as a swallow!
To the river of Peace, and its solacing shades,
To the haunts of my lost ones in heavenly glades,
      With strong aspirations
      Their pinions' vibrations
        I follow.

O heart! be thou patient!
    Though here I am stationed
      A season in durance,
The chain of the world I will cheerfully wear;
For, spanning my soul like a rainbow, I bear
      With the yoke of my lowly
      Condition, a holy
        Assurance,—

That never in vain
Does the spirit maintain
Her eternal allegiance:
Though suffering and yearning, like Infancy learning
Its lesson, we linger; then skyward returning,
On plumes fully grown
We depart to our own
Native regions!

MIDSUMMER

AROUND this lovely valley rise
The purple hills of Paradise.

Oh, softly on yon banks of haze
Her rosy face the Summer lays!

Becalmed along the azure sky,
The argosies of cloud-land lie,
Whose shores, with many a shining rift,
Far off their pearl-white peaks uplift.

Through all the long midsummer day
The meadow sides are sweet with hay.
I seek the coolest sheltered seat
Just where the field and forest meet,
Where grow the pine trees tall and bland,
The ancient oaks austere and grand,
And fringy roots and pebbles fret
The ripples of the rivulet.

I watch the mowers as they go
Through the tall grass, a white-sleeved row;
With even stroke their scythes they swing,
In tune their merry whetstones ring;
Behind the nimble youngsters run
And toss the thick swaths in the sun;
The cattle graze; while, warm and still,
Slopes the broad pasture, basks the hill,
And bright, when summer breezes break,
The green wheat crinkles like a lake.

The butterfly and humble-bee
Come to the pleasant woods with me;
Quickly before me runs the quail,
The chickens skulk behind the rail,
High up the lone wood-pigeon sits,
And the wood-pecker pecks and flits.
Sweet woodland music sinks and swells,
The brooklet rings its tinkling bells,
The swarming insects drone and hum,
The partridge beats his throbbing drum.
The squirrel leaps among the boughs,
And chatters in his leafy house.
The oriole flashes by; and, look!
Into the mirror of the brook,
Where the vain bluebird trims his coat,
Two tiny feathers fall and float.

As silently, as tenderly,
The down of peace descends on me.
Oh, this is peace! I have no need
Of friend to talk, of book to read:
A dear Companion here abides;
Close to my thrilling heart He hides;
The holy silence is His voice:
I lie and listen and rejoice.

AT SEA

THE night is made for cooling shade,
    For silence, and for sleep;
And when I was a child I laid
My hands upon my breast and prayed,
    And sank to slumbers deep:
Childlike as then, I lie to-night,
And watch my lonely cabin light.

Each movement of the swaying lamp
    Shows how the vessel reels:
As o'er her deck the billows tramp,
And all her timbers strain and cramp,
    With every shock she feels,
It starts and shudders, while it burns,
And in its hingèd socket turns.

Now swinging slow, and slanting low,
  It almost level lies;
And yet I know, while to and fro
I watch the seeming pendule go
  With restless fall and rise,
The steady shaft is still upright,
Poising its little globe of light.

O hand of God! O Lamp of Peace!
  O Promise of my soul!—
Though weak and tossed, and ill at ease,
Amid the roar of smiting seas,
  The ship's convulsive roll,
I own, with love and tender awe,
Yon perfect type of faith and law!

A heavenly trust my spirit calms,
  My soul is filled with light;
The ocean sings his solemn psalms,
The wild winds chant: I cross my palms,
  Happy as if, to-night,
Under the cottage roof, again
I heard the soothing summer rain.

Rose Terry Cooke

A THANKSGIVING

I BRING my hymn of thankfulness
  To Thee, dear Lord, to-day;
Though not for joys Thy name I bless,
  And not for gifts I pray.
The griefs that know not man's redress
  Before Thy feet I lay.

Master! I thank Thee for the sin
  That taught mine eyes to see
What depths of loving lie within
  The heart that broke for me;
What patience human want can win
  From God's divinity.

I thank Thee for the blank despair,
    When friend and love forsake,
That taught me how Thy cross to bear,
    Who bore it for my sake,
And showed my lonely soul a prayer
    That from Thy lips I take.

I thank Thee for the life of grief
    I share with all below,
Wherein I learn the sure relief
    My brother's heart to know,
And in the wisdom taught of pain
    To soothe and share his woe.

I thank Thee for the languid years
    Of loneliness and pain,
When flesh and spirit sowed in tears,
    But scattered not in vain ;
For trust in God and faith in man
    Sprang up beneath the rain.

I thank Thee for my vain desires,
    That no fulfilment knew ;
For life's consuming, cleansing fires,
    That searched me through and through,
Till I could say to Him : ' Forgive !
    They know not what they do.'

What fulness of my earthly store,
    What shine of harvest sun,
What ointment on Thy feet to pour,
    What honored race to run,
What joyful song of thankfulness,
    Here ended or begun,
Shall mate with mine, who learn so late
    To know Thy will is done?

REST

*Oh! spare me, that I may recover strength before I go hence
and be no more.*—Ps. xxxix. 13.

FOLD up thy hands, my weary soul,
    Sit down beside the way !
Thou hast at last a time to rest,
    At last a holiday.

Thy lingering life of weariness,
  Thy time of toil and tears,
A little space may grant thee grace
  To overcome thy fears—

A bright access of patient peace,
  Not rapture, nor delight;
But even as sounds of labor cease
  Before the hush of night;

Or as the storm that all day long
  Has wailed, and raged, and wept,
Nor ceased its force nor changed its course,
  While slow the daylight crept;

But suddenly, before the sun
  Drops down behind the hills,
A clear, calm shining parts the cloud
  And all the ether fills;

Or as the sweet and steadfast shore
  To them that sail the sea;
Or home to them that ply the oar,
  Or leave captivity.

Like any child that cries itself
  On mother's breast to sleep,
Lord, let me lie a little while,
  Till slumber groweth deep;

So deep that neither love nor life
  Shall stir its calm repose—
Beyond the stress of mortal strife,
  The strain of mortal woes.

Spare me this hour to sleep, before
  Thy sleepless bliss is given;
Give me a day of rest on earth,
  Before the work of heaven!

Ellen Clementine Howarth

THE PASSION FLOWER

I PLUCKED it in an idle hour,
  And placed it in my book of prayer,
'Tis not the only passion flower
  That hath been crushed and hidden there.
And now through floods of burning tears
  My withered bloom once more I see,
And I lament the long, long years,
  The wasted years, afar from Thee.

My flower is emblem of the bright
  'First fervor' that my spirit knew,
A dream of beauty, joy and light—
  Now pale and dead it meets my view.
What is there left of dream or flower
  But ashes? Take, I pray, from me,
All my vain thoughts of fame and power,
  And draw my spirit nearer Thee.

Charles Gordon Ames

UNDER THE CLOUD

O BEAUTEOUS things of earth!
  I cannot feel your worth
      To-day.

O kind and constant friend!
Our spirits cannot blend
      To-day.

O Lord of truth and grace!
I cannot see Thy face
      To-day.

A shadow on my heart
Keeps me from all apart
      To-day.

Yet something in me knows
How fair creation glows
  To-day.

And something makes me sure
That love is not less pure
  To-day.

And that th' Eternal Good
Minds nothing of my mood
  To-day.

For when the sun grows dark
A sacred, secret spark
  Shoots rays.

Fed from a hidden bowl
A Lamp burns in my soul
  All days.

ATHANASIA

THE ship may sink,
 And I may drink
A hasty death in the bitter sea;
  But all that I leave
  In the ocean-grave
Can be slipped and spared, and no loss to me.

  What care I,
  Though falls the sky,
And the shrivelling earth to a cinder turn?
  No fires of doom
  Can ever consume
What never was made nor meant to burn.

  Let go the breath,
  There is no death
To the living soul, nor loss, nor harm.
  Not of the clod
  Is the life of God;
Let it mount, as it will, from form to form.

HIDDEN LIFE

SINCE Eden, it keeps the secret!
    Not a flower beside it knows
To distil from the day the fragrance
    And beauty that flood the rose.

Silently speeds the secret
    From the loving eye of the sun
To the willing heart of the flower:
    The life of the twain is one.

Folded within my being,
    A wonder to me is taught,
Too deep for curious seeing
    Or fathom of sounding thought,

Of all sweet mysteries holiest!
    Faded are rose and sun!
The Highest hides in the lowliest;
    My Father and I are one.

UNSEEN

HOW do the rivulets find their way?
    How do the flowers know the day,
And open their cups to catch the ray?

I see the germ to the sunlight reach,
And the nestlings know the old bird's speech;
I do not see who is there to teach.

I see the hare from the danger hide,
And the stars through the pathless spaces ride;
I do not see that they have a guide.

He is Eyes for All who is eyes for the mole;
All motion goes to the rightful goal;
O God! I can trust for the human soul.

Albert Laighton

TO MY SOUL

GUEST from a holier world,
    Oh, tell me where the peaceful valleys lie!
Down in the ark of life, when thou shalt fly,
    Where will thy wings be furled?

Where is thy native nest?
Where the green pastures that the blessed roam?
Impatient dweller in thy clay-built home,
    Where is thy heavenly rest?

On some immortal shore,
Some realm away from earth and time, I know;
A land of bloom, where living waters flow,
    And grief comes nevermore.

Faith turns my eyes above;
Day fills with floods of light the boundless skies;
Night watches calmly with her starry eyes
    All tremulous with love.

And, as entranced I gaze,
Sweet music floats to me from distant lyres:
I see a temple, round whose golden spires
    Unearthly glory plays!

Beyond those azure deeps
I fix thy home,—a mansion kept for thee
Within the Father's house, whose noiseless key
    Kind Death, the warder, keeps!

Martha Perry Lowe

HONOR ALL MEN

GREAT Master! teach us how to hope in man:
    We lift our eyes upon his works and ways,
And disappointment chills us as we gaze,
Our dream of him so far the truth outran,
So far his deeds are ever falling short.

And then we fold our graceful hands, and say,
  'The world is vulgar.' Didst Thou turn away,
O Sacred Spirit, delicately wrought!
Because the humble souls of Galilee
  Were tuned not to the music of Thine own,
  And chimed not to the pulsing undertone
Which swelled Thy loving bosom like a sea?
Shame Thou our coldness, most Benignant Friend,
  When we so daintily do condescend.

WORK

LORD, send us forth among Thy fields to work!
  Shall we for words and names contending be,
  Or lift our garments from the dust we see,
And all the noonday heat and burden shirk?
The fields are white for harvest, shall we stay
  To find a bed of roses for the night,
  And watch the far-off cloud that comes to sight,
Lest it should burst in showers upon our way?
Fling off, my soul, thy grasping self, and view
  With generous ardor all thy brothers' need;
  Fling off thy thoughts of golden ease, and weed
A corner of thy Master's vineyard too.
  The harvest of the world is great indeed,
O Jesus! and the laborers are few.

Emily Dickinson

THE CHARIOT

BECAUSE I could not stop for Death,
  He kindly stopped for me;
The carriage held but just ourselves
  And Immortality.

We slowly drove, he knew no haste,
  And I had put away
My labor, and my leisure too,
  For his civility.

We passed the school where children played,
  Their lessons scarcely done ;
We passed the fields of gazing grain,
  We passed the setting sun.

We paused before a house that seemed
  A swelling of the ground ;
The roof was scarcely visible,
  The cornice but a mound.

Since then 'tis centuries, but each
  Feels shorter than the day
I first surmised the horses' heads
  Were toward eternity.

CERTAINTY

I NEVER saw a moor,
    I never saw the sea ;
Yet know I how the heather looks,
  And what a wave must be.

I never spoke with God,
  Nor visited in heaven ;
Yet certain am I of the spot
  As if the chart were given.

A DIALOGUE

DEATH is a dialogue between
    The spirit and the dust ;
' Dissolve,' says Death. The spirit, ' Sir,
  I have another trust.'

Death doubts it, argues from the ground ;
  The spirit turns away,
Just laying off, for evidence,
  An overcoat of clay.

SETTING SAIL

EXULTATION is the going
    Of an inland soul to sea,—
Past the houses, past the headlands,
    Into deep eternity!

Bred as we, among the mountains,
    Can the sailor understand
The divine intoxication
    Of the first league out from land?

AFTER DEATH

THE bustle in a house
    The morning after death
Is solemnest of industries
    Enacted upon earth,—

The sweeping up the hearth,
    And putting love away
We shall not want to use again
    Until eternity.

NEEDLESS FEAR

AFRAID? Of whom am I afraid?
    Not Death; for who is he?
The porter of my father's lodge
    As much abasheth me.

Of life? 'Twere odd I fear a thing
    That comprehendeth me
In one or more existences
    At Deity's decree.

Of resurrection? Is the east
    Afraid to trust the morn
With her fastidious forehead?
    As soon impeach my crown!

NOT IN VAIN

IF I can stop one heart from breaking,
    I shall not live in vain;
If I can ease one life the aching,
    Or cool one pain,
Or help one fainting robin
    Unto his nest again,
I shall not live in vain.

TIME

LOOK back on Time with kindly eyes,
    He doubtless did his best;
How softly sinks his trembling sun
    In human nature's west.

THE BATTLE-FIELD

THEY dropped like flakes, they dropped like stars,
    Like petals from a rose,
When suddenly across the June
    A wind with fingers goes.

They perished in the seamless grass,—
    No eye could find the place;
But God on His repealless list
    Can summon every face.

VANISHED

SHE died,—this was the way she died;
    And when her breath was done,
Took up her simple wardrobe
    And started for the sun.

Her little figure at the gate
    The angels must have spied,
Since I could never find her
    Upon the mortal side.

PRAYER

AT least to pray is left, is left.
O Jesus! in the air
I know not which Thy chamber is,—
I'm knocking everywhere.

Thou stirrest earthquake in the south,
And maelstrom in the sea;
Say, Jesus Christ of Nazareth,
Hast Thou no arm for me?

THE FOLD

LET down the bars, O Death!
The tired flocks come in
Whose bleating ceases to repeat,
Whose wandering is done.

Thine is the stillest night,
Thine the securest fold;
Too near thou art for seeking thee,
Too tender to be told.

THE MARTYRS

THROUGH the straight pass of suffering
The martyrs ever trod,
Their feet upon temptation,
Their faces upon God.

A stately shriven company,
Convulsion playing round,
Harmless as streaks of meteor
Upon a planet's bound.

Their faith the everlasting troth;
Their expectation fair;
The needle to the north degree
Wades so, through polar air.

Elizabeth Lloyd Howell

MILTON'S PRAYER OF PATIENCE

I AM old and blind!
　　Men point at me as smitten by God's
　　　　frown;
Afflicted and deserted of my kind,
　　Yet am I not cast down.

I am weak, yet strong;
I murmur not that I no longer see;
Poor, old, and helpless, I the more belong,
　　Father supreme! to Thee.

All-merciful One!
When men are furthest, then art Thou most near;
When friends pass by, my weaknesses to shun,
　　Thy chariot I hear.

Thy glorious face
Is leaning toward me; and its holy light
Shines in upon my lonely dwelling-place,
　　And there is no more night.

On my bended knee
I recognize Thy purpose clearly shown:
My vision Thou hast dimmed, that I may see
　　Thyself,—Thyself alone.

I have naught to fear;
This darkness is the shadow of Thy wing;
Beneath it I am almost sacred; here
　　Can come no evil thing.

Oh, I seem to stand
Trembling, where foot of mortal ne'er hath been,
Wrapped in that radiance from the sinless land,
　　Which eye hath never seen!

Visions come and go:
Shapes of resplendent beauty round me throng;
From angel lips I seem to hear the flow
　　Of soft and holy song.

It is nothing now,
When heaven is opening on my sightless eyes
When airs from Paradise refresh my brow,
That earth in darkness lies.

In a purer clime
My being fills with rapture,—waves of thought
Roll in upon my spirit,—strains sublime
Break over me unsought.

Give me now my lyre!
I feel the stirrings of a gift divine:
Within my bosom glows unearthly fire,
Lit by no skill of mine.

Paul Hamilton Hayne

CHRISTIAN EXALTATION

O CHRISTIAN soldier! shouldst thou rue
Life and its toils, as others do,—
Wear a sad frown from day to day,
And garb thy soul in hodden-gray?
Oh! rather shouldst thou smile elate,
Unquelled by sin, unawed by hate,—
Thy lofty-statured spirit dress
In moods of royal stateliness;—
For say, what service so divine
As that, ah! warrior heart, of thine,
High pledged alike through gain or loss,
To thy brave banner of the cross?

Yea! what hast *thou* to do with gloom,
Whose footsteps spurn the conquered tomb?
Thou, that through dreariest dark canst see
A smiling immortality?

Leave to the mournful, doubting slave,
Who deems the whole wan earth a grave,
Across whose dusky mounds forlorn
Can rise no resurrection morn,
The sombre mien, the funeral weed,
That darkly match so dark a creed;

But be *thy* brow turned bright on all,
Thy voice like some clear clarion call,
Pealing o'er life's tumultuous van
The key-note of the hopes of man,
While o'er thee flames through gain, through loss,—
That fadeless symbol of the cross !

THE MASK OF DEATH

IN youth, when blood was warm and fancy high,
   I mocked at Death. How many a quaint conceit
I wove about his veilèd head and feet,
Vaunting aloud, '*Why need we dread to die?*'
But now, enthralled by deep solemnity,
Death's pale, phantasmal shade I darkly greet ;
Ghostlike it haunts the earth, it haunts the street,
Or drearier makes drear midnight's mystery.
Ah, soul-perplexing vision ! oft I deem
That antique myth is true which pictured Death
A masked and hideous form all shrank to see ;
But at the last slow ebb of mortal breath,
Death, his mask melting like a nightmare dream,
Smiled,—heaven's High-Priest of Immortality.

Helen Hunt Jackson

'*NOT AS I WILL*'

BLINDFOLDED and alone I stand,
   With unknown thresholds on each hand ;
The darkness deepens as I grope,
Afraid to fear, afraid to hope :
Yet this one thing I learn to know
Each day more surely as I go,
That doors are opened, ways are made,
Burdens are lifted or are laid,
By some great law unseen and still,
Unfathomed purpose to fulfil,
        ' Not as I will.'

Blindfolded and alone I wait;
Loss seems too bitter, gain too late;
Too heavy burdens in the load
And too few helpers on the road;
And joy is weak and grief is strong,
And years and days so long, so long:
Yet this one thing I learn to know
Each day more surely as I go,
That I am glad the good and ill
By changeless law are ordered still,
  ' Not as I will.'

' Not as I will': the sound grows sweet
Each time my lips the words repeat.
' Not as I will': the darkness feels
More safe than light when this thought steals
Like whispered voice to calm and bless
All unrest and all loneliness.
' Not as I will,' because the One
Who loved us first and best has gone
Before us on the road, and still
For us must all His love fulfil,
  ' Not as we will.'

DOUBT

THEY bade me cast the thing away,
 They pointed to my hands all bleeding,
They listened not to all my pleading;
 The thing I meant I could not say;
 I knew that I should rue the day
If once I cast that thing away.

I grasped it firm, and bore the pain;
 The thorny husks I stripped and scattered;
If I could reach its heart, what mattered
 If other men saw not my gain,
 Or even if I should be slain?
I knew the risks; I chose the pain.

O, had I cast that thing away,
I had not found what most I cherish,
A faith without which I should perish,—
The faith which, like a kernel, lay
Hid in the husks which on that day
My instinct would not throw away!

GLIMPSES

AS when on some great mountain-peak we stand,
  In breathless awe beneath its dome of sky,
Whose multiplied horizons seem to lie
Beyond the bounds of earthly sea and land,
We find the circled space too vast, too grand,
And soothe our thoughts with restful memory
Of sudden sunlit glimpses we passed by
Too quickly, in our feverish demand
To reach the height,—
                    So, darling, when the brink
Of highest heaven we reach at last, I think
Even that great gladness will grow yet more glad,
As we, with eyes that are no longer sad,
Look back, while Life's horizons slowly sink,
To some swift moments which on earth we had.

SPINNING

LIKE a blind spinner in the sun,
  I tread my days;
I know that all the threads will run
      Appointed ways;
I know each day will bring its task,
And, being blind, no more I ask.

I do not know the use or name
    Of that I spin;
I only know that some one came
      And laid within
My hand the thread, and said, 'Since you
Are blind, but one thing you can do.'

Sometimes the threads so rough and fast
    And tangled fly,
I know wild storms are sweeping past,
    And fear that I
Shall fall; but dare not try to find
A safer place, since I am blind.

I know not why, but I am sure
    That tint and place
In some great fabric to endure
    Past time and race
My threads will have; so from the first,
Though blind, I never felt accurst.

I think, perhaps, this trust has sprung
    From one short word
Said over me when I was young,—
    So young, I heard
It, knowing not that God's name signed
My brow, and sealed me His, though blind.

But whether this be seal or sign
    Within, without,
It matters not,—the bond divine
    I never doubt.
I know He set me here, and still,
And glad, and blind, I wait His will.

But listen, listen, day by day,
    To hear their tread
Who bear the finished web away,
    And cut the thread,
And bring God's message in the sun,
'Thou poor, blind spinner, work is done.'

Saxe Holm

THE ANGEL OF PAIN

ANGEL of Pain, I think thy face
    Will be, in all the heavenly place,
The sweetest face that I shall see,
The swiftest face to smile on me.

All other angels faint and tire;
Joy wearies, and forsakes desire;
Hope falters face to face with fate,
And dies because it cannot wait;
And Love cuts short each loving day,
Because fond hearts cannot obey
The subtlest law which measures bliss
By what it is content to miss.

But thou, O loving, faithful Pain—
Hated, reproached, rejected, slain—
Dost only closer cling and bless
In sweeter, stronger steadfastness.
Dear, patient angel, to thine own
Thou comest, and art never known
Till late, in some lone twilight place
The light of thy transfigured face
Sudden shines out, and speechless, they
Know they have walked with Christ all day.

THE LOVE OF GOD

LIKE a cradle, rocking, rocking,
   Silent, peaceful, to and fro,—
Like a mother's sweet looks dropping
   On the little face below,—
Hangs the green earth, swinging, turning,
   Jarless, noiseless, safe and slow;
Falls the light of God's face, bending
   Down and watching us below.

And as feeble babes that suffer,
   Toss and cry, and will not rest,
Are the ones the tender mother
   Holds the closest, loves the best;
So when we are weak and wretched,
   By our sins weighed down, distressed,
Then it is that God's great patience
   Holds us closest, loves us best.

O great Heart of God! whose loving
   Cannot hindered be nor crossed;
Will not weary, will not even
   In our death itself be lost—

Love divine! of such great loving
  Only mothers know the cost,—
Cost of love, which all love passing,
  Gave a Son to save the lost.

A HYMN

I CANNOT think but God must know
  About the thing I long for so;
I know He is so good, so kind,
I cannot think but He will find
Some way to help, some way to show
Me to the thing I long for so.

I stretch my hand,—it lies so near:
It looks so sweet, it looks so dear.
'Dear Lord,' I pray, 'oh, let me know
If it is wrong to want it so.'
He only smiles,—He does not speak;
My heart grows weaker and more weak,
With looking at the thing so dear,
Which lies so far and yet so near.

Now, Lord, I leave at Thy loved feet
This thing which looks so near, so sweet,
I will not seek, I will not long,—
I almost fear I have been wrong.
I'll go and work the harder, Lord,
And wait till by some loud, clear word
Thou callest me to Thy loved feet,
To take this thing, so dear, so sweet.

THE GOSPEL OF MYSTERY

GOOD tidings every day.
  God's messengers ride fast.
We do not hear one half they say,
There is such noise on the highway,
Where we must wait till they ride past.

Their banners blaze and shine
With Jesus Christ's dear name
  And story, how by God's design
  He saves us, in His love divine,
And lifts us from our sin and shame.

Their music fills the air,
Their songs sing all of heaven;
  Their ringing trumpet-peals declare
  What crowns to souls who fight and dare
And win, shall presently be given.

Their hands throw treasures round
Among the multitude.
  No pause, no choice, no count, no bound,
  No questioning how men are found,
If they be evil or be good.

But all the banners bear
Some words we cannot read;
  And mystic echoes in the air,
  Which borrow from the song no share,
In sweetness all the songs exceed.

And of the multitude,
No man but in his hand
  Holds some great gift misunderstood,
  Some treasure, for whose use or good
His ignorance sees no demand.

These are the tokens lent
By immortality;
  Birth-marks of our divine descent;
  Sureties of ultimate intent,
God's gospel of Eternity.

Good tidings every day.
The messengers ride fast.
  Thanks be to God for all they say;
  There is such noise on the highway,
Let us keep still while they ride past.

Louisa May Alcott

TRANSFIGURATION

MYSTERIOUS Death! who in a single hour
　　Life's gold can so refine;
　　　And by thy art divine
Change mortal weakness to immortal power!

Bending beneath the weight of eighty years,
　　Spent with the noble strife
　　　Of a victorious life,
We watched her fading heavenward, through our tears.

But, ere the sense of loss our hearts had wrung,
　　A miracle was wrought,
　　　And swift as happy thought
She lived again, brave, beautiful, and young.

Age, Pain, and Sorrow dropped the veils they wore,
　　And showed the tender eyes
　　　Of angels in disguise,
Whose discipline so patiently she bore.

The past years brought their harvest rich and fair,
　　While Memory and Love
　　　Together fondly wove
A golden garland for the silver hair.

How could we mourn like those who are bereft,
　　When every pang of grief
　　　Found balm for its relief
In counting up the treasure she had left?—

Faith that withstood the shocks of toil and time,
　　Hope that defied despair,
　　　Patience that conquered care,
And loyalty whose courage was sublime;

The great deep heart that was a home for all,
　　Just, eloquent and strong,
　　　In protest against wrong;
Wide charity that knew no sin, no fall;

The Spartan spirit that made life so grand,
      Mating poor daily needs
      With high, heroic deeds,
That wrested happiness from Fate's hard hand.

We thought to weep, but sing for joy instead,
      Full of the grateful peace
      That followed her release;
For nothing but the weary dust lies dead.

Oh noble woman! never more a queen
      Than in the laying down
      Of sceptre and of crown,
To win a greater kingdom yet unseen,

Teaching us how to seek the highest goal,
      To earn the true success;
      To live, to love, to bless,
And make death proud to take a royal soul.

Edmund Clarence Stedman

'THE UNDISCOVERED COUNTRY'

COULD we but know
    The land that ends our dark uncertain
        travel,
Where lie those happier hills and meadows low,—
Ah, if beyond the spirit's inmost cavil,
    Aught of that country could we surely know,
      Who would not go?

Might we but hear
The hovering angels' high imagined chorus,
    Or catch, betimes, with wakeful eyes and clear
One radiant vista of the realm before us,—
    With one rapt moment given to see and hear,
      Ah, who would fear?

Were we quite sure
To find the peerless friend who left us lonely,
Or there, by some celestial stream as pure,
To gaze in eyes that here were love-lit only,—
This weary mortal coil, were we quite sure,
Who would endure?

THE DISCOVERER

I HAVE a little kinsman
    Whose earthly summers are but three,
And yet a voyager is he
Greater than Drake or Frobisher,
Than all their peers together!
He is a brave discoverer,
And, far beyond the tether
Of them who seek the frozen pole,
Has sailed where the noiseless surges roll.
Ay, he has travelled whither
A winged pilot steered his bark
Through the portals of the dark,
Past hoary Mimir's well and tree,
Across the unknown sea.

Suddenly, in his fair young hour,
Came one who bore a flower,
And laid it in his dimpled hand
    With this command:
'Henceforth thou art a rover!
Thou must make a voyage far,
Sail beneath the evening star,
And a wondrous land discover.'
With his sweet smile innocent
Our little kinsman went.

Since that time no word
From the absent has been heard.
    Who can tell
How he fares, or answer well
What the little one has found
Since he left us, outward bound?

O 2

Would that he might return!
Then should we learn
From the pricking of his chart
How the skyey roadways part.
Hush! does not the baby this way bring,
To lay beside this severed curl,
Some starry offering
Of chrysolite or pearl?

Ah, no! not so!
We.may follow on his track,
But he comes not back.
        And yet I dare aver
He is a brave discoverer
Of climes his elders do not know.
He has more learning than appears
On the scroll of twice three thousand years,
More than in the groves is taught,
Or from furthest Indies brought;
He knows, perchance, how spirits fare,—
What shapes the angels wear,
What is their guise and speech
In those lands beyond our reach,—
And his eyes behold
Things that shall never, never be to mortal
        hearers told.

Nancy Priest Wakefield

HEAVEN

THE city's shining towers we may not see
    With our dim earthly vision;
For Death the silent warder, keeps the key
    That opes the gates Elysian.

But sometimes, when adown the western sky
    A fiery sunset lingers,
Its golden 'gates swing inward noiselessly,
    Unlocked by unseen fingers.

And while they stand a moment half ajar,
    Gleams from the inner glory
Stream brightly through the azure vault afar,
    And half reveal the story.

O land unknown! O land of love divine!
    Father, all wise, eternal!
O guide these wandering, way-worn feet of mine
    Into those pastures vernal!

Phillips Brooks

THE CHILD OF BETHLEHEM

O LITTLE town of Bethlehem,
    How still we see thee lie!
Above thy deep and dreamless sleep
    The silent stars go by;
Yet in thy dark streets shineth
    The everlasting light;
The hopes and fears of all the years
    Are met in thee to-night!

For Christ is born of Mary;
    And gathered all above,
While mortals sleep, the angels keep
    Their watch of wondering love.
O morning stars! together
    Proclaim the holy birth,
And praises sing to God the King,
    And peace to men on earth!

How silently, how silently,
    The wondrous gift is given!
So God imparts to human hearts
    The blessings of His heaven.
No ear may hear His coming;
    But in this world of sin,
Where meek souls will receive Him, still
    The dear Christ enters in.

O holy Child of Bethlehem !
    Descend to us, we pray ;
Cast out our sin and enter in—
    Be born in us to-day !
We hear the Christmas angels
    The great glad tidings tell ;
Oh, come to us, abide with us,
    Our Lord Emmanuel !

George Arnold

JUBILATE

GRAY distance hid each shining sail,
    By ruthless breezes borne from me ;
And, lessening, fading, faint and pale,
    My ships went forth to sea.

Where misty breakers rose and fell
    I stood and sorrowed hopelessly ;
For every wave had tales to tell
    Of wrecks far out at sea.

To-day, a song is on my lips :
    Earth seems a paradise to me :
For God is good, and lo, my ships
    Are coming home from sea !

IN THE DARK *

ALL moveless stand the ancient cedar-trees
    Along the drifted sandhills where they grow :
And from the dark west comes a wandering breeze,
    And waves them to and fro.

A murky darkness lies along the sand,
    Where bright the sunbeams of the morning shone,
And the eye vainly seeks by sea and land
    Some light to rest upon.

* See note.

No large pale star its glimmering vigil keeps ;
  An inky sea reflects an inky sky,
And the dark river, like a serpent, creeps
  To where its black piers lie.

Strange salty odors through the darkness steal,
  And, through the dark, the ocean-thunders roll ;
Thick darkness gathers, stifling, till I feel
  Its weight upon my soul.

I stretch my hands out in the empty air ;
  I strain my eyes into the heavy night ;
Blackness of darkness !—Father, hear my prayer !
  Grant me to see the light !

Harriet McEwen Kimball

THE GUEST

*Behold, I stand at the door, and knock ; if any man hear My voice,
and open the door, I will come in to him, and will sup with him ;
and he with Me.*

SPEECHLESS Sorrow sat with me ;
    I was sighing wearily,
Lamp and fire were out : the rain
Wildly beat the window-pane.
In the dark we heard a knock,
And a hand was on the lock ;
One in waiting spake to me,
        Saying sweetly,
' I am come to sup with thee ! '

All my room was dark and damp ;
' Sorrow,' said I, ' trim the lamp ;
Light the fire, and cheer thy face ;
Set the guest-chair in its place.'
And again I heard the knock ;
In the dark I found the lock :—
' Enter ! I have turned the key !
        Enter, Stranger !
Who art come to sup with me.'

Opening wide the door He came,
But I could not speak His name;
In the guest-chair took His place;
But I could not see His face!
When my cheerful fire was beaming,
When my little lamp was gleaming,
And the feast was spread for three,
    Lo! my Master
Was the Guest that supped with me!

THE FEAST-TIME OF THE YEAR

THIS is the feast-time of the year,
  When hearts grow warm and home more dear;
When autumn's crimson torch expires
To flash again in winter fires;
And they who tracked October's flight
Through woods with gorgeous hues bedight,
In charmèd circle sit and praise
The goodly log's triumphant blaze.

This is the feast-time of the year,
When Plenty pours her wine of cheer,
And even humble boards may spare
To poorer poor a kindly share;
While bursting barns and granaries know
A richer, fuller overflow,
And they who dwell in golden ease
Bless without toil, yet toil to please.

This is the feast-time of the year:
The blessed Advent draweth near.
Let rich and poor together break
The bread of love for Christ's sweet sake,
Against the time when rich and poor
Must ope for Him a common door,
Who comes a guest, yet makes a feast,
And bids the greatest and the least.

ALL'S WELL

THE day is ended. Ere I sink to sleep,
  My weary spirit seeks repose in Thine ;
Father, forgive my trespasses, and keep
      This little life of mine.

With loving-kindness curtain Thou my bed,
And cool in rest my burning pilgrim feet ;
Thy pardon be the pillow for my head ;
      So shall my rest be sweet.

At peace with all the world, dear Lord, and Thee,
No fears my soul's unwavering faith can shake ;
All 's well, whichever side the grave for me
      The morning light may break.

John James Piatt

GLOW-WORM AND STAR

A GOLDEN twinkle in the wayside grass,
  See the lone glow-worm, buried deep in dew,
Brightening and lightening the low darkness through,
Close to my feet, that by its covert pass ;
And, in the little pool of recent rain,
O'erhung with tremulous grasses, look, how bright,
Filling the drops along each blade with light,
Yon great white star, some system's quickening brain,
Whose voyage through that still deep is never done,
Makes its small mirror by this gleam of earth !
O soul, with wonders where thy steps have trod,
Which is most wondrous, worm or mirrored sun?
. . . The Mighty One shows in everything one birth ;
The worm's a star as high from thee in God.

A SONG OF CONTENT

THE eagle nestles near the sun;
  The dove's low nest for me!—
The eagle's on the crag: sweet one,
  The dove's in our green tree.
For hearts that beat like thine and mine,
  Heaven blesses humble earth;
The angels of our heaven shall shine
  The angels of our hearth!

TRANSFIGURATION

CRIMSONING the woodlands dumb and hoary,
  Bleak with long November winds and rains,
Lo, at sunset breathes a sudden glory,
  Breaks a fire on all the western panes!

Eastward far I see the restless splendor
  Shine through many a window-lattice bright;
Nearer all the farm-house gables render
  Flame for flame, and meet in breathless light.

Many a mansion, many a cottage lowly,
  Lost in radiance, palpitates the same,
At the torch of beauty strange and holy,
  All transfigured in the evening flame.

Luminous, within, a marvelous vision,—
  Things familiar half-unreal show;
In the effluence of Land Elysian,
  Every bosom feels a holier glow.

Faces lose, as at some wondrous portal,
  Earthly masks, and heavenly features wear;
Many a mother like a saint immortal,
  Folds her child, a haloed angel fair.

Sarah M. B. Piatt

THE GIFT OF TEARS

THE legend says: In Paradise
    God gave the world to man.   Ah me!
The woman lifted up her eyes:
    'Woman I have but tears for thee.'
But tears? And she began to shed,
Thereat, the tears that comforted.

(No other beautiful woman breathed,
    No rival among men had he.
The seraph's sword of fire was sheathed,
    The golden fruit hung on the tree.
Her lord was lord of all the earth,
Wherein no child had wailed its birth.)

'Tears to a bride?' 'Yea, therefore tears.'
    'In Eden?' 'Yea, and tears therefore.'
Ah, bride in Eden, there were fears
    In the first blush your young cheek wore,
Lest that first kiss had been too sweet,
Lest Eden withered from your feet!

Mother of women! Did you see
    How brief your beauty, and how brief,
Therefore, the love of it must be,
    In that first garden, that first grief?
Did those first drops of sorrow fall
To move God's pity for us all?

Oh, sobbing mourner by the dead—
    One watcher at the grave grass-grown!
Oh, sleepless for some darling head
    Cold-pillowed on the prison-stone,
Or wet with drowning seas! He knew,
Who gave the gift of tears to you!

THE ANSWER OF THE GARDENER

HE leant, at sunset, on his spade.
　　(Oh, but the child was sweet to see,
The one who in the orchard played!)
　　He called: 'I've planted you a tree!'

The boy looked at it for a while,
　　Then at the radiant woods below;
And said, with wonder in his smile—
　　'Why don't you put the leaves on, though?'

The gardener, with a reverent air,
　　Lifted his eyes, took off his hat—
'The Other Man, the One up there,'
　　He answered, 'He must see to that.'

FAITH

'YES, God is good, I'm told. You see,
　　I cannot read. But, then,
I can believe. He's good to me,
He is, and good to men.
They say He sends us sorrow, too.
The world would be too sweet
To leave, if this should not be true.'
—('The world the moth can eat.')

'WHEN SAW WE THEE?'

THEN shall He answer how He lifted up,
　　In the cathedral there, at Lille, to me
The same still mouth that drank the Passion-cup,
　　And how I turned away and did not see.

How—oh, that boy's deep eyes and withered arm!
　　In a mad Paris street, one glittering night,
Three times drawn backward by His beauty's charm,
　　I gave Him—not a farthing for the sight.

How, in that shadowy temple at Cologne,
    Through all the mighty music, I did wring
The agony of His last mortal moan
    From that blind soul I gave not anything.

And how at Bruges, at a beggar's breast,
    There by the windmill where the leaves whirled so,
I saw Him nursing, passed Him with the rest,
    Followed by His starved mother's stare of woe.

But, my Lord Christ, Thou knowest I had not much,
    And fain must keep that which I had for grace
To look, forsooth, where some dead painter's touch
    Had left Thy thorn-wound or Thy Mother's face.

Therefore, O my Lord Christ, I pray of Thee
    That of Thy great compassion Thou wilt save,
Laid up from moth and rust, somewhere, for me,
    High in the heavens—the coins I never gave.

A DREAM'S AWAKENING

SHUT in a close and dreary sleep,
    Lonely and frightened and oppressed,
I felt a dreadful serpent creep,
    Writhing and crushing, o'er my breast.

I woke, and knew my child's sweet arm,
    As soft and pure as flakes of snow,
Beneath my dream's dark, hateful charm,
    Had been the thing that tortured so.

And in the morning's dew and light
    I seemed to hear an angel say,
'The pain that stings in time's low night
    May prove God's love in higher day.'

WE TWO

GOD'S will is—the bud of the rose for your hair,
    The ring for your hand and the pearl for your
        breast;
God's will is—the mirror that makes you look fair.
    No wonder you whisper: 'God's will is the best.'

But what if God's will were the famine, the flood?—
    And were God's will the coffin shut down in your
        face?—
And were God's will the worm in the fold of the bud,
    Instead of the picture, the light, and the lace?

Were God's will the arrow that flieth by night,
    Were God's will the pestilence walking by day,
The clod in the valley, the rock on the height—
    I fancy 'God's will' would be harder to say.

God's will is—your own will? What honor have you
    For having your own will, awake or asleep?
Who praises the lily for keeping the dew,
    When the dew is so sweet for the lily to keep?

God's will unto me is not music or wine.
    With helpless reproaching, with desolate tears,
God's will I resist, for God's will is divine;
    And I—shall be dust to the end of my years.

God's will is—not mine. Yet one night I shall lie
    Very still at His feet, where the stars may not shine.
'Lo! I am well pleased,' I shall hear from the sky;
    Because—it is God's will I do, and not mine.

Louise Chandler Moulton

LONG IS THE WAY

LONG is the way, O Lord!
    My steps are weak:
I listen for Thy word,—
    When wilt Thou speak?

Must I still wander on
    'Mid noise and strife;
Or go as Thou hast gone,
    From life to Life?

SOME DAY OR OTHER

SOME day or other I shall surely come
    Where true hearts wait for me ;
Then let me learn the language of that home
    While here on earth I be,
Lest my poor lips for want of words be dumb
    In that High Company.

LOVER AND FRIEND HAST THOU PUT FAR FROM ME

I HEAR the soft September rain intone,
    And cheerful crickets chirping in the grass,—
I bow my head, I, who am all alone ;
    The light winds see, and shiver as they pass.

No other thing is so bereft as I,—
    The rain-drops fall, and mingle as they fall,—
The chirping cricket knows his neighbor nigh,—
    Leaves sway responsive to the light wind's call.

But Friend and Lover Thou hast put afar,
    And left me only Thy great, solemn sky,—
I try to pierce beyond the farthest star
    To search Thee out, and find Thee ere I die ;

Yet dim my vision is, or Thou dost hide
    Thy sacred splendor from my yearning eyes :
Be pitiful, O God, and open wide
    To me, bereft, Thy heavenly Paradise.

Give me one glimpse of that sweet, far-off rest,—
    Then I can bear Earth's solitude again ;
My soul, returning from that heavenly quest,
    Shall smile, triumphant, at each transient pain.

Nor would I vex my heart with grief or strife,
    Though Friend and Lover Thou hast put afar,
If I could see, through my worn tent of Life,
    The steadfast shining of Thy morning star.

SELFISH PRAYER

HOW we, poor players on Life's little stage,
   Thrust blindly at each other in our rage,
Quarrel and fret, and rashly dare to pray
To God to help us on our selfish way.

We think to move Him with our prayer and praise,
To serve our needs; as in the old Greek days
Their gods came down and mingled in the fight
With mightier arms the flying foe to smite.

The laughter of those gods pealed down to men,
For heaven was but earth's upper story then,
Where goddesses about an apple strove,
And the high gods fell humanly in love.

We own a God whose presence fills the sky,—
Whose sleepless eyes behold the worlds roll by;
Shall not His memory number, one by one,
The sons of men, who call them each His son?

QUESTION

DEAR and blessèd dead ones, can you look and
   listen
  To the sighing and the moaning down here below?
Does it make a discord in the hymns of heaven,—
  The discord that jangles in the Life you used to
    know?

When we pray our prayers to the great God above
   you,
  Does the echo of our praying ever glance aside your
    way?
Do you know the thing we ask for, and wish that you
   could give it,
  You, whose hearts ached with wishing in your own
    little day?

Are your ears deaf with praises, you blessed dead of
heaven,
  And your eyes blind with glory, that you cannot see
  our pain ?
If you saw, if you heard, you would weep among the
angels,
  And the praises and the glory would be for you in
  vain.

Yet He listens to our praying, the great God of pity,
  As He fills with pain the measure of our Life's little
  day,—
Could He bear to sit and shine there, on His white
throne in heaven,
  But that He sees the end, while we only see the way ?

AN OPEN DOOR

> *City, of thine a single, simple door*
> *By some new Power reduplicate must be*
> *Even yet my life-porch in eternity.*
> DANTE GABRIEL ROSSETTI.

THAT longed-for door stood open, and he passed
    On through the star-sown fields of light, and stayed
  Before its threshold, glad and unafraid,
Since all that Life or Death could do at last
Was over, and the hour so long forecast
  Had brought his footsteps thither. Undismayed
  He entered. Were his lips on her lips laid ?
God knows. They met, and their new day was vast.

Night shall not darken it, nor parting blight :
  'Whatever is to know,' they know it now :
  He comes to her with laurels on his brow,
Hero and conqueror from his life's fierce fight,
And Longing is extinguished in Delight,—
  'I still am I,' his eyes say,—'Thou art thou ! '

COME UNTO ME

I HEAR the low voice call that bids me come,—
　Me, even me, with all my grief opprest,
　With sins that burden my unquiet breast,
And in my heart the longing that is dumb,
Yet beats forever, like a muffled drum,
　For all delights whereof I, dispossest,
　Pine and repine, and find nor peace nor rest
This side the haven where He bids me come.

He bids me come and lay my sorrows down,
　And have my sins washed white by His dear grace ;
He smiles—what matter, then, though all men frown?
　Naught can assail me, held in His embrace ;
And if His welcome home the end may crown,
　Shall I not hasten to that heavenly place?

IN MID-OCEAN

ACROSS this sea I sail, and do not know
　What hap awaits me on its farther side,—
　In these long days what dear hope may have died;
What sweet, accustomed joy I must forgo ;
What new acquaintance make with unguessed woe
　(I, who with sorrow have been long allied),
　Or what blest gleam of joy yet undescried
Its tender light upon my way will throw.

Thus over Death's unsounded sea we sail,
　Toward a far, unmapped, unpictured shore,
Unwitting what awaits us, bliss or bale,
　Like the vast multitude that went before,
Scourged on by the inexorable gale
　The everlasting mystery to explore.

HELP THOU MY UNBELIEF !

BECAUSE I seek Thee not, oh seek Thou me !
　Because my lips are dumb, oh hear the cry
I do not utter as Thou passest by,
And from my life-long bondage set me free !

Because content I perish, far from Thee,
  Oh seize me, snatch me from my fate, and try
  My soul in Thy consuming fire! Draw nigh
And let me, blinded, Thy salvation see.

If I were pouring at Thy feet my tears,
  If I were clamoring to see Thy face,
    I should not need Thee, Lord, as now I need,
Whose dumb, dead soul knows neither hopes nor fears,
  Nor dreads the outer darkness of this place—
    Because I seek not, pray not, give Thou heed!

AT END

AT end of Love, at end of Life,
    At end of Hope, at end of Strife,
At end of all we cling to so—
The sun is setting—must we go?

At dawn of Love, at dawn of Life,
At dawn of Peace that follows Strife,
At dawn of all we long for so—
The sun is rising—let us go.

LOVE'S RESURRECTION DAY

ROUND among the quiet graves,
    When the sun was low,
Love went grieving,—Love who saves:
    Did the sleepers know?

At his touch the flowers awoke,
    At his tender call
Birds into sweet singing broke,
    And it did befall

From the blooming, bursting sod
    All Love's dead arose,
And went flying up to God
    By a way Love knows.

P 2

ON HOMEWARD WING

FROM the soft south the constant bird comes back,
    Faith-led, to find the welcome of the Spring
In the old boughs whereto she used to cling,
Before she sought the unknown southward track:
Above the Winter and the storm-cloud's wrack
    She hears the prophecy of days that bring
    The Summer's pride, and plumes her homeward wing
To seek again the joys that exiles lack.

Shall I of little faith, less brave than she,
    Set forth unwillingly my goal to find,
    Go home from exile with reluctant mind,
Distrust the steadfast stars I cannot see,
    And doubt the heavens because my eyes are blind?
Nay! Give me faith, like wings, to soar to Thee!

FOR EASTER MORNING

THE glad Dawn sets his fires upon the hills,
    Then floods the valleys with his golden light,
And, triumphing o'er all the hosts of night,
The waiting world with new-born rapture thrills:
And, hark! I seem to hear a song which fills
    The trembling air of earth with heaven's delight,
    And straight uplifts, with its celestial might,
Souls faint with longing, compassed round with ills.

'Christ, Christ is risen!' the unseen singers sing:
    'Christ, Christ is risen!' the echoing hosts reply --
The whist wind feels a passing seraph's wing,
    And holds its breath while shining ones go by:
'Christ, Christ is risen!'—loud let the anthem ring;
    He lives—He loves—He saves—we need not die.

'FAIN WOULD I CLIMB'

FAIN would I climb the heights that lead to God,
　　But my feet stumble and my steps are weak—
　Warm are the valleys, and the hills are bleak:
Here, where I linger, flowers make soft the sod,
But those far heights that martyr feet have trod
　　Are sharp with flints, and from the farthest peak
　　The still, small voice but faintly seems to speak,
While here the drowsy lilies dream and nod.

I have dreamed with them, till the night draws nigh
　　In which I cannot climb: still high above,
In the blue vastness of the awful sky,
　　Those unscaled peaks my fatal weakness prove—
Those shining heights that I must reach, or die
　　Afar from God, unquickened by His love.

THE SONG OF THE STARS

IN those high heavens, wherein the fair stars flower,
　　They do God's praises sound from night till morn,
　And when the smiling day is newly born
Chant, each to each, His glory and His power—
Then silent wait, through Day's brief triumph hour,
　　Watching till Night shall come again, with scorn
　　Of those chameleon splendors that adorn
Day's death, and then before his victor cower.

Forever to immortal ears they sing—
　　These shining stars that praise their Maker's grace—
And from far world to world their anthems ring:
　　They shine and sing because they see His face—
We, cowards, dread the vision Death shall bring,
　　The waking rapture, and the fair, far place.

Harriet Prescott Spofford

FIRST AND LAST

JUST come from heaven, how bright and fair
    The soft locks of the baby's hair,
As if the unshut gates still shed
The shining halo round his head!

Just entering heaven, what sacred snows
Upon the old man's brow repose!
For there the opening gates have strown
The glory from the great white throne.

WITNESSES

WHENEVER my heart is heavy,
    And life seems sad as death,
A subtle and marvelous mockery
    Of all who draw their breath,
And I weary of thronèd injustice,
    The rumor of outrage and wrong,
And I doubt if God rules above us,
    And I cry, O Lord, how long,
How long shall sorrow and evil
    Their forces around them draw!
Is there no power in Thy right hand?
    Is there no life in Thy law?

Then at last the blazing brightness
    Of day forsakes its height,
Slips like a splendid curtain
    From the awful and infinite night;
And out of the depths of distance,
    The gulfs of purple space,
The stars steal, slow and silent,
    Each in its ancient place,—
Each in its armor shining,
    The hosts of heaven arrayed,
And wheeling through the midnight,
    As they did when the world was made.

And I lean out among the shadows
  Cast by that far white gleam,
And I tremble at the murmur
  Of one mote in the mighty beam,
As the everlasting squadrons
  Their fated influence shed,
While the vast meridians sparkle
  With the glory of their tread.
That constellated glory
  The primal morning saw,
And I know God moves to His purpose,
  And still there is life in His law!

DAYS OF REST

STILL Sundays, rising o'er the world,
  Have never failed to bring their calm,
While from their tranquil wings unfurled,
  On the tired heart distilling balm,
A purer air bathes all the fields,
  A purer gold the generous sky;
The land a hallowed silence yields,
  All things in mute, glad worship lie,—
All, save where careless innocence
  In the great Presence sports and plays,
A wild bird whistles, or the wind
  Tosses the light snow from the sprays.

For life renews itself each week,
  Each Sunday seems to crown the year;
The fair earth rounds as fresh a cheek
  As though just made another sphere.
The shadowy film that sometimes breathes
  Between our thought and heaven disparts,
The quiet hour so brightly wreathes
  Its solemn peace about our hearts,
And Nature, whether sun or shower
  Caprices with her soaring days,
Rests conscious, in a happy sense,
  Of the wide smile that lights her ways.

Theodore Tilton

IN GOD'S ACRE

I

THOU art alive, O grave.
      Thou with thy living grass,
Blown of all winds that pass,—
Thou with thy daisies white,
Dewy at morn and night,—
Thou on whose granite stone
Greenly the moss has grown,—
Thou on whose holy mound,
Through the whole summer round,
Sweetly the roses thrive,—
Thou art alive!
O grave, thou art alive!

II

Answer me, then, O grave,—
Yea, from thy living bloom
Speak to me, O green tomb,—
Say if the maid I know,
Sepulchred here below,—
Say if the sweet white face,
Hidden in this dark place,—
Say, if the hair of gold
Buried amid thy mould,—
Say, O thou grave, her bed,—
Is my love dead?
O say, are the dead dead?

Washington Gladden

ULTIMA VERITAS

IN the bitter waves of woe,
      Beaten and tossed about
By the sullen winds that blow
      From the desolate shores of doubt,—

When the anchors that faith had cast
  Are dragging in the gale,
I am quietly holding fast
  To the things that cannot fail:

I know that right is right;
  That it is not good to lie;
That love is better than spite,
  And a neighbor than a spy;

I know that passion needs
  The leash of a sober mind;
I know that generous deeds
  Some sure reward will find;

That the rulers must obey;
  That the givers shall increase;
That Duty lights the way
  For the beautiful feet of Peace;—

In the darkest night of the year,
  When the stars have all gone out,
That courage is better than fear,
  That faith is truer than doubt;

And fierce though the fiends may fight,
  And long though the angels hide,
I know that Truth and Right
  Have the universe on their side;

And that somewhere, beyond the stars,
  Is a Love that is better than fate;
When the night unlocks her bars
  I shall see Him, and I will wait.

Thomas Bailey Aldrich

MIRACLES

SICK of myself and all that keeps the light
  Of the blue skies away from me and mine.
I climb this ledge, and by this wind-swept pine
Lingering, watch the coming of the night.

'Tis ever a new wonder to my sight:
Men look to God for some mysterious sign,
For other stars than those that nightly shine,
For some unnatural symbol of His might:—
Would'st see a miracle as grand as those
The Prophets wrought of old in Palestine?
Come watch with me the shaft of fire that glows
In yonder west; the fair, frail palaces,
The fading alps and archipelagoes,
And great cloud-continents of sunset seas.

SLEEP

WHEN to soft sleep we give ourselves away,
    And in a dream as in a fairy bark
Drift on and on through the enchanted dark
To purple daybreak—little thought we pay
To that sweet better world we know by day.
We are clean quit of it, as is a lark
So high in heaven no human eye can mark
The thin swift pinion cleaving through the gray.
Till we awake ill fate can do no ill,
The resting heart shall not take up again
The heavy load that yet must make it bleed;
For this brief space the loud world's voice is still,
No faintest echo of it brings us pain.
How will it be when we shall sleep indeed?

KNOWLEDGE

KNOWLEDGE—who hath it? Nay, not thou,
    Pale student, pondering thy futile lore!
A little space it shall be thine, as now
'Tis his whose funeral passes at thy door:
Last night a clown that scarcely knew to spell—
Now he knows all. O wondrous miracle!

Celia Thaxter

A SONG OF EASTER

SING, children, sing!
　　And the lily censers swing;
Sing that life and joy are waking and that Death no
　　more is king.
Sing the happy, happy tumult of the slowly brightening
　　spring;
　　　　Sing, little children, sing!

Sing, children, sing!
Winter wild has taken wing.
Fill the air with the sweet tidings till the frosty echoes
　　ring!
Along the eaves the icicles no longer glittering cling;
And the crocus in the garden lifts its bright face to
　　the sun,
And in the meadows softly the brooks begin to run;
And the golden catkins swing
In the warm airs of the spring;
　　　　Sing, little children, sing!

Sing, children, sing!
The lilies white you bring
In the joyous Easter morning for hope are blossoming;
And as the earth her shroud of snow from off her breast
　　doth fling,
So may we cast our fetters off in God's eternal spring.
So may we find release at last from sorrow and from pain,
So may we find our childhood's calm, delicious dawn again.
Sweet are your eyes, O little ones, that look with smiling
　　grace,
Without a shade of doubt or fear into the Future's face!
Sing, sing in happy chorus, with joyful voices tell
That death is life, and God is good, and all things shall
　　be well;
That bitter days shall cease
In warmth and light and peace,—
That winter yields to spring,—
　　　　Sing, little children, sing!

'THE SUNRISE NEVER FAILED US YET'

UPON the sadness of the sea
    The sunset broods regretfully;
From the far lonely spaces, slow
Withdraws the wistful afterglow.

So out of life the splendor dies;
So darken all the happy skies;
So gathers twilight, cold and stern;
But overhead the planets burn;

And up the East another day
Shall chase the bitter dark away;
What though our eyes with tears be wet!
The sunrise never failed us yet.

The blush of dawn may yet restore
Our light and hope and joy once more:
Sad soul, take comfort, nor forget
That sunrise never failed us yet!

THE SANDPIPER

ACROSS the narrow beach we flit,
    One little sandpiper and I,
And fast I gather, bit by bit,
The scattered drift-wood bleached and dry.
The wild waves reach their hands for it,
The wild wind raves, the tide runs high,
As up and down the beach we flit,—
One little sandpiper and I.

Above our heads the sullen clouds
Scud black and swift across the sky;
Like silent ghosts in misty shrouds
Stand out the white light-houses high.
Almost as far as eye can reach
I see the close-reefed vessels fly,
As fast we flit along the beach,—
One little sandpiper and I.

I watch him as he skims along
Uttering his sweet and mournful cry.
He starts not at my fitful song,
Or flash of fluttering drapery.
He has no thought of any wrong;
He scans me with a fearless eye.
Stanch friends are we, well tried and strong,
The little sandpiper and I.

Comrade, where wilt thou be to-night,
When the loosed storm breaks furiously?
My driftwood fire will burn so bright!
To what warm shelter canst thou fly?
I do not fear for thee, though wroth
The tempest rushes through the sky:
For are we not God's children both,
Thou, little sandpiper, and I.

William Winter

THE ANGEL DEATH

COME with a smile, when come thou must,
    Evangel of the world to be,
And touch and glorify this dust,—
    This shuddering dust, that now is me—
    And from this prison set me free!

Long in those awful eyes I quail,
    That gaze across the grim profound:
Upon that sea there is no sail,
    Nor any light nor any sound
    From the far shore that girds it round:

Only—two still and steady rays
    That those twin orbs of doom o'ertop;
Only—a quiet, patient gaze
    That drinks my being, drop by drop,
    And bids the pulse of nature stop.

Come with a smile, auspicious friend,
  To usher in the eternal day!
Of these weak terrors make an end,
  And charm the paltry chains away
  That bind me to this timorous clay!

And let me know my soul akin
  To sunrise, and the winds of morn,
And every grandeur that has been
  Since this all-glorious world was born,—
  Nor longer droop in my own scorn.

Come, when the way grows dark and chill!
  Come, when the baffled mind is weak,
And in the heart that voice is still,
  Which used in happier days to speak,
  Or only whispers, sadly meek.

Come with a smile that dims the sun!
  With pitying heart and gentle hand!
And waft me, from my vigil done,
  To peace, that waits on thy command,
  In some mysterious better land.

EGERIA

THE star I worship shines alone,
  In native grandeur set apart;
Its light, its beauty, all my own,
  And imaged only in my heart.

The flower I love lifts not its face
  For other eyes than mine to see;
And, having lost that sacred grace,
  'Twould have no other charm for me.

The hopes I bear, the joys I feel,
  Are silent, secret, and serene;
Pure is the shrine at which I kneel,
  And purity herself my queen.

I would not have an impious gaze
  Profane the altar where are laid
My hopes of nobler, grander days,
  By heaven inspired, by earth betrayed.

I would not have the noontide sky
    Pour down its bold, obtrusive light
Where all the springs of feeling lie,
    Deep in the soul's celestial night.

Far from the weary strife and noise,
    The tumult of the great to-day,
I guard my own congenial joys,
    And keep my own sequestered way.

For all that world is cursed with care;
    Has nothing holy, nothing dear,
No light, no music anywhere,—
    It will not see, it will not hear.

But Thou, Sweet Spirit, viewless Power,
    Whom I have loved and trusted long,—
In pleasure's day, in sorrow's hour,—
    Muse of my life and of my song;

Breathe softly, Thou, with peaceful voice,
    In my soul's temple, vast and dim!
In Thy own perfect joy rejoice,
    With morning and with evening hymn!

And though my hopes around me fall
    Like rain-drops in a boundless sea,
I will not think I lose them all
    While yet I keep my trust in Thee!

Mary Frances Butts

TRUST

BUILD a little fence of trust
    Around to-day;
Fill the space with loving work,
    And therein stay;
Look not through the sheltering bars
    Upon to-morrow;
God will help thee bear what comes
    Of joy or sorrow.

William Dean Howells

A THANKSGIVING

LORD, for the erring thought
  Not into evil wrought;
Lord, for the wicked will
Betrayed and baffled still;
For the heart from itself kept,
Our thanksgiving accept.

For ignorant hopes that were
Broken to our blind prayer;
For pain, death, sorrow, sent
Unto our chastisement;
For all loss of seeming good,
Quicken our gratitude!

CALVARY

IF He could doubt on His triumphant cross,
  How much more I, in the defeat and loss
Of seeing all my selfish dreams fulfilled,
Of having lived the very life I willed,
Of being all that I desired to be?
My God, my God! Why hast Thou forsaken me?

WHAT SHALL IT PROFIT?

IF I lay waste, and wither up with doubt
  The blessed fields of heaven where once my faith
Possessed itself serenely safe from death;
If I deny the things past finding out;
Or if I orphan my own soul of One
That seemed a Father, and make void the place
Within me where He dwelt in power and grace,
What do I gain by that I have undone?

Francis Bret Harte

THE TWO SHIPS

AS I stand by the cross on the lone mountain's crest,
    Looking over the ultimate sea;
In the gloom of the mountain a ship lies at rest,
    And one sails away from the lea:
One spreads its white wings on a far-reaching tract,
    With pennant and sheet flowing free;
One hides in the shadow with sails laid aback,—
    The ship that is waiting for me!

But lo! in the distance the clouds break away,
    The Gate's glowing portals I see; *
And I hear from the outgoing ship in the bay
    The song of the sailors in glee.
So I think of the luminous footprints that bore
    The comfort o'er dark Galilee,
And wait for the signal to go to the shore,
    To the ship that is waiting for me.

THE ANGELUS

HEARD AT THE MISSION DOLORES, 1868 *

BELLS of the Past, whose long-forgotten music
    Still fills the wide expanse,
Tingeing the sober twilight of the Present
    With color of romance:

I hear your call, and see the sun descending
    On rock and wave and sand,
As down the coast the Mission voices blending
    Girdle the heathen land.

Within the circle of your incantation
    No blight nor mildew falls;
Nor fierce unrest, nor lust, nor low ambition
    Passes those airy walls.

* See note.

Borne on the swell of your long waves receding,
    I touch the farther Past,—
I see the dying glow of Spanish glory,
    The sunset dream, and last,

Before me rise the dome-shaped Mission towers,
    The white Presidio ;
The swart commander in his leathern jerkin,
    The priest in stole of snow.

Once more I see Portala's cross uplifting
    Above the setting sun ;
And past the headland, northward, slowly drifting
    The freighted galleon.

O solemn bells ! whose consecrated masses
    Recall the faith of old,—
O tinkling bells ! that lulled with twilight music
    The spiritual fold !

Your voices break and falter in the darkness,—
    Break, falter, and are still ;
And veiled and mystic, like the Host descending,
    The sun sinks from the hill !

John Burroughs

WAITING

SERENE, I fold my hands and wait,
    Nor care for wind or tide or sea ;
I rave no more 'gainst time or fate,
    For, lo ! my own shall come to me.

I stay my haste, I make delays,
    For what avails this eager pace ?
I stand amid the eternal ways,
    And what is mine shall know my face.

Asleep, awake, by night or day,
    The friends I seek are seeking me;
No wind can drive my bark astray,
    Nor change the tide of destiny.

What matter if I stand alone?
    I wait with joy the coming years;
My heart shall reap where it has sown,
    And garner up its fruit of tears.

The waters know their own, and draw
    The brook that springs in yonder height,
So flows the good with equal law
    Unto the soul of pure delight.

The stars come nightly to the sky:
    The tidal wave unto the sea;
Nor time, nor space, nor deep, nor high,
    Can keep my own away from me.

Seth Curtis Beach

THE INSPIRATION OF THE SPIRIT

MYSTERIOUS Presence, source of all,—
    The world without, the soul within,—
Fountain of life, O hear our call,
    And pour Thy living waters in.

Thou breathest in the rushing wind,
    Thy Spirit stirs in leaf and flower;
Nor wilt Thou from the willing mind
    Withhold Thy light, and love, and power.

Thy hand unseen to accents clear
    Awoke the psalmist's trembling lyre,
And touched the lips of holy seer
    With flame from Thine own altar fire.

That touch divine still, Lord, impart,
    Still give the prophet's burning word;
And, vocal in each waiting heart,
    Let living psalms of praise be heard.

Edna Dean Proctor

PRAYERS FOR THE DEAD

NAY! I will pray for them until I go
    To their far realm beyond the strait of death!
For, past the deeps and all the winds that blow,
Somewhere within God's silences I know
    My yearning heart, my prayers with sobbing breath,
Will find and bring them gladness! Drear and slow
Would dawn my days, were they not followed so
    With perfect love that never varieth!

Does the fond wife, when mists hide wave and lea,
    Forget her fisher's safety to implore,
Till the lost bark that holds her joy in fee,
    Blithe, through the billows, comes again to shore? —
Our vanished ones but sail a vaster sea,
    And there, as here, God listens evermore.

THE PERFECT DAY

THE blast has swept the clouds away,
    The gloom, the mist, the rain;
Serene and blue is all the sky,
Save for a white cloud floating high,
A lone, celestial argosy
    That dares the azure main;
And, light as wafts of Eden blow,
The zephyrs wander to and fro.

What do I care that yester-night
    The wind was loud and chill?
Now earth is lapt in sunny calm;
The woods, the fields, exhale their balm;
And breeze and brook and bird a psalm
    Sing sweet, by vale and hill, —
What do I care that skies were cold?
To-day all heaven is flushed with gold.

O when the blast of death has blown
    The clouds of time away,
So may the shadows of our years—
The gloom of doubts and grief and fears
And dark regrets and bitter tears—
    Fade in God's perfect day!
And seem as slight and brief and vain
As yester-evening's mist and rain.

Henry Ames Blood

PRO MORTUIS

FOR the dead and for the dying;
    For the dead that once were living,
And the living that are dying,
    Pray I to the All-Forgiving;

For the dead who yester journeyed;
    For the living who, to-morrow,
Through the Valley of the Shadow,
    Must all bear the world's great sorrow;

For the immortal, who, in silence,
    Have already crossed the portal;
For the mortal, who, in silence,
    Soon shall follow the immortal.

Keep Thine arms round all, O Father!—
    Round lamenting and lamented;
Round the living and repenting,
    Round the dead who have repented.

Keep Thine arms round all, O Father!
    That are left or that are taken;
For they all are needy, whether
    The forsaking or forsaken.

Mary Mapes Dodge

THE TWO MYSTERIES *

WE know not what it is, dear, this sleep so deep
and still;
The folded hands, the awful calm, the cheek so pale
and chill;
The lids that will not lift again, though we may call
and call,
The strange, white solitude of peace that settles over all.

We know not what it means, dear, this desolate heart-
pain,—
This dread to take our daily way, and walk in it again.
We know not to what other sphere the loved who leave
us go;
Nor why we're left to wonder still; nor why we do not
know.

But this we know: our loved and dead, if they should
come this day,—
Should come and ask us, 'What is life?' not one of us
could say.
Life is a mystery as deep as ever death can be;
Yet, oh, how sweet it is to us, this life we live and see!

Then might they say,—these vanished ones,—and blessèd
is the thought!—
'So death is sweet to us, beloved, though we may tell
you naught;
We may not tell it to the quick,—this mystery of death,—
Ye may not tell us, if ye would, the mystery of breath.'

The child who enters life comes not with knowledge
or intent,
So those who enter death must go as little children sent.
Nothing is known, but I believe that God is overhead;
And as life is to the living, so death is to the dead.

* See note.

Margaret E. Sangster

IN GALILEE

THE Master walked in Galilee,
  Across the hills and by the sea,
And in whatever place He trod,
He felt the passion of a God.

The twelve who deemed Him King of men,
Longed for the conquering hour, when
The peasant's robe without a seam
Should be the purple of their dream.

Yet daily from His lips of love
Fell words their thoughts as far above
As wisdom's utmost treasure, piled
Upon the stammering of a child.

Like frost on flower, like blight on bloom,
His speech to them of cross and tomb;
Nor could their grieving spirits see
One gleam of hope in Galilee.

What booted it that He should rise,
Were death to hide Him from their eyes?
What meant the promised throne divine
Were earth to be an empty shrine?

Low drooped the skies above the land,
Too dull the Lord to understand.
Alas! as slow of heart are we,
Abiding oft in Galilee.

Charlotte Fiske Bates Rogé

SATISFIED

LIFE is unutterably dear,
  God makes to-day so fair;
Though heaven is better,—being here
  I long not to be there.

The weights of life are pressing still,
  Not one of them may fall;
Yet such strong joys my spirit fill,
  That I can bear them all.

Though Care and Grief are at my side,
  There would I let them stay,
And still be ever satisfied
  With beautiful To-day!

EVIL THOUGHT

A FORM not always dark, but ever dread,
  That sometimes haunts the holiest of all,—
God's audience-room, the chamber of the dead,
  He ventures here, to woo or to appal!

When the sou. sits with every portal wide,
  Joyful to drink the air and light of God,
This dark one rushes through with rapid stride,
  Leaving the print of evil where he trod.

Sometimes he enters like a thief at night;
  And breaking in upon the stillest hour
Startles the soul to tremble with affright,
  Lest she be pinioned by so foul a power.

Again we see his shadow, feel his tread,
  And just escape that strange and captive touch;
Perhaps by some transfixing wonder led,
  We look till drawn within his very clutch.

O valorous souls! so strong to meet the foe,
  O timid souls! yet brave in flight of wing,
Secure and happy ones who seldom know
  The agony this visitant can bring,—

Have mercy on your brothers housed so ill,
  Too weak or blinded any force to wield;
Judging their deeds, this fiend remember still:
  Christ pity those who cannot use His shield!

John White Chadwick

A PRAYER FOR UNITY

ETERNAL Ruler of the ceaseless round
  Of circling planets singing on their way;
Guide of the nations from the night profound
  Into the glory of the perfect day;
Rule in our hearts that we may ever be
Guided, and strengthened, and upheld by Thee.

We are of Thee, the children of Thy love,
  The brothers of Thy well-belovèd Son;
Descend, O Holy Spirit! like a dove,
  Into our hearts, that we may be as one,—
As one with Thee, to whom we ever tend;
As one with Him, our Brother, and our Friend.

We would be one in hatred of all wrong,
  One in our love of all things sweet and fair,
One with the joy that breaketh into song,
  One with the grief that trembles into prayer,
One in the power that makes Thy children free,
To follow Truth, and thus to follow Thee.

Oh! clothe us with Thy heavenly armor, Lord,—
  Thy trusty shield, Thy sword of love divine.
Our inspiration be Thy constant word;
  We ask no victories that are not Thine.
Give or withhold, let pain or pleasure be,
Enough to know that we are serving Thee.

AULD LANG SYNE

IT singeth low in every heart,
  We hear it each and all,—
A song of those who answer not,
  However we may call;
They throng the silence of the breast,
  We see them as of yore,—
The kind, the brave, the true, the sweet,
  Who walk with us no more.

'Tis hard to take the burden up,
  When these have laid it down;
They brightened all the joy of life,
  They softened every frown;
But, oh! 'tis good to think of them
  When we are troubled sore!
Thanks be to God that such have been,
  Though they are here no more.

More home-like seems the vast unknown,
  Since they have entered there;
To follow them were not so hard,
  Wherever they may fare;
They cannot be where God is not,
  On any sea or shore;
Whate'er betides, Thy love abides,
  Our God, for evermore.

IN JUNE

I show you a mystery.

O FRIEND, your face I cannot see,
    Your voice I cannot hear,
But for us both breaks at our feet
  The flood-tide of the year;
The summer-tide all beautiful
  With fragrance, and with song
Sung by the happy-hearted birds
  To cheer the months along.

And so the mystery I show
  Is this, all simple sweet:
Because God's summer-tide so breaks
  At yours and at my feet,
We're not so very far apart
  As it at first would seem;
We're near each other *in the Lord;*
  The miles are all a dream.

William Channing Gannett

'CONSIDER THE LILIES, HOW THEY GROW'

HE hides within the lily
   A strong and tender care,
That wins the earth-born atoms
   To glory of the air;
He weaves the shining garments
   Unceasingly and still,
Along the quiet waters,
   In niches of the hill.

We linger at the vigil
   With Him who bent the knee
To watch the old-time lilies
   In distant Galilee;
And still the worship deepens
   And quickens into new,
As brightening down the ages
   God's secret thrilleth through.

O Toiler of the lily,
   Thy touch is in the Man!
No leaf that dawns to petal
   But hints the angel-plan.
The flower-horizons open!
   The blossom vaster shows!
We hear Thy wide worlds echo,—
   See how the lily grows.

Shy yearnings of the savage,
   Unfolding thought by thought,
To holy lives are lifted,
   To visions fair are wrought;
The races rise and cluster,
   And evils fade and fall,
Till chaos blooms to beauty,
   Thy purpose crowning all!

THE SECRET PLACE OF THE MOST HIGH

THE Lord is in His Holy Place
   In all things near and far!
Shekinah of the snowflake, He,
   And Glory of the star,
And Secret of the April land
   That stirs the field to flowers,
Whose little tabernacles rise
   To hold Him through the hours.

He hides Himself within the love
   Of those whom we love best;
The smiles and tones that make our homes
   Are shrines by Him possessed;
He tents within the lonely heart,
   And shepherds every thought;
We find Him not by seeking far,—
   We lose Him not, unsought.

Our art may build its Holy Place,
   Our feet on Sinai stand,
But Holiest of Holies knows
   No tread, no touch of hand;
The listening soul makes Sinai still
   Wherever we may be,
And in the vow, 'Thy will be done!'
   Lies all Gethsemane.

IN LITTLES

A LITTLE House of Life,
   With many noises rife,
     Noises of joy and crime;
A little gate of birth,
Through which I slipped to Earth
     And found myself in Time.

And there, not far before,
Another little door,
     One day to swing so free!
None pauses there to knock,
No other hand tries lock,—
     It knows, and waits for me.

From out what Silent Land
I came, on Earth to stand
 And learn life's little art,
Is not in me to say:
I know I did not stray,—
 Was *sent*; to come, my part.

And down what Silent Shore
Beyond yon little door
 I pass, I cannot tell;
I know I shall not stray,
Nor ever lose the way,—
 Am *sent*; and all is well.

WHERE DID IT GO?

WHERE did yesterday's sunset *go*,
 When it faded down the hills so slow,
And the gold grew dim, and the purple light
Like an army with banners passed from sight?
Will its flush go into the golden-rod,
Its thrill to the purple aster's nod,
Its crimson fleck the maple-bough,
And the Autumn-glory begin from now?

 Deeper than flower-fields sank the glow
 Of the silent pageant passing slow.

It flushed all night in many a dream,
It thrilled in the folding hush of prayer,
It glided into a poet's song,
It is setting still in a picture rare;
It changed by the miracle none can see
To the shifting lights of a symphony;
And in resurrections of faith and hope
The glory died on the shining slope.

 For it left its light on the hills and seas
 That rim a thousand memories.

THE HIGHWAY

Whatever road I take joins the highway that leads to Thee.

WHEN the night is still and far,
    Watcher from the shadowed deeps!
When the morning breaks its bar,
    Life that shines and wakes and leaps!
When old Bible-verses glow,
    Starring all the deep of thought,
Till it fills with quiet dawn
    From the peace our years have brought,—
        Sun within both skies, we see
        How all lights lead back to Thee!

'Cross the field of daily work
    Run the footpaths, leading—where?
Run they east or run they west,
    One way all the workers fare.
Every awful thing of earth,—
    Sin and pain and battle-noise;
Every dear thing,—baby's birth,
    Faces, flowers, or lovers' joys,—
        Is a wicket-gate, where we
        Join the great highway to Thee!

Restless, restless, speed we on,—
    Whither in the vast unknown?
Not to you and not to me
    Are the sealèd orders shown:
But the Hand that built the road,
    And the Light that leads the feet,
And this inward restlessness,
    Are such invitation sweet,
        That where I no longer see,
        Highway still must lead to Thee!

IN TWOS

SOMEWHERE in the world there hide
    Garden-gates that no one sees,
Save they come in happy twos,—
    Not in ones, nor yet in threes.

But from every maiden's door
  Leads a pathway straight and true;
Map and survey know it not,—
  He who finds, finds room for two!

Then they see the garden-gates!
  Never skies so blue as theirs,
Never flowers so many-sweet,
  As for those who come in pairs.

Round and round the alleys wind:
  Now a cradle bars the way,
Now a little mound, behind,—
  So the two go through the day.

When no nook in all the lanes
  But has heard a song or sigh,
Lo! another garden-gate
  Opens as the two go by.

In they wander, knowing not;
  'Five and Twenty!' fills the air
With a silvery echo low,
  All about the startled pair.

Happier yet *these* garden-walks;
  Closer, heart to heart, they lean;
Stiller, softer, falls the light;
  Few the twos, and far between.

Till, at last, as on they pass
  Down the paths so well they know,
Once again at hidden gates
  Stand the two; they enter slow.

Golden Gates of 'Fifty Years,'
  May *our* two your latchet press!
Garden of the Sunset Land,
  Hold their dearest happiness!

Then a quiet walk again:
  Then a wicket in the wall:
Then one, stepping on alone,—
  Then two at the Heart of All!

MARY'S MANGER-SONG

SLEEP, my little Jesus,
    On Thy bed of hay,
While the shepherds homeward
    Journey on the way!
Mother is Thy shepherd,
    And will vigil keep;
O, did the angels wake Thee?
    Sleep, my Jesus, sleep!

Sleep, my little Jesus,
    While Thou art my own!
Ox and ass Thy neighbors,—
    Shalt Thou have a throne?
Will they call me blessèd?
    Shall I stand and weep?
O, be it far, Jehovah!
    Sleep, my Jesus, sleep!

Sleep, my little Jesus,
    Wonder-baby mine!
Well the singing angels
    Greet Thee as divine.
Through my heart, as heaven,
    Low the echoes sweep
Of Glory to Jehovah!
    Sleep, my Jesus, sleep!

Frederick Lucian Hosmer

FOUND

They that know Thy name will put their trust in Thee.

O NAME, all other names above,
    What art Thou not to me,
Now I have learned to trust Thy love
    And cast my care on Thee!

What is our being but a cry,
　A restless longing still,
Which Thou alone canst satisfy,
　Alone Thy fulness fill!

Thrice blessèd be the holy souls
　That lead the way to Thee,
That burn upon the martyr-rolls
　And lists of prophecy.

And sweet it is to tread the ground
　O'er which their faith hath trod;
But sweeter far, when Thou art found,
　The soul's own sense of God!

The thought of Thee all sorrow calms;
　Our anxious burdens fall;
His crosses turn to triumph-palms,
　Who finds in God his all.

PASSING UNDERSTANDING

The peace of God that passeth all understanding.

MANY things in life there are
　　Past our 'understanding' far,
And the humblest flower that grows
Hides a secret no man knows.

All unread by outer sense
Lies the soul's experience;
Mysteries around us rise,
We, the deeper mysteries!

Who hath scales to weigh the love
That from heart to heart doth move,
The divine unrest within,
Or the keen remorse for sin?

Who can map those tracks of light
Where the fancy wings its flight,
Or to outer vision trace
Thought's mysterious dwelling-place?

Who can sound the silent sea,
Where, with sealèd orders, we
Voyage from birth's forgotten shore
Toward the unknown land before?

While we may so little scan
Of Thy vast creation's plan,
Teach us, O our God, to be
Humble in our walk with Thee!

May we trust, through ill and good,
Thine unchanging Fatherhood,
And our highest wisdom find
In the reverent heart and mind!

Clearer vision shall be ours,
Larger wisdom, ampler powers,
And the meaning yet appear
Of what passes knowledge here.

ON THE MOUNT

NOT always on the mount may we
    Rapt in the heavenly vision be;
The shores of thought and feeling know
The Spirit's tidal ebb and flow.

Lord, it is good abiding here—
We cry, the heavenly Presence near;
The vision vanishes, our eyes
Are lifted into vacant skies!

Yet hath one such exalted hour
Upon the soul redeeming power,
And in its strength through after days
We travel our appointed ways;

Till all the lowly vale grows bright,
Transfigured in remembered light,
And in untiring souls we bear
The freshness of the upper air.

The mount for vision,—but below
The paths of daily duty go,
And nobler life therein shall own
The pattern on the mountain shown.

MY DEAD

I CANNOT think of them as dead
  Who walk with me no more;
Along the path of life I tread
  They have but gone before.

The Father's house is mansioned fair
  Beyond my vision dim;
All souls are His, and, here or there,
  Are living unto Him.

And still their silent ministry
  Within my heart hath place,
As when on earth they walked with me,
  And met me face to face.

Their lives are made forever mine;
  What they to me have been
Hath left henceforth its seal and sign
  Engraven deep within.

Mine are they by an ownership
  Nor time nor death can free;
For God hath given to Love to keep
  Its own eternally.

A PSALM OF TRUST

I LITTLE see, I little know,
  Yet can I fear no ill;
He who hath guided me till now
  Will be my leader still.

No burden yet was on me laid
  Of trouble or of care,
But He my trembling step hath stayed,
  And given me strength to bear.

I came not hither of my will
   Or wisdom of mine own :
That Higher Power upholds me still,
   And still must bear me on.

I knew not of this wondrous earth,
   Nor dreamed what blessings lay
Beyond the gates of human birth
   To glad my future way.

And what beyond this life may be
   As little I divine,—
What love may wait to welcome me,
   What fellowships be mine.

I know not what beyond may lie,
   But look, in humble faith,
Into a larger life to die,
   And find new birth in death.

He will not leave my soul forlorn ;
   I still must find Him true,
Whose mercies have been new each morn
   And every evening new.

Upon His providence I lean,
   As lean in faith I must:
The lesson of my life hath been
   A heart of grateful trust.

And so my onward way I fare
   With happy heart and calm,
And mingle with my daily care
   The music of my psalm.

THE INDWELLING GOD

O that I knew where I might find Him.

GO not, my soul, in search of Him,
   Thou wilt not find Him there,—
Or in the depths of shadow dim,
   Or heights of upper air.

For not in far-off realms of space
  The Spirit hath its throne;
In every heart it findeth place
  And waiteth to be known.

Thought answereth alone to thought,
  And Soul with soul hath kin;
The outward God he findeth not,
  Who finds not God within.

And if the vision come to thee
  Revealed by inward sign,
Earth will be full of Deity
  And with His glory shine!

Thou shalt not want for company,
  Nor pitch thy tent alone;
The indwelling God will go with thee,
  And show thee of His own.

O gift of gifts, O grace of grace
  That God should condescend
To make thy heart His dwelling-place,
  And be thy daily Friend!

Then go not thou in search of Him,
  But to thyself repair;
Wait thou within the silence dim,
  And thou shalt find Him there.

THE MYSTERY OF GOD

O THOU, in all Thy might so far,
  In all Thy love so near,
Beyond the range of sun and star,
  And yet beside us here,—

What heart can comprehend Thy name,
  Or, searching, find Thee out,
Who art within, a quickening Flame,
  A Presence round about?

Yet though I know Thee but in part,
  I ask not, Lord, for more :
Enough for me to know Thou art,
  To love Thee and adore.

O sweeter than aught else besides,
  The tender mystery
That like a veil of shadow hides
  The Light I may not see !

And dearer than all things I know
  Is childlike faith to me,
That makes the darkest way I go
  An open path to Thee.

Charlotte Mellen Packard

VESPERS

O SHADOW in a sultry land !
  We gather to thy breast,
Whose love, enfolding like the night
  Brings quietude and rest,
Glimpse of the fairer life to be,
  In foretaste here possessed !

From aimless wanderings we come,
  From drifting to and fro ;
The wave of being mingles deep
  Amid its ebb and flow ;
The grander sweep of tides serene
  Our spirits yearn to know.

That which the garish day had lost,
  The twilight vigil brings,
While softlier the vesper bell
  Its silver cadence rings,—
The sense of an immortal trust,
  The brush of angel wings.

Drop down behind the solemn hills,
    O Day with golden skies !
Serene above its fading glow
    Night, starry crowned, arise !
So beautiful may heaven be,
    When life's last sunbeam dies.

George McKnight

LIVE WHILE YOU LIVE

A VIEW of present life is all thou hast !
    Oblivion's cloud, like a high-reaching wall,
Conceals thy former being, and a pall
Hangs o'er the gate through which thou'lt soon have
        passed.
Dost chafe, in these close bounds imprisoned fast ?
Perhaps thy spirit's memory needs, withal,
Such limits, lest vague dimness should befall
Its records of a life-duration vast ;
And artfully thy sight may be confined
While thou art dwelling on this earthly isle,
That its exceeding beauty may the while
Infuse itself within thy growing mind,
And fit thee, in some future state sublime,
Haply, to grasp a wider range of time.

KINSHIP

So light, yet sure, the bond that binds the world.

I FOUND beside a meadow brooklet bright,
    Spring flowers whose tranquil beauty seemed to give
Glad answers as to whence and why we live.
With pleased delay I lingered while I might,
Because I thought when they were out of sight,
No more of joy from them I should receive.

But now I know absence cannot bereave
Their loveliness of power to give delight;
For still my soul with theirs glad converse holds,
Through sense more intimate and blessed than seeing;
A bond of kindred that includes all being,
Our lives in conscious union now infolds:
And oh, to me it is enough of bliss
To know I am, and that such beauty is.

IN UNISON

MAY nevermore a selfish wish of mine
Grow to a deed, unless a greater care
For others' welfare in the incitement share.
O Nature, let my purposes combine,
Henceforth, in conscious unison with thine,—
To spread abroad God's gladness, and declare
In living form what is forever fair—
Meekly to labor in thy great design,
Oh, let my little life be given whole!
If so, by action or by suffering,
Joy to my fellow-creatures I may bring,
Or, in the lowly likeness of my soul,
To beautiful creation's countless store
One form of beauty may be added more.

EUTHANASIA

SEEING our lives by Nature now are led
In an appointed way so tenderly;
So often lured by Hope's expectancy;
So seldom driven by scourging pain and dread;
And though by destiny so limited
Insuperably, our pleasant paths seem free:—
May we not trust it ever thus shall be?
That when we come the lonely vale to tread,
Leading away into the unknown night,
Our Mother then, kindly persuasive still,
Shall gently temper the reluctant will?
So, haply, we shall feel a strange delight,
Even that dreary way to travel o'er,
And the mysterious realm beyond explore.

Sophie Winthrop Weitzel

LOVE'S OPPORTUNITY

EARLY they came, yet they were come too late;
 The tomb was empty; in the misty dawn
Angels sat watching, but the Lord was gone.
Beyond earth's clouded day-break far was He,
Beyond the need of their sad ministry;
Regretful stood the three, with doubtful breast,
Their gifts unneeded and in vain their quest.

The spices—were they wasted? Legend saith
That, flung abroad on April's gentle breath,
They course the earth, and evermore again
In Spring's sweet odors they come back to men.
The tender thought! Be sure He held it dear;
He came to them with words of highest cheer,
And mighty joy expelled their hearts' brief fear.

Yet happier that morning—happier yet—
I count that other woman in her home,
Whose feet impatient all too soon had come,
Who ventured chill disfavor at the feast,
'Mid critics' murmur sought that lowliest Guest,
Broke her rare vase, its fragrant wealth outpoured,
And gave her gift aforehand to her Lord.

THE STAR AT DAWN

A STEALING glory, still, intent and sure,
 And one fair star left on the flushing sky;
(It is a time of birth, an opening door,
 A moment full of possibility;
 None knows how great a thing this day may see.)

'Twas night that lit that fair star, dark-browed night,
 And still it burns, paled but before the sun;
Pure through the darkness beamed its steadfast light.
 When sunshine conquers shade, when night is gone,
 Its tender radiance to the day is won.

So thou, dear grace of patience, in the soul
  Dost keep brave vigil through the shadowed hour;
Joy comes,—the morning! swift the mists unroll;
  The full day dawns, thy faithful watch is o'er;
Not that thy light is less, but heaven's is more.

LAWS AND LAW

MIGHTY man's will, and sweeps a world-wide arc;
  Great Nature's arm swings free in Titan curve;
Holding them both, with tense and tireless nerve,
Eternal Love moves onward to its mark.

FROM ONE WHO WENT AWAY IN HASTE

SWEET friends, I could not speak before I went,
  We could not wait—the messenger and I;
Will you guess all—with love's clear vision bent
  On that poor past, with eyes that search the sky?
Some things I would have done, some words have said;
  Swift had my feet on those last errands run.
Once more I would have said, 'I love you,'—plead
  Once more forgiveness for the good undone.
And do I hear a whisper, 'Ah, forgive,
  Forgive us any tenderness forgot'?
Hush, dearest pleader, where to-day I live
  Love's depth drowns all; the things that were are not.
Of all the wondrous tale anon we'll talk,
And on some sunny height together walk.

Nora Perry

A PRAYER

ANOINT my eyes that I may see
  Through all this sad obscurity,
This worldly mist that dims my sight,
These crowding clouds that hide the light.

Full vision, as perhaps have they
Who walk beyond the boundary way,
I do not seek, I do not ask,
But only this,—that through the mask,

Which centuries of soil and sin
Have fashioned for us, I may win
A clearer sight to show me where
Truth walks with faith divine and fair.

Minot Judson Savage

MYSTERY

O WHY are darkness and thick cloud
   Wrapped close for ever round the throne of God?
Why is our pathway still in mystery trod?
None answers, though we call aloud.

    The seedlet of the rose,
      While still beneath the ground,
    Think you it ever knows
      The mystery profound
Of its own power of birth and bloom,
Until it springs above its tomb?

    The caterpillar crawls
      Its mean life in the dust,
    Or hangs upon the walls
      A dead aurelian crust;
Think you the larva ever knew
Its gold-winged flight before it flew?

    When from the port of Spain
      Columbus sailed away,
    And down the sinking main
      Moved toward the setting day,
Could any words have made him see
The new worlds that were yet to be?

The boy with laugh and play
Fills out his little plan,
Still lisping, day by day,
Of how he'll be a man;
But can you to his childish brain
Make aught of coming manhood plain?

Let heaven be just above us,
Let God be e'er so nigh,
Yet howso'er He love us,
And howe'er much we cry,
There is no speech that can make clear
The thing 'that doth not yet appear.'

'Tis not that God loves mystery.
The things beyond us we can never know,
Until up to their lofty height we grow,
And finite grasps infinity.

James Herbert Morse

LABOR AND LIFE

HOW to labor and find it sweet:
How to get the good red gold
That veinèd hides in the granite fold
Under our feet—
The good red gold that is bought and sold,
Raiment to man, and house, and meat!

And how, while delving, to lift the eye
To the far-off mountains of amethyst,
The rounded hills, and the intertwist
Of waters that lie
Calm in the valleys, or that white mist
Sailing across a soundless sky.

Mary Anne Lathbury

THE DYING DAY

DAY is dying in the west;
   Heaven is touching earth with rest:
Wait and worship while the night
Sets her evening lamps alight
      Through all the sky.

Lord of life, beneath the dome
Of the universe, Thy home,
Gather us who seek Thy face
To the fold of Thy embrace,
      For Thou art nigh.

While the deepening shadows fall,
Heart of Love, enfolding all,
Through the glory and the grace
Of the stars that veil Thy face
      Our hearts ascend.

When, forever from our sight
Pass the stars—the day—the night,
Lord of angels, on our eyes
Let eternal morning rise,
      And shadows end.

THE BREAD OF LIFE

BREAK Thou the bread of life,
   Dear Lord, to me;
As Thou didst break the loaves
   Beside the sea;
Beyond the sacred page
   I seek Thee, Lord;
My spirit pants for Thee,
   O living Word!

Bless Thou the truth, dear Lord,
  To me—to me—
As Thou didst bless the bread
  By Galilee;
Then shall all bondage cease,
  All fetters fall;
And I shall find my peace,
  My all-in-all.

Edward Rowland Sill

A MORNING THOUGHT

WHAT if some morning, when the stars were paling,
    And the dawn whitened, and the East was clear,
Strange peace and rest fell on me from the presence
  Of a benignant Spirit standing near:

And I should tell him, as he stood beside me,
  'This is our Earth—most friendly Earth, and fair;
Daily its sea and shore through sun and shadow
  Faithful it turns, robed in its azure air:

'There is blest living here, loving and serving,
  And quest of truth, and serene friendships dear;
But stay not Spirit! Earth has one destroyer—
  His name is Death: flee, lest he find thee here!'

And what if then, while the still morning brightened,
  And freshened in the elm the Summer's breath,
Should gravely smile on me the gentle angel,
  And take my hand and say, 'My name is Death.'

HOME

THERE lies a little city in the hills;
    White are its roofs, dim is each dwelling's door,
And peace with perfect rest its bosom fills.

There the pure mist, the pity of the sea,
Comes as a white, soft hand, and reaches o'er
And touches its still face most tenderly.

Unstirred and calm, amid our shifting years,
Lo! where it lies, far from the clash and roar,
With quiet distance blurred, as if thro' tears.

O heart, that prayest so for God to send
Some loving messenger to go before
And lead the way to where thy longings end,

Be sure, be very sure, that soon will come
His kindest angel, and through that still door
Into the Infinite love will lead thee home.

LIFE

FORENOON and afternoon and night,—Forenoon
And afternoon, and night,—
Forenoon, and—what!
The empty song repeats itself. No more?
Yea, that is Life: make this forenoon sublime,
This afternoon a psalm, this night a prayer,
And Time is conquered, and thy crown is won.

THE FUTURE

WHAT may we take into the vast Forever?
That marble door
Admits no fruit of all our long endeavor,
No fame-wreathed crown we wore,
No garnered lore.

What can we bear beyond the unknown portal?
No gold, no gains
Of all our toiling: in the life immortal
No hoarded wealth remains,
Nor gilds, nor stains.

Naked from out that far abyss behind us
We entered here:
No word came with our coming, to remind us
What wondrous world was near,
No hope, no fear.

Into the silent, starless Night before us,
    Naked we glide:
No hand has mapped the constellations o'er us,
    No comrade at our side,
    No chart, no guide.

Yet fearless toward that midnight, black and hollow,
    Our footsteps fare:
The beckoning of a Father's hand we follow—
    His love alone is there,
    No curse, no care.

THE FOOL'S PRAYER

THE royal feast was done; the King
    Sought some new sport to banish care,
And to his jester cried: 'Sir Fool,
    Kneel now, and make for us a prayer!

The jester doffed his cap and bells,
    And stood the mocking court before;
They could not see the bitter smile
    Behind the painted grin he wore.

He bowed his head, and bent his knee
    Upon the monarch's silken stool,
His pleading voice arose: 'O Lord,
    Be merciful to me, a fool!

'No pity, Lord, could change the heart
    From red with wrong to white as wool;
The rod must heal the sin: but Lord,
    Be merciful to me, a fool!

' 'Tis not by guilt the onward sweep
    Of truth and right, O Lord, we stay;
'Tis by our follies that so long
    We hold the earth from heaven away.

' These clumsy feet, still in the mire,
    Go crushing blossoms without end;
These hard, well-meaning hands we thrust
    Among the heart-strings of a friend.

'The ill-timed truth we might have kept—
  Who knows how sharp it pierced and stung?
The word we had not sense to say—
  Who knows how grandly it had rung?

'Our faults no tenderness should ask,
  The chastening stripes must cleanse them all:
But for our blunders—oh, in shame
  Before the eyes of heaven we fall.

'Earth bears no balsam for mistakes;
  Men crown the knave, and scourge the tool
That did his will; but Thou, O Lord,
  Be merciful to me, a fool!'

The room was hushed; in silence rose
  The King, and sought his gardens cool,
And walked apart, and murmured low,
  'Be merciful to me, a fool!'

OPPORTUNITY

THIS I beheld, or dreamed it in a dream:—
    There spread a cloud of dust along a plain;
And underneath the cloud, or in it, raged
A furious battle, and men yelled, and swords
Shocked upon swords and shields. A prince's banner
Wavered, then staggered backward, hemmed by foes.
A craven hung along the battle's edge,
And thought, 'Had I a sword of keener steel—
That blue blade that the king's son bears,—but this
Blunt thing!'—he snapt and flung it from his hand,
And lowering crept away and left the field.

Then came the king's son, wounded, sore bestead,
And weaponless, and saw the broken sword,
Hilt-buried in the dry and trodden sand,
And ran and snatched it, and with battle-shout
Lifted afresh he hewed his enemy down,
And saved a great cause that heroic day.

Joaquin Miller

HOPE

WHAT song is well sung not of sorrow?
　What triumph well won without pain?
What virtue shall be and not borrow
　Bright lustre from many a stain?

What birth has there been without travail?
　What battle well won without blood?
What good shall earth see without evil
　Ingarner'd as chaff with the good?

Lo! the Cross set in rocks by the Roman,
　And nourish'd by blood of the Lamb,
And water'd by tears of the woman,
　Has flourish'd, has spread like a palm;

Has spread in the frosts and far regions
　Of snows in the North, and South sands
Where never the tramp of his legions
　Was heard, or reach'd forth his red hands.

Be thankful: the price and the payment,
　The birth, the privations and scorn,
The Cross, and the parting of raiment,
　Are finish'd. The star brought us morn.

THE LAST SUPPER

*And when they had sung an hymn they went out into the
Mount of Olives.*

WHAT song sang the twelve with the Saviour
　When finish'd the sacrament wine?
Were they bow'd and subdued in behavior,
　Or bold, as made bold with a sign?

Were tne nairy breasts strong and defiant?
　Were the naked arms brawny and strong?
Were the bearded lips lifted reliant,
　Thrust forth and full sturdy with song?

What sang they? What sweet song of Zion,
  With Christ in their midst like a crown?
While here sat Saint Peter, the lion;
  And there like a lamb, with head down,

Sat Saint John, with his silken and raven
  Rich hair on his shoulders, and eyes
Lifting up to the faces unshaven
  Like a sensitive child's in surprise.

Was the song as strong fishermen swinging
  Their nets full of hope to the sea?
Or low, like the ripple-wave singing
  Sea-songs on their loved Galilee?

Were they sad with foreshadow of sorrows,
  Like the birds that sing low when the breeze
Is tip-toe with a tale of to-morrow,—
  Of earthquakes and sinking of seas?

Ah! soft was their song as the waves are,
  That fall in low musical moans;
And sad I should say as the winds are,
  That blow by the white gravestones.

Sidney Lanier

A BALLAD OF TREES AND THE MASTER

INTO the woods my Master went,
  Clean forspent, forspent,
Into the woods my Master came,
  Forspent with love and shame.
But the olives they were not blind to Him,
The little gray leaves were kind to Him,
The thorn-tree had a mind to Him,
  When into the woods He came.

Out of the woods my Master went,
And He was well-content.
Out of the woods my Master came,
  Content with death and shame.

When Death and Shame would woo Him last,
From under the trees they drew him last;
'Twas on a tree they slew Him—last
When out of the woods He came.

IN ABSENCE

LET no man say, *He at his lady's feet*
   Lays worship that to heaven alone belongs;
Yea, swings the incense that for God is meet
   In flippant censers of light lover's songs.
Who says it knows not God, nor love, nor thee;
   For love is large as is yon heavenly dome:
In love's great blue, each passion is full free
   To fly his favorite flight and build his home.
Did e'er a lark with skyward-pointing beak
   Stab by mischance a level-flying dove?
Wife-love flies level, his dear mate to seek:
   God-love darts straight into the skies above.
Crossing the windage of each other's wings
But speeds them both upon their journeyings.

MY SPRINGS

IN the heart of the Hills of Life, I know
   Two springs that with unbroken flow
Forever pour their lucent streams
Into my soul's far Lake of Dreams.

Not larger than two eyes, they lie
Beneath the many-changing sky,
And mirror all of life and time,—
Serene and dainty pantomime,

Shot through with lights of stars and dawns,
And shadowed sweet by ferns and fawns,—
Thus heaven and earth together vie
Their shining depths to sanctify.

Always when the large Form of Love
Is hid by storms that rage above,
I gaze in my two springs and see
Love in his very verity.

Always when Faith with stifling stress
Of grief hath died in bitterness,
I gaze in my two springs and see
A Faith that smiles immortally.

Always when Charity and Hope,
In darkness bounden, feebly grope,
I gaze in my two springs and see
A Light that sets my captives free.

Always, when Art on perverse wing
Flies where I cannot hear him sing,
I gaze in my two springs and see
A charm that brings him back to me.

When Labor faints, and Glory fails,
And coy Reward in sighs exhales,
I gaze in my two springs and see
Attainment full and heavenly.

O Love, O Wife, thine eyes are they,—
My springs from out whose shining gray
Issue the sweet celestial streams
That feed my life's bright Lake of Dreams.

Oval and large and passion-pure,
And gray and wise and honor-sure;
Soft as a dying violet-breath
Yet calmly unafraid of death;

Thronged, like two dove-cotes of gray doves,
With wife's and mother's and poor-folks' loves,
And home-loves and high glory-loves,
And science loves and story-loves,

And loves for all that God and man
In art or nature make or plan,
And lady-loves for spidery lace
And broideries and supple grace,

And diamonds and the whole sweet round
Of littles that large life compound,
And loves for God and God's bare truth,
And loves for Magdalen and Ruth.

Dear eyes, dear eyes and rare complete—
Being heavenly-sweet and earthly-sweet,—
I marvel that God made you mine,
For when He frowns, 'tis then ye shine!

WEDDING HYMN

THOU God, whose high, eternal love
    Is the only blue sky of our life,
Clear all the heaven that bends above
    The life-road of this man and wife.

May these two lives be but one note
    In the world's strange-sounding harmony,
Whose sacred music e'er shall float
    Through every discord up to Thee.

As when from separate stars two beams
    Unite to form one tender ray:
As when two sweet but shadowy dreams
    Explain each other in the day:

So may these two dear hearts one light
    Emit, and each interpret each.
Let an angel come and dwell to-night
    In this dear double-heart, and teach!

THE MARSHES OF GLYNN

*   *   *   *   *   *

AS the marsh-hen secretly builds on the watery sod,
    Behold, I will build me a nest on the greatness of
        God:
I will fly in the greatness of God as the marsh-hen flies,
In the freedom that fills all the space 'twixt the marsh
        and the skies:
By so many roots as the marsh-grass sends in the sod
I will heartily lay me a-hold on the greatness of God:
Oh, like to the greatness of God is the greatness within
The range of the marshes, the liberal marshes of Glynn.

May Louise Riley Smith

SOMETIME

SOMETIME, when all life's lessons have been learned,
　And sun and stars forevermore have set,
The things which our weak judgments here have spurned,
　The things o'er which we grieved with lashes wet,
Will flash before us, out of life's dark night,
　As stars shine most in deeper tints of blue;
And we shall see how all God's plans are right,
　And how what seems reproof was love most true.

And we shall see how, while we frown and sigh,
　God's plans go on as best for you and me;
How, when we called, He heeded not our cry,
　Because His wisdom to the end could see.
And e'en as prudent parents disallow
　Too much of sweet to craving babyhood,
So God, perhaps, is keeping from us now
　Life's sweetest things, because it seemeth good.

And if sometimes, commingled with life's wine,
　We find the wormwood, and rebel and shrink,
Be sure a wiser hand than yours or mine
　Pours out this potion for our lips to drink;
And if some friend we love is lying low,
　Where human kisses cannot reach his face,
Oh, do not blame the loving Father so,
　But wear your sorrow with obedient grace!

And you shall shortly know that lengthened breath
　Is not the sweetest gift God sends His friend,
And that, sometimes, the sable pall of death
　Conceals the fairest boon His love can send.
If we could push afar the gates of life,
　And stand within, and all God's workings see,
We could interpret all this doubt and strife,
　And for each mystery could find a key.

But not to-day. Then be content, poor heart!
　God's plans like lilies pure and white unfold;
We must not tear the close-shut leaves apart,
　Time will reveal the calyxes of gold.

And if, through patient toil, we reach the land
  Where tired feet, with sandals loosed, may rest,
When we shall clearly know and understand,
  I think that we will say, ' God knew the best ! '

Charles Munroe Dickinson

A MORNING MIRACLE

As Christ stands close to both God and sin,
So earth meets heaven where the skies begin;
But the air is so pure though faint and thin,
It keeps the earthly out and the heavenly in.

THE river lifts its morning mist,
  An incense-offering to the sun ;
Through countless threads of amethyst
  And gold and silver, finely spun,
It trembles upward through the skies,
As slowly as a soul might rise,
Until it felt the magnet-power of Paradise.

'Tis of the earth, but out of it
  Has been distilled each earthly trace ;
The watchful skies alone transmit
  The pure through their transparent space ;
The earthy back to the earth is given ;
No longer a part of the river even,
The heavenly alone ascendeth to heaven.

Francis Howard Williams

AN ANSWER

I QUESTIONED : *Why is evil on the Earth ?*
  A sage for answer struck a chord, and lo !
I found the harmony of little worth
  To teach my soul the truth it longed to know.

He struck again ; a saddened music, rife
  With wisdom, in my ear an answer poured :
Sin is the jarring semitone of life,—
  The needed minor in a perfect chord.

LOVE CAME TO ME

LOVE came to me when I was young;
  He brought me songs, he brought me flowers;
Love wooed me lightly, trees among,
  And dallied under scented bowers;
And loud he carolled: 'Love is King!'
For he was riotous as spring,
  And careless of the hours,—
    When I was young.

Love lingered near when I grew old;
  He brought me light from stars above;
And consolations manifold;
  He fluted to me like a dove;
And Love leaned out of Paradise,
And gently kissed my faded eyes,
  And whispered, 'God is Love,'—
    When I grew old.

Richard Watson Gilder

THE SOWER

I

A SOWER went forth to sow;
  His eyes were dark with woe;
He crushed the flowers beneath his feet,
Nor smelt the perfume, warm and sweet,
That prayed for pity everywhere.
He came to a field that was harried
By iron, and to heaven laid bare;
He shook the seed that he carried
O'er that brown and bladeless place.
He shook it, as God shakes the hail
Over a doomèd land,
When lightnings interlace
The sky and the earth, and his wand
Of love is a thunder-flail.
  Thus did that Sower sow;
His seed was human blood,
And tears of women and men.

And I, who near him stood,
Said: 'When the crop comes, then
There will be sobbing and sighing,
Weeping and wailing and crying,
Flame, and ashes, and woe.'

II

It was an autumn day
When next I went that way.
And what, think you, did I see?
What was it that I heard,
What music was in the air?
The song of a sweet-voiced bird?
Nay—but the songs of many,
Thrilled through with praise and prayer.
Of all those voices not any
Were sad of memory;
But a sea of sunlight flowed,
A golden harvest glowed,
And I said: 'Thou only art wise,
God of the earth and skies!
And I praise Thee, again and again,
For the Sower whose name is Pain.'

'THERE IS NOTHING NEW UNDER THE SUN'

THERE is nothing new under the sun;
    There is no new hope or despair;
The agony just begun
    Is as old as the earth and the air.
My secret soul of bliss
    Is one with the singing stars,
And the ancient mountains miss
    No hurt that my being mars.

I know as I know my life,
    I know as I know my pain,
That there is no lonely strife,
    That he is mad who would gain
A separate balm for his woe,
    A single pity and cover;
The one great God I know
    Hears the same prayer over and over.

I know it, because at the portal
　Of heaven I bowed and cried,
And I said: 'Was ever a mortal
　Thus crowned and crucified!
My praise thou hast made my blame;
　My best thou hast made my worst;
My good thou hast turned to shame;
　My drink is a flaming thirst.'

But scarce my prayer was said
　Ere from that place I turned;
I trembled, I hung my head,
　My cheek, shame-smitten, burned;
For there where I bowed down
　In my boastful agony,
I thought of Thy cross and crown—
　O Christ, I remembered Thee.

AFTER-SONG

THROUGH love to light! Oh, wonderful the way
　That leads from darkness to the perfect day!
From darkness and from sorrow of the night
To morning that comes singing o'er the sea.
Through love to light! through light, O God, to Thee,
Who art the love of love, the eternal light of light!

MORNING AND NIGHT

THE mountain that the morn doth kiss
　Glad greets its shining neighbor;
Lord! heed the homage of our bliss,
　The incense of our labor.

Now the long shadows eastward creep,
　The golden sun is setting;
Take, Lord! the worship of our sleep,
　The praise of our forgetting.

TEMPTATION

NOT alone in pain and gloom
   Does the abhorrèd tempter come;
Not in light alone and pleasure
Proffers he the poisoned measure.
When the soul doth rise
Nearest to its native skies,
There the exalted spirit finds,
Borne upon the heavenly winds,
Satan, in an angel's guise,
With voice divine and innocent eyes.

'EACH MOMENT HOLY IS'

EACH moment holy is, for out from God
   Each moment flashes forth a human soul.
Holy each moment is, for back to Him
Some wandering soul each moment home returns.

FATHER AND CHILD

BENEATH the deep and solemn midnight sky,
   At this last verge and boundary of time
I stand, and listen to the starry chime
That sounds to the inward ear, and will not die.
Now do the thoughts that daily hidden lie
   Arise, and live in a celestial clime,—
   Unutterable thoughts, most high, sublime,
Crossed by one dread that frights mortality.
Thus, as I muse, I hear my little child
   Sob in its sleep within the cottage near—
   My own dear child! Gone is that mortal doubt!
The Power that drew our lives forth from the wild
   Our Father is; we shall to Him be dear,
   Nor from His universe be blotted out!

HOLY LAND

THIS is the earth He walked on: not alone
  That Asian country keeps the sacred stain;
Ah, not alone the far Judæan plain,
Mountain and river! Lo, the sun that shone
On Him, shines now on us; when day is gone
  The moon of Galilee comes forth again,
  And lights our path as His; an endless chain
Of years and sorrows makes the round world one.
The air we breathe, He breathed,—the very air
  That took the mold and music of His high
And God-like speech. Since then shall mortal dare
  With base thought front the ever sacred sky—
Soil with foul deed the ground whereon He laid,
In holy death, His pale immortal head!

THE SONG OF A HEATHEN

SOJOURNING IN GALILEE A.D. 32

IF Jesus Christ is a man,—
  And only a man,—I say
That of all mankind I cleave to Him,
  And to Him will I cleave alway.

If Jesus Christ is a God,—
  And the only God,—I swear
I will follow Him through heaven and hell,
  The earth, the sea, and the air!

A MADONNA OF FRA LIPPO LIPPI

NO heavenly maid we here behold,
  Though round her brow a ring of gold;
This baby, solemn-eyed and sweet,
Is human all from head to feet.

Together close her palms are prest
In worship of that godly guest;
But glad her heart and unafraid,
While on her neck His hand is laid.

Two children, happy, laughing, gay,
Uphold the little child in play;
Not flying angels these, what though
Four wings from their four shoulders grow.

Fra Lippo, we have learned from thee
A lesson of humanity;
To every mother's heart forlorn,
In every house the Christ is born.

John Banister Tabb

THE PASCHAL MOON

THY face is whitened with remembered woe;
    For thou alone, pale satellite, didst see,
  Amid the shadows of Gethsemane,
The mingled cup of sacrifice o'erflow;
Nor hadst the power of utterance to show
    The wasting wound of silent sympathy,
    Till sudden tides, obedient to thee,
Sobbed, desolate in weltering anguish, low.

The holy night returneth year by year;
    And while the mystic vapors from thy rim
Distil the dews, as from the Victim there
    The red drops trickled in the twilight dim,
The ocean's changeless threnody we hear,
    And gaze upon thee as thou didst on Him.

EASTER

LIKE a meteor, large and bright,
    Fell a golden seed of light
On the field of Christmas night
    When the Babe was born;
Then 'twas sepulchred in gloom
Till above His holy tomb
Flashed its everlasting bloom—
    Flower of Easter morn.

THE PLAYMATES

WHO are thy playmates, boy?
'My favorite is Joy,
Who brings with him his sister Peace, to stay
The livelong day.
I love them both; but he
Is most to me.'

And where thy playmates now,
O man of sober brow?
'Alas! dear Joy, the merriest, is dead.
But I have wed
Peace; and our babe, a boy,
New-born, is Joy.'

NEKROS

LO! all thy glory gone!
God's masterpiece undone!
The last created and the first to fall;
The noblest, frailest, godliest of all.

Death seems the conqueror now,
And yet his victor thou:
The fatal shaft, its venom quench'd in thee,
A mortal raised to immortality.

Child of the humble sod,
Wed with the breath of God,
Descend! for with the lowest thou must lie—
Arise! thou hast inherited the sky.

ALTER EGO

THOU art to me as is the sea
Unto the shell;
A life whereof I breathe, a love
Wherein I dwell.

THE SUNBEAM

A LADDER from the Land of Light,
    I rest upon the sod,
Whence dewy angels of the Night
    Climb back again to God.

CONFIDED

A NOTHER lamb, O Lamb of God, behold,
    Within this quiet fold,
Among Thy Father's sheep
I lay to sleep!
A heart that never for a night did rest
Beyond its mother's breast.
Lord, keep it close to Thee,
Lest waking it should bleat and pine for me!

THE INCARNATION

S AVE through the flesh Thou wouldst not come to me—
    The flesh, wherein Thy strength my weakness found,
A weight to bow Thy Godhead to the ground,
And lift to heaven a lost humanity.

TO THE CHRIST

T HOU hast on earth a Trinity,—
    Thyself, my fellow-man, and me;
When one with him, then one with Thee;
Nor, save together. Thine are we.

EARTH'S TRIBUTE

F IRST the grain, and then the blade—
    The one destroyed, the other made;
Then stalk and blossom, and again
The gold of newly minted grain.

So Life, by Death the reaper cast
To earth, again shall rise at last;
For 'tis the service of the sod
To render God the things of God.

RESURRECTION

ALL that springeth from the sod
    Tendeth upwards unto God;
All that cometh from the skies
Urging it anon to rise.

Winter's life-delaying breath
Leaveneth the lump of death,
Till the frailest fettered bloom
Moves the earth, and bursts the tomb.

Welcome, then, Time's threshing-pain
And the furrows where each grain,
Like a Samson, blossom-shorn,
Waits the resurrection morn.

Elizabeth Stuart Phelps

FEELING THE WAY

FEELING the way,—and all the way uphill;
    But on the open summit, calm and still,
The feet of Christ are planted; and they stand
In view of all the quiet land.

Feeling the way,—and though the way is dark,
The eyelids of the morning yet shall mark
Against the East the shining of His face,
At peace upon the lighted place.

Feeling the way,—and if the way is cold,
What matter?—since upon the fields of gold
His breath is melting; and the warm winds sing
While rocking summer days for Him.

LEARNING TO PRAY

MY inmost soul, O Lord, to Thee
  Leans like a growing flower
Unto the light. I do not know
  The day nor blessed hour
When that deep-rooted, daring growth
  We call the heart's desire
Shall burst and blossom to a prayer
  Within the sacred fire
Of Thy great patience ; grow so pure,
  So still, so sweet a thing
As perfect prayer must surely be.
  And yet my heart will sing
Because Thou seem'st sometimes so near,
  Close-present God ! to me.
It seems I could not have a wish
  That was not shared by Thee ;
It seems I cannot be afraid
  To speak my longings out,
So tenderly Thy gathering love
  Enfolds me round about ;
It seems as if my heart would break,
  If, living on the light,
I should not lift to Thee at last
  A bud of flawless white.
And yet, O helpless heart ! how sweet
  To grow, and bud, and say :
The flower, however marred or wan,
  Shall not be cast away.

Sarah Chauncey Woolsey

HE THAT BELIEVETH SHALL NOT MAKE HASTE

THE aloes grow upon the sand,
  The aloes thirst with parching heat ;
Year after year they wait and stand,
  Lonely and calm, and front the beat
  Of desert winds, and still a sweet
And subtle voice thrills all their veins :

'Great patience wins; it still remains,
After a century of pains,
   For you to bloom and be complete.

'I grow upon a thorny waste,
   Hot noontide lies on all the way,
And with its scorching breath makes haste,
   Each freshening dawn, to burn and slay;
   Yet patiently I bide and stay,
Knowing the secret of my fate.
The hour of bloom, dear Lord, I wait,
Come when it will, or soon or late,
   A hundred years is but a day.'

LABORARE EST ORARE

HOW infinite and sweet, Thou everywhere
   And all-abounding Love, Thy service is!
Thou liest an ocean round my world of care,
My petty every-day; and fresh and fair
   Pour Thy strong tides through all my crevices,
Until the silence ripples into prayer.

That Thy full glory may abound, increase,
   And so Thy likeness shall be formed in me,
I pray; the answer is not rest or peace,
But charges, duties, wants, anxieties,
   Till there seems room for everything but Thee,
And never time for anything but these.

And I should fear, but lo! amid the press,
   The whirl and hum and pressure of my day,
I hear Thy garment s sweep, Thy seamless dress,
And close beside my work and weariness
   Discern Thy gracious form, not far away,
But very near, O Lord, to help and bless.

The busy fingers fly, the eyes may see
   Only the glancing needle which they hold,
But all my life is blossoming inwardly,
And every breath is like a litany,
   While through each labor, like a thread of gold,
Is woven the sweet consciousness of Thee!

Edgar Fawcett

MY LITTLE ONE

GOD bless my little one! how fair
   The mellow lamplight gilds his hair,
Loose on the cradle-pillow there,
   God bless my little one!

God love my little one! as clear,
Cool sunshine holds the first green spear
On April meadows, hold him dear.
   God love my little one!

When these fond lips are mute, and when
I slumber, not to wake again,
God bless, God guard, God love him then,
   My little one! Amen.

Henry Augustin Beers

PSYCHE

AT evening in the port she lay,
   A lifeless block with canvas furled;
But silently at peep of day
Spread her white wings and skimmed away,
And, rosy in the dawn's first ray,
   Sank down behind the rounding world.

So hast thou vanished from our side,
   Dear bark, that from some far bright strand,
Anchored awhile on life's dull tide;
Then, lifting spirit-pinions wide,
In heaven's own orient glorified,
   Steered outward seeking Holy Land.

John Vance Cheney

THE HAPPIEST HEART

WHO drives the horses of the sun
 Shall lord it but a day;
Better the lowly deed were done,
 And kept the humble way.

The rust will find the sword of fame,
 The dust will hide the crown;
Ay, none shall nail so high his name
 Time will not tear it down.

The happiest heart that ever beat
 Was in some quiet breast
That found the common daylight sweet,
 And left to heaven the rest.

TEARS

NOT in the time of pleasure
 Hope doth set her bow;
But in the sky of sorrow,
 Over the vale of woe.

Through gloom and shadow look we
 On beyond the years:
The soul would have no rainbow
 Had the eyes no tears.

FAITH

NO help in all the stranger-land,
 O fainting heart, O failing hand?
There's a morning and a noon,
And the evening cometh soon.

The way is endless, friendless? No;
God sitteth high to see below;
There's a morning and a noon,
And the evening cometh soon.

Look yonder on the purpling west:
Ere long the glory and the rest.
There's a morning and a noon,
And the evening cometh soon.

Emma Lazarus

HOPE

HER languid pulses thrill with sudden hope,
   That will not be forgot nor cast aside,
And life in statelier vistas seems to ope,
   Illimitably lofty, long, and wide.
What doth she know? She is subdued and mild,
Quiet and docile 'as a weanèd child.'

If grief came in such unimagined wise,
   How may joy dawn? In what undreamed-of hour
May the light break with splendor of surprise,
   Disclosing all the mercy and the power?—
A baseless hope, yet vivid, keen, and bright,
As the wild lightning in the starless night.

She knows not whence it came, nor where it passed,
   But it revealed, in one brief flash of flame,
A heaven so high, a world so rich and vast,
   That, full of meek contrition and mute shame,
In patient silence hopefully withdrawn,
She bows her head, and bides the certain dawn.

PATIENCE

THE passion of despair is quelled at last;
   The cruel sense of undeservèd wrong,
The wild self-pity, these are also past;
   She knows not what may come, but she is strong;
She feels she hath not aught to lose nor gain,
Her patience is the essence of all pain.

As one who sits beside a lapsing stream,
   She sees the flow of changeless day by day,
Too sick and tired to think, too sad to dream,
   Nor cares how soon the waters slip away,
Nor where they lead; at the wise God's decree,
She will depart or 'bide indifferently.

There is a deeper pathos in the mild
  And settled sorrow of the quiet eyes,
Than in the tumults of the anguish wild,
  That made her curse all things beneath the skies;
No question, no reproaches, no complaint,
Hers is the holy calm of some meek saint.

GIFTS

'O WORLD-GOD, give me wealth!' the Egyptian
      cried.
  His prayer was granted. High as heaven, behold
Palace and Pyramid; the brimming tide
  Of lavish Nile washed all his land with gold.
Armies of slaves toiled ant-wise at his feet,
World-circling traffic roared through mart and street,
His priests were gods, his spice-balmed kings en-
      shrined
  Set death at naught in rock-ribbed charnels deep.
Seek Pharaoh's race to-day, and ye shall find
  Rust and the moth, silence and dusty sleep.

'O World-God, give me beauty!' cried the Greek.
  His prayer was granted. All the earth became
Plastic and vocal to his sense; each peak,
  Each grove, each stream, quick with Promethean flame,
Peopled the world with imaged grace and light.
The lyre was his, and his the breathing might
Of the immortal marble, his the play
  Of diamond-pointed thought and golden tongue.
Go seek the sunshine-race, ye find to-day
  A broken column and a lute unstrung.

'O World-God, give me power!' the Roman cried.
  His prayer was granted. The vast world was chained
A captive to the chariot of his pride.
  The blood of myriad provinces was drained
To feed that fierce, insatiable red heart;
Invulnerably bulwarked every part
With serried legions, and with close-meshed Code;
  Within, the burrowing worm had gnawed its home.
A roofless ruin stands where once abode
  The imperial race of everlasting Rome.

'O Godhead, give me Truth!' the Hebrew cried.
　His prayer was granted; he became the slave
Of the Idea, a pilgrim far and wide,
　Cursed, hated, spurned, and scourged with none to save.
The Pharaohs knew him, and when Greece beheld,
　His wisdom wore the hoary crown of Eld.
Beauty he hath forsworn, and wealth and power.
　Seek him to-day, and find in every land
No fire consumes him, neither floods devour;
　Immortal through the lamp within his hand.

Arlo Bates

IN SHADOW

OH, egotism of agony! While we
　　Weep thus sore-stricken, filling earth with moan,
　The feet of those we love, through ways unknown,
Brought into lands of living light may be.

E'en our tear-blinded eyes can dimly see
　What heights are reached by sorrow's paths alone,
　Where heavenly joy and radiance shall atone;
For gloom and woe have held us utterly;

And sure our dead, loftier of soul, and now
　Free from the weakness human sight doth mar,
Must death with power and vision new endow.

If we, blind, groping, feel the truth afar,
　They wear its very radiance on their brow.
Death takes a rush-light, but he gives a star!

Mrs. Robert G. Howland

REQUIESCAM *

I LAY me down to sleep,
　With little thought or care,
Whether my waking find
　Me here or there.

* See note.

A bowing, burdened head,
That only asks to rest,
Unquestioning, upon
    A loving breast.

My good right hand forgets
Its cunning now.
To march the weary march
    I know not how.

I am not eager, bold,
Nor strong—all that is past;
I am ready not to do
    At last, at last.

My half day's work is done,
And this is all my part;
I give a patient God
    My patient heart,—

And grasp His banner still,
Though all its blue be dim;
These stripes, no less than stars,
    Lead after Him.

Oscar Fay Adams

WITH A PRAYER-BOOK

IN Common Prayer our hearts ascend
    To that white throne where angels bend.
Now grant, O Lord, that those who call
Themselves by Thy dear name may all
Show forth Thy praise in lives that tend

To noble purpose, lofty end,
And unto us Thy blessing lend
    As low upon our knees we fall
                In Common Prayer.

In this dear Book past ages blend
Their voice with ours; we do commend
  Our souls, in doubt and sin-held thrall,
  To His fond care, and cot and hall
Alike to Him petitions send
      In Common Prayer.

Nathan Haskell Dole

IN THE OLD COUNTRY CHURCH

IS it a dream? Am I once more a child?
  In this old church I worshipped long ago!
Again I feel the strange delightful glow
That filled my young heart with a radiance mild,
While from the organ-loft the tones, beguiled
  By skilful hands, harmoniously flow,
  Now swelling high, now welling faint and low,
As though harsh discords all were reconciled!

Outside, the graceful elm-boughs softly sway;
  Thro' open windows breathes the summer breeze;
And in the hush before the people pray
  I hear the murmur of a myriad bees.
Is it a dream? Am I a child to-day?
  It verily seems so, as I bow my knees!

Ah! golden hours of childhood gone for ever!
  My brown-eyed, quiet little maiden there,
  Who feels but knows not what is meant by prayer,
The time must come when she too will endeavor
Her weary heart from sad to-days to sever,
  To lift the burden of a present care;
  Then will she to the Father's house repair
To find sure comfort! May it fail her never!

The summer breeze will sweep the cloudless sky;
  The yellow bees will hum among the elms;
The mellow organ-tones will swell and sigh;
The priest will speak his words of counsel sweet
To guide the wandering soul to heavenly realms;
And thus each age its marvels doth repeat.

Eugene Field

CHRISTMAS EVE

OH, hush thee, little Dear-my-Soul,
  The evening shades are falling,—
Hush thee, my dear, dost thou not hear
  The voice of the Master calling?

Deep lies the snow upon the earth,
  But all the sky is ringing
With joyous song, and all night long
  The stars shall dance, with singing.

Oh, hush thee, little Dear-my-Soul,
  And close thine eyes in dreaming,
And angels fair shall lead thee where
  The singing stars are beaming.

A Shepherd calls His little lambs,
  And He longeth to caress them;
He bids them rest upon His breast,
  That His tender love may bless them.

So, hush thee, little Dear-my-Soul,
  Whilst evening shades are falling,
And above the song of the heavenly throng
  Thou shalt hear the Master calling.

THE DEAD BABE

LAST night, as my dear babe lay dead,
  In agony I knelt and said:
    'O God! What have I done,
Or in what wise offended Thee,
That Thou shouldst take away from me
    My little son?

'Upon the thousand useless lives,
Upon the guilt that vaunting thrives,
    Thy wrath were better spent!
Why shouldst Thou take my little son—
Why shouldst Thou vent Thy wrath upon
    This innocent?'

Last night, as my dear babe lay dead,
Before mine eyes the vision spread
    Of things that *might* have been;
Licentious riot, cruel strife,
Forgotten prayers, a wasted life
    Dark red with sin!

Then, with sweet music in the air,
I saw another vision there:
    A Shepherd in whose keep
A little lamb—my little child!
Of worldly wisdom undefiled,
    Lay fast asleep!

Last night, as my dear babe lay dead,
In those two messages I read
    A wisdom manifest;
And, though my arms be childless now,
I am content—to Him I bow
    Who knoweth best.

BETHLEHEM-TOWN

As I was going to Bethlehem-town,
  Upon the earth I cast me down
All underneath a little tree,
That whispered in this wise to me:
'Oh, I shall stand on Calvary
And bear what burthen saveth thee!'

As up I fared to Bethlehem-town,
I met a shepherd coming down,
And thus he quoth: 'A wondrous sight
Hath spread before mine eyes this night,—
An angel host, most fair to see,
That sung full sweetly of a tree
That shall uplift on Calvary
What burthen saveth you and me!'

And as I gat to Bethlehem-town,
Lo! wise men came that bore a crown.
'Is there,' cried I, 'in Bethlehem
A King shall wear this diadem?'

'Good sooth,' they quoth, 'and it is He
That shall be lifted on the tree,
And freely shed on Calvary
What blood redeemeth us and thee!'

Unto a Child in Bethlehem-town
The wise men came and brought the crown;
And while the Infant smiling slept,
Upon their knees they fell and wept;
But, with her Babe upon her knee,
Naught recked that Mother of the tree
That should uplift on Calvary
What burthen saveth all and me.

Again I walk in Bethlehem-town,
And think on Him that wears the crown.
I may not kiss His feet again,
Nor worship Him as did I then;
My King hath died upon the tree,
And hath outpoured on Calvary
What blood redeemeth you and me!

THE PEACE OF CHRISTMAS-TIME

DEAREST, how hard it is to say
  That all is for the best,
Since, sometimes, in a grievous way
  God's will is manifest.

See with what hearty, noisy glee
  Our little ones to-night
Dance round and round our Christmas-tree
  With pretty toys bedight.

Dearest, one voice they may not hear,
  One face they may not see,—
Ah, what of all this Christmas cheer
  Cometh to you and me?

Cometh before our misty eyes
  That other little face;
And we clasp, in tender, reverent wise,
  That love in the old embrace.

Dearest, the Christ-Child walks to-night,
  Bringing His peace to men;
And He bringeth to you and to me the light
  Of the old, old years again:

Bringeth the peace of long ago,
  When a wee one clasped your knee
And lisped of the morrow,—dear one, you know,—
  And here come back is he!

Dearest, 'tis sometimes hard to say
  That all is for the best,
For, often in a grievous way,
  God's will is manifest.

But in the grace of this holy night
  That bringeth us back our child,
Let us see that the ways of God are right,
  And so be reconciled.

THE THREE KINGS OF COLOGNE

FROM out Cologne there came three kings
  To worship Jesus Christ their King.
To Him they sought, fine herbs they brought,
  And many a beauteous golden thing;
They brought their gifts to Bethlehem town,
And in that manger set them down.

Then spake the first king, and he said,
  'O Child, most heavenly, bright, and fair!
I bring this crown to Bethlehem town
  For Thee, and only Thee, to wear;
So give a heavenly crown to me
When I shall come at last to Thee!'

The second then, 'I bring Thee here
  This royal robe, O Child!' he cried;
'Of silk 'tis spun, and such an one
  There is not in the world beside;
So in the day of doom requite
Me with a heavenly robe of white!'

The third king gave his gift, and quoth:
  'Spikenard and myrrh to Thee I bring,
And with these twain would I most fain
  Anoint the body of my King;
So may their incense sometime rise
To plead for me in yonder skies!'

Thus spake the three kings of Cologne,
  That gave their gifts, and went their way;
And now kneel I in prayer hard by
  The cradle of the Child to-day;
Nor crown, nor robe, nor spice I bring
As offering unto Christ, my King.

Yet have I brought a gift the Child
  May not despise, however small;
For here I lay my heart to-day,
  And it is full of love to all.
Take Thou the poor but loyal thing,
My only tribute, Christ, my King!

Charles Francis Richardson

WISDOM

A CANDLE in the night
    But little space makes bright;
And when the skylark sings
He soars on fading wings.

Thus wisdom may not see
The things that distant be;
Nor may its eager ear
The world's far secrets hear.

But God exists; what more
Lies hid in learned lore?
My duty well I know;
Has life aught else to show?

God's works and ways I see,
God's wisdom teaches me;
I seek no other guide,
If He be by my side.

PEACE

IF sin be in the heart,
    The fairest sky is foul, and sad the summer
        weather,
The eye no longer sees the lambs at play together,
The dull ear cannot hear the birds that sing so sweetly,
And all the joy of God's good earth is gone completely,
    If sin be in the heart.

If peace be in the heart,
The wildest winter storm is full of solemn beauty,
The midnight lightning flash but shows the path of duty,
Each living creature tells some new and joyous story,
The very trees and stones all catch a ray of glory.
    If peace be in the heart.

LOVE

IF suddenly upon the street
    My gracious Saviour I should meet,
And He should say, 'As I love thee,
What love hast thou to offer Me?'
Then what could this poor heart of mine
Dare offer to that heart divine?

His eye would pierce my outward show,
His thought my inmost thought would know;
And if I said, 'I love Thee, Lord,'
He would not heed my spoken word,
Because my daily life would tell
If verily I loved Him well.

If on the day or in the place
Wherein He met me face to face,
My life could show some kindness done,
Some purpose formed, some work begun
For His dear sake, then it were meet
Love's gift to lay at Jesus' feet.

JUSTICE

A HUNDRED noble wishes fill my heart,
    I long to help each soul in need of aid;
In all good works my zeal would have its part,
    Before no weight of toil it stands afraid.

But noble wishes are not noble deeds,
    And he does least who seeks to do the whole;
Who works the best, his simplest duties heeds,
    Who moves the world, first moves a single soul.

Then go, my heart, thy plainest work begin,
    Do first not what thou canst, but what thou must;
Build not upon a corner-stone of sin,
    Nor seek great works until thou first be just.

Maurice Francis Egan

MAURICE DE GUÉRIN

THE old wine filled him, and he saw, with eyes
    Anoint of Nature, fauns and dryads fair
Unseen by others; to him maidenhair
And waxen lilacs, and those birds that rise
A-sudden from tall reeds at slight surprise,
Brought charmèd thoughts; and in earth everywhere
He, like sad Jaques, found a music rare
As that of Syrinx to old Grecians wise.
A pagan heart, a Christian soul had he,
He followed Christ, yet for dead Pan he sighed,
Till earth and heaven met within his breast;
As if Theocritus in Sicily
Had come upon the Figure crucified,
And lost his gods in deep Christ-given rest.

A QUESTION

FROM thy whole life take all the sweetest days
    Of earthly joy; take love before it cools;
Take words far-brought by all the learnèd schools
Since man first thought; then take the brightest rays
Which poets limnèd with their rose-flushed tools;
Take heart-wrung music chastened with strict rules
Of greatest masters; and in all thy ways
Find things that make men only pleasure's fools.
Take these; beside them lay one heart-felt prayer;
Take these; beside them lay one little deed—
One simple act done for the great Christ-Heart—
And all earth's fairest toys like graspless air
To it will be; this being, then what need
To strive for things that will, with time, depart?

WE CONQUER GOD

O WORLD, great world, now thou art all my own,
    In the deep silence of my soul I stay
The current of thy life, though the wild day
Surges around me, I am all alone;—
Millions of voices rise, yet my weak tone
Is heard by Him who is the Light, the Way,
All Life, all Truth, the center of Love's ray;
Clamor, O Earth, the Great God hears my moan!
Prayer is the talisman that gives us all,
We conquer God by force of His own love,
He gives us all; when prostrate we implore—
The Saints must listen; prayers pierce Heaven's wall;
The humblest soul on earth, when mindful of
Christ's promise, is the greatest conqueror.

COLUMBUS THE WORLD-GIVER

WHO doubts has met defeat ere blows can fall;
    Who doubts must die with no palm in his hand;
Who doubts shall never be of that high band
Which clearly answer—Present! to Death's call·
For Faith is life, and, though a funeral pall
Veil our fair Hope, and on our promised land
A mist malignant hang, if Faith but stand
Among our ruins, we shall conquer all.

O faithful soul, that knew no doubting low;
O Faith incarnate, lit by Hope's strong flame,
And led by Faith's own cross to dare all ill
And find our world!—but more than this we owe
To thy true heart; thy pure and glorious name
Is one clear trumpet call to Faith and Will.

FRA ANGELICO

ART is true art when art to God is true,
  And only then: to copy Nature's work
Without the chains that run the whole world through
Gives us the eye without the lights that lurk
In its clear depths: no soul, no truth is there.
Oh, praise your Rubens and his fleshly brush!
Oh, love your Titian and his carnal air!
Give me the trilling of a pure-toned thrush,
And take your crimson parrots. Artist-saint!
O Fra Angelico, your brush was dyed
In hues of opal, not in vulgar paint;
You showed to us pure joys for which you sighed,
Your heart was in your work, you never feigned:
You left us here the Paradise you gained!

PERPETUAL YOUTH

'TIS said there is a fount in Flower Land,—
  De Leon found it,—where Old Age away
Throws weary mind and heart, and fresh as day
Springs from the dark and joins Aurora's band:
This tale, transformed by some skilled trouvère's wand
From the old myth in a Greek poet's lay,
Rests on no truth. Change bodies as Time may,
Souls do not change, though heavy be his hand.
Who of us needs this fount? What soul is old?
Age is a mask,—in heart we grow more young,
For in our winters we talk most of spring;
And as we near, slow-tottering, God's safe fold,
Youth's loved ones gather nearer;—though among
The seeming dead, youth's songs more clear they sing.

Annie Trumbull Slosson

A CHRISTMAS CAROL

WHERE are you going, my little children,
   Soft-eyed Zillah, and brown-faced Seth,
Little David with cheek so ruddy,
   Dark-haired, slender Elizabeth?

What are the burdens you carry with you,
   Poised on the head and swung in the hand;
What is the song from your red lips ringing,
   What is your errand, you little band?

'Sirs, as you know, we are Hebrew children,
   I am Zillah, and this is Seth;
Here is David, our little brother,
   And this our sister Elizabeth.

'Our father's sheep are on yonder hillside,
   He cares for us and he watches them;
We left our home in the early morning,
   And go our way into Bethlehem.

'Surely you know that the Blessèd Baby,
   Greeted by angels with songs of joy,
Is lying there with His gentle Mother,
   And we are going to see the Boy.

'Here in our baskets are gifts we bring Him,
   All to lay at His little feet;
Amber honey our bees have gathered,
   Milk from our goats so white and sweet;

'Cakes of our figs, and grapes that are purple,
   Olives plucked from our own old trees;
Savory herbs, and fragrant spices,
   All we bring Him on bended knees.

'See, this is wool so soft and so fleecy,
   Purple dyes that a king might wear;
Skins of the goat, and the ram, and the badger,
   All for the Baby that's sleeping there.

'Here are shells from the Red Sea brought us,
  Here are feathers all bright and gay;
Tell us, good sirs, had ever a baby
  Fairer gifts than we bring to-day?

'Seth gives his dove, though he loves it dearly;
  David these shells for the Holy Boy;
Elizabeth wove Him this pretty basket,
  But I have only this little toy,—

'Two sticks of olive-wood, carved by my father,
  One standing up and one crossing it—so;
We have little to offer, we poor little children,
  But we give all we can, and we sing as we go.'

Singing they went with their simple treasures,
  Sweet rang their voices o'er valley and hill,
'Glory, oh, glory to God in the highest,
  Peace upon earth, and to men good-will.'

Still they went singing, these Hebrew children,
  Soft-eyed Zillah and brown-faced Seth;
Little David with cheek so ruddy,
  Dark-haired, slender Elizabeth.

A CHILD'S EASTER

HAD I been there, when Christ, our Lord, lay sleeping
    Within that tomb in Joseph's garden fair,
I would have watched all night beside my Saviour—
        Had I been there.

Close to the hard, cold stone my soft cheek pressing,
I should have thought my head lay on His breast;
And dreaming that His dear arms were about me,
        Have sunk to rest.

All thro' the long, dark night when others slumbered,
Close, close beside Him still I would have stayed,
And, knowing how He loved the little children,
        Ne'er felt afraid.

'To-morrow,' to my heart I would have whispered,
'I will rise early in the morning hours,
And wand'ring o'er the hillside I will gather
        The fairest flowers;

'Tall, slender lilies (for my Saviour loved them,
And tender words about their beauty spake),
And golden buttercups, and glad-eyed daisies,
    But just awake;

'"Grass of the field" in waving, feath'ry beauty,
He clothed it with that grace, so fair but brief,
Mosses all soft and green, and crimson berry,
    With glossy leaf.

'While yet the dew is sparkling on the blossoms,
I'll gather them and lay them at His feet,
And make the blessèd place where He is sleeping
    All fair and sweet.

'The birds will come, I know, and sing above Him,
The sparrows whom He cared for when awake,
And they will fill the air with joyous music
    For His dear sake.'

And, thinking thus, the night would soon be passing,
Fast drawing near that first glad Easter light.
Ah, Lord, if I could but have seen Thee leaving
    The grave's dark night!

I would have kept so still, so still, and clasping
My hands together as I do in prayer,
I would have knelt, reverent, but oh, so happy!—
    Had I been there.

Perhaps He would have bent one look upon me;
Perhaps in pity for that weary night,
He would have laid on my uplifted forehead
    A touch so light;

And all the rest of life I should have felt it,
A sacred sign upon my brow imprest,
And ne'er forgot that precious, lonely vigil,
    So richly blest.

Dear Lord, thro' death and night I was not near Thee;
But in Thy risen glory can rejoice,
So, loud and glad in song this Easter morning,
    Thou'lt hear my voice.

James Whitcomb Riley

THE PRAYER PERFECT

DEAR Lord! kind Lord!
  Gracious Lord! I pray
Thou wilt look on all I love
  Tenderly to day!
Weed their hearts of weariness;
  Scatter every care
Down a wake of angel-wings
  Winnowing the air.

Bring unto the sorrowing
  All release from pain;
Let the lips of laughter
  Overflow again;
And with all the needy
  O divide, I pray,
This vast treasure of content
  That is mine to-day!

THE KINGLY PRESENCE

BY the splendor in the heavens, and the hush upon
    the sea,
And the majesty of silence reigning over Galilee,—
We feel Thy Kingly presence, and we humbly bow the
    knee,
And lift our hearts and voices in gratefulness to Thee.

Thy Messenger has spoken, and our doubts have fled
    and gone
As the dark and spectral shadows of the night before
    the dawn;
And in the kindly shelter of the Light around us drawn,
We would nestle down for ever on the breast we lean
    upon.

You have given us a Shepherd—you have given us a
    Guide,
And the light of heaven grew dimmer when you sent
    Him from your side,—
But He comes to lead Thy children where the gates
    will open wide
To welcome His returning, when His works are glorified.

By the splendor in the heavens, and the hush upon
    the sea,
And the majesty of silence reigning over Galilee,—
We feel Thy Kingly presence, and we humbly bow the
    knee
And lift our hearts and voices in gratefulness to Thee.

THE BEAUTIFUL CITY

THE Beautiful City! forever
    Its rapturous praises resound;
We fain would behold it—but never
    A glimpse of its glory is found:
We slacken our lips at the tender
    White breasts of our mothers to hear
Of its marvelous beauty and splendor:—
    We see—but the gleam of a tear!

Yet never the story may tire us,
    First graven in symbols of stone—
Rewritten on scrolls of papyrus,
    And parchment, and scattered and blown
By the winds of the tongues of all nations,
    Like a litter of leaves wildly whirled
Down the rack of a hundred translations,
    From the earliest lisp of the world.

We compass the earth and the ocean,
    From the Orient's uttermost light,
To where the last ripple in motion
    Lips hem of the skirt of the night,—
But the Beautiful City evades us—
    No spire of it glints in the sun—
No glad-bannered battlement shades us,
    When all our long journey is done.

Where lies it ? We question and listen ;
  We lean from the mountain, or mast,
And see but dull earth or the glisten
  Of seas inconceivably vast :
The dust of the one blurs our vision,
  The glare of the other our brain—
Nor city nor island Elysian
  In all of the land or the main !

We kneel in dim fanes where the thunders
  Of organs tumultuous roll,
And the longing heart listens and wonders,
  And the eyes look aloft from the soul ;
But the chanson grows fainter and fainter,
  Swoons wholly away and is dead ;
And our eyes only reach where the painter
  Has dabbled a saint overhead.

The Beautiful City ! O mortal,
  Fare hopefully on in thy quest,
Pass down through the green grassy portal
  That leads to the Valley of Rest,
There first passed the One who, in pity
  Of all thy great yearning, awaits
To point out the Beautiful City,
  And loosen the trump at the gates.

THE DEAD WIFE

ALWAYS I see her in a saintly guise
  Of lilied raiment, white as her own brow
When first I kissed the tear-drops to the eyes
  That smile forever now.

Those gentle eyes ! They seem the same to me,
  As, looking through the warm dews of mine own,
I see them gazing downward patiently
  Where, lost and all alone

In the great emptiness of night, I bow
  And sob aloud for one returning touch
Of the dear hands that, heaven having now,
  I need so much—so much !

Ellen Mackay Hutchinson

UNDER THE STARS

O NIGHT, look down through cloud and star
  Upon our fret and pain!
Bid all the dreams that day denies
  Bloom into faith again!
In silvery shades of shadow come,
And take earth's weary children home!

Sweet teacher, wiser than the schools,
  Thy speechless lessons bring!
The rebel soul, the aching heart,
  The will like broken wing,
Make ready for a stiller night,
And for a dearer Morning Light!

Edith Matilda Thomas

*What shall I say? He hath both spoken unto me, and Himself
hath done it: I shall go softly all my years in the bitterness of my
soul.*— Isa. xxxviii. 15.

THE QUIET PILGRIM

WHEN on my soul in nakedness
  His swift avertless hand did press,
Then I stood still, nor cried aloud,
  Nor murmured low in ashes bowed;
And, since my woe is utterless,
  To supreme quiet I am vowed;
Afar from me be moan and tears,—
I shall go softly all my years.

Whenso my quick light-sandalled feet
Bring me where joys and pleasures meet,
  I mingle with their throng at will;
  They know me not an alien still,
Since neither words nor ways unsweet
  Of storèd bitterness I spill;
Youth shuns me not, nor gladness fears,—
I shall go softly all my years.

Whenso I come where griefs convene,
And in my ear their cry is keen;
　They know me not, as on I glide,
　That with Arch Sorrow I abide.
They haggard are, and dropped of mien,
　And round their brows have cypress tied;
Such shows I leave to light Grief's peers,—
I shall go softly all my years.

Yea, softly! heart of hearts unknown,
Silence hath speech that passeth moan,
　More piercing-keen than breathèd cries
　To such as heed, made sorrow-wise.
But save this voice without a tone,
　That runs before me to the skies,
And rings above Thy ringing spheres,
Lord, I go softly all my years.

'IF STILL THEY LIVE, WHOM TOUCH NOR SIGHT'

IF still they live, whom touch nor sight
　　Nor any subtlest sense can prove,
Though dwelling past our day and night,
　　At farthest star's remove,—

Oh, not because these skies they change
For upper deeps of sky unknown,
Shall that which made them ours grow strange,
　　For spirit holds its own;

Whether it pace this earth around,
Or cross, with printless, buoyant feet,
The unreverberant Profound
　　That hath no name nor mete!

'OFT HAVE I WAKENED ERE THE SPRING OF DAY'

OFT have I wakened ere the spring of day,
　　And from my window looking forth have found
All dim and strange the long-familiar ground,
But soon I saw the mist glide slow away,

And leave the hills in wonted green array,
While from the stream-sides and the fields around
Rose many a pensive day-entreating sound,
And the deep-breasted woodlands seemed to pray.

Will it be even so when first we wake
Beyond the Night in which are merged all nights,—
The soul sleep-heavy and forlorn will ache,
Deeming herself midst alien sounds and sights?
Then will the gradual Day with comfort break
Along the old deeps of being, the old heights?

William Ordway Partridge

THE MASTER'S WORK

THE hands that do God's work are patient hands,
　　And quick for toil, though folded oft in prayer;
They do the unseen work they understand
　　And find—no matter where.

The feet that follow His must be swift feet,
For time is all too short, the way too long;
Perchance they will be bruised, but falter not,
　　For love shall make them strong.

The lips that speak God's words must learn to wear
Silence and calm, although the pain be long;
And, loving so the Master, learn to share
　　His agony and wrong.

CHANGE

THE dearest things in this fair world must change;
　　Thy senses hurry on to sure decay;
Thy strength will fail, the pain seem no more strange,
　　While love more feebly cheers the misty way.
What then remains above the task of living?
　　Is there no crown where that rude cross hath pressed?
Yes, God remains, His own high glory giving
　　To light thy lonely path, to make it blest.

Yea, God remains, though suns are daily dying,—
　A gracious God, who marks the sparrow's fall;
He listens while thine aching heart is sighing;
　He hears and answers when His children call;
His love shall fill the void when death assails,—
The one, eternal God, who never fails.

Carl Spencer

THE KING'S SHIPS

GOD hath so many ships upon the sea!
　His are the merchant-men that carry treasure,
The men-of-war, all bannered gallantly,
　The little fisher-boats and barks of pleasure.
On all this sea of time there is not one
That sailed without the glorious name thereon.

The winds go up and down upon the sea,
　And some they lightly clasp, entreating kindly,
And waft them to the port where they would be;
　And other ships they buffet long and blindly.
The cloud comes down on the great sinking deep,
And on the shore the watchers stand and weep.

And God hath many wrecks within the sea;
　Oh, it is deep! I look in fear and wonder;
The wisdom throned above is dark to me,
　Yet it is sweet to think His care is under;
That yet the sunken treasure may be drawn
Into His storehouse when the sea is gone.

So I, that sail in peril on the sea,
　With my beloved, whom yet the waves may cover,
Say: God hath more than angels' care of me,
　And larger share than I in friend and lover!
Why weep ye so, ye watchers on the land?
This deep is but the hollow of His hand!

George Edward Woodberry *

SODOMA'S CHRIST SCOURGED

I SAW in Siena pictures,
  Wandering wearily;
I sought not the names of the masters,
  Nor the works men care to see;
But once in a low-ceiled passage
  I came on a place of gloom,
Lit here and there with halos
  Like saints within the room.
The pure, serene, mild colors
  The early artists used
Had made my heart grow softer,
  And still on peace I mused.
Sudden I saw the Sufferer,
  And my frame was clenched with pain;
Perchance no throe so noble
  Visits my soul again.
Mine were the stripes of the scourging;
  On my thorn-pierced brow blood ran;
In my breast the deep compassion
  Breaking the heart for man.
I drooped with heavy eyelids,
  Till evil should have its will;
On my lips was silence gathered;
  My waiting soul stood still.
I gazed, nor knew I was gazing;
  I trembled, and woke to know
Him whom they worship in heaven
  Still walking on earth below.
Once have I borne His sorrows
  Beneath the flail of fate!
Once in the woe of His passion,
  I felt the soul grow great!
I turned from my dead Leader;
  I passed the silent door;
The gray-walled street received me;
  On peace I mused no more.

* See note.

Willis Boyd Allen

'WITH YOU ALWAY'

WHY seek ye for Jehovah
  Mid Sinai's awful smoke?
The burning bush now shelters
A sparrow's humble folk;
The curve of God's sweet heaven
Is the curve of the leaf of oak;
The Voice that stilled the tempest
To the little children spoke,—
The bread of life eternal
Is the bread He blessed and broke.

UNTO THE PERFECT DAY

A MORNING-GLORY* bud, entangled fast
  Amid the meshes of its winding stem,
Strove vainly with the coils about it cast,
  Until the gardener came and loosened them.

A suffering human life entangled lay
  Among the tightening coils of its own past;
The Gardener came, the fetters fell away,
  The life unfolded to the sun at last.

Anna Jane Granniss

THE SAINTS' MESSENGER

IF I knew it now, how strange it would seem,
  To think, to know, ere another day
I should have passed over the silent way,
And my present life become as a dream;
  But what if that step should usher me
Right into the sinless company
  Of the saints in heaven.

* Convolvulus.

I'll carefully watch the door of my lips
　As I talk with my comrades to-day,
　And think a little before I say,
To see that no careless expression slips,
　Which I should find would so ill compare
　With the holy converse uttered there,
　　By the saints in heaven.

If they let me in—Oh, how sweet, how strange,
　The thought that before a new day dawn,
　I may put the incorruptible on,—
That beautiful garment, the robe of change!
　And walk and talk with that happy throng,
　Perhaps join my voice in the 'new, new song,'
　　With the saints in heaven.

But I fear I should be poorly meet
　To mingle much with the saints at all;
　My earthly service would seem so small—
Just going of errands on tired feet;
　But, oh! how blest, if it were my share
　To be the trusted messenger there,
　　For the saints in heaven!

With holy missives to take and bring,
　Sometime, perhaps, it would come to be
　That some pure saint would commission me
To carry his message straight to the King:
　And the King His answer would defer,
　To turn and smile on the messenger
　　Of His saints in heaven!

MY GUEST

THE day is fixed that there shall come to me
　　A strange mysterious guest;
The time I do not know, he keeps the date,
So all I have to do is work and wait,
　　And keep me at my best,
And do my common duties patiently.

I've often wondered if that day would break
      Brighter than other days
That I might know, or wrapped in some strange gloom;
And if he'd find me waiting in my room,
      Or busy with life's ways,
With tired hands, and weary eyes that ache.

For many years I've known that he would come,
      And so have watched for him;
And sometimes even said, 'He will come soon!'
Yet mornings pass followed by afternoon,
      With twilights dusk and dim,
And silent night-times, when the world is dumb.

But he *will* come, and find me here or there,
      It does not matter when,
For when he comes, I know that he will take
In his these very hands of mine that ache,
      (They will be idle then,)
Just folded may be, with a silent prayer.

Yes, he whom I expect has been called Death,
      And once he is my guest,
Nothing disturbs of what has been, or is;
I'll leave the world's loud company for his,
      As that which seemeth best,
And none may hear the tender words he saith.

So we pass out, my royal guest and I,
      As noiseless as he came;
For naught will do but I must go with him,
And leave the house I've lived in closed and dim,
      It only bears my name—
I've known I should not need it, by and by.

And so I sleep and wake, I toil and rest,
      Knowing when he shall come,
My Elder Brother will have sent for me,
Bidding him say that they especially
      Have need of me at home;
And so, I shall go gladly with my guest.

Margaret Wade Deland

HYMN

O PATIENT Christ! when long ago
　　O'er old Judea's rugged hills
Thy willing feet went to and fro,
　　To find and comfort human ills—
　　　　Did once Thy tender, earnest eyes
　　　　Look down the solemn centuries,
　　　　And see the smallness of our lives?

Souls struggling for the victory,
　　And martyrs, finding death was gain,
Souls turning from the Truth and Thee,
　　And falling deep in sin and pain—
　　　　Great heights and depths were surely seen,
　　　　But, oh! the dreary waste between—
　　　　Small lives, not base perhaps, but mean:

Their selfish efforts for the right,
　　Or cowardice that keeps from sin;
Content to only see the height
　　That nobler souls will toil to win!
　　　　Oh, shame, to think Thine eyes should see
　　　　The souls contented just to be—
　　　　The lives too small to take in Thee.

Lord, let this thought awake our shame,
　　That blessèd shame that stings to life,
Rouse us to live for Thy dear name,
　　Arm us with courage for the strife!
　　　　O Christ! be patient with us still;
　　　　Dear Christ! remember Calvary's hill—
　　　　Our little lives with purpose fill!

LOVE AND DEATH

A LAS! that men must see
　　Love, before Death!
Else they content might be
　　With their short breath;
　　　　Aye, glad, when the pale sun
　　　　Showed restless Day was done,
　　　　And endless Rest begun.

Glad, when with strong, cool hand
  Death clasped their own,
And with a strange command,
    Hushed every moan;
      Glad to have finished pain,
      And labor wrought in vain,
      Blurred by Sin's deepening stain.

But Love's insistent voice
  Bids Self to flee—
'Live that I may rejoice,
  Live on for me!'
    So, for Love's cruel mind,
    Men fear this Rest to find,
    Nor know great Death is kind!

DOUBT

O DISTANT Christ! the crowded, darkening years
  Drift slow between Thy gracious face and me;
My hungry heart leans back to look for Thee,
But finds the way set thick with doubts and fears.

My groping hands would touch Thy garment's hem,
  Would find some token Thou art walking near;
  Instead they clasp but empty darkness drear,
And no diviner hands reach out to them!

Sometimes my listening soul, with bated breath,
  Stands still to catch a footfall by my side,
  Lest, haply, my earth-blinded eyes but hide
Thy stately figure, leading Life and Death;

My straining eyes, O Christ, but long to mark
  A shadow of Thy presence, dim and sweet,
  Or far-off light to guide my wandering feet,
Or hope for hands prayer-beating 'gainst the dark.

O Thou! unseen by me, that like a child
  Tries in the night to find its mother's heart,
  And weeping, wanders only more apart,
Not knowing in the darkness that she smiled—

Thou, all unseen, dost hear my tired cry,
  As I, in darkness of a half belief,
  Grope for Thy heart, in love and doubt and grief:
O Lord! speak soon to me—'Lo, here am I!'

EASTER MUSIC

BLOW, golden trumpets, sweet and clear,
    Blow soft upon the perfumed air;
Bid the sad earth to join your song,
'To Christ does victory belong!'

Oh, let the winds your message bear
To every heart of grief and care;
Sound through the world the joyful lay,
'Our Christ hath conquered Death to-day!'

On cloudy wings let glad words fly
Through the soft blue of echoing sky:
Ring out, O trumpets, sweet and clear,
'Through Death immortal Life is here!'

Ina Donna Coolbrith

IN BLOSSOM TIME

IT'S O my heart, my heart,
  To be out in the sun and sing!
To sing and shout in the fields about,
  In the balm and the blossoming.

Sing loud, O bird in the tree;
  O bird, sing loud in the sky,
And honey-bees blacken the clover seas:
  There are none of you glad as I.

The leaves laugh low in the wind,
  Laugh low with the wind at play;
And the odorous call of the flowers all
  Entices my soul away!

For O but the world is fair, is fair:
  And O but the world is sweet!
I will out in the gold of the blossoming mould,
  And sit at the Master's feet.

And the love my heart would speak,
  I would fold in the lily's rim,
That the lips of the blossom, more pure and meek,
  May offer it up to Him.

Then sing in the hedgerow green, O thrush,
  O skylark, sing in the blue;
Sing loud, sing clear, that the King may hear,
  And my soul shall sing with you!

A PRAYER

O SOUL! however sweet
    The goal to which I hasten with swift feet—
If just within my grasp,
  I reach, and joy to clasp,
And find there one whose body I must make
  A footstool for that sake,
Though ever and for evermore denied,
  Grant me to turn aside!

O howsoever dear
The love I long for, seek, and find anear—
  So near, so dear, the bliss
  Sweetest of all that is,
If I must win by treachery or art,
  Or wrong one other heart,
Though it should bring me death, my soul, that day
  Grant me to turn away!

  That in the life so far
And yet so near, I be without a scar
Of wounds dealt others; greet with lifted eyes
  The pure of Paradise!
  So I may never know
The agony of tears I caused to flow!

Tudor Jenks

A CHRISTMAS SONG

WHEN mother-love makes all things bright,
  When joy comes with the morning light,
When children gather round their tree,
    Thou Christmas Babe,
    We sing of Thee!

When manhood's brows are bent in thought
To learn what men of old have taught,
When eager hands seek wisdom's key,
    Wise Temple Child,
    We learn of Thee!

When doubts assail, and perils fright,
When, groping blindly in the night,
We strive to read life's mystery,
    Man of the Mount,
    We turn to Thee!

When shadows of the valley fall,
When sin and death the soul appal,
One light we through the darkness see—
    Christ on the Cross,
    We cry to Thee!

And when the world shall pass away,
And dawns at length the perfect day,
In glory shall our souls made free,
    Thou God enthroned,
    Then worship Thee!

Charles Henry Crandall

WAITING

AS little children in a darkened hall
  At Christmas-tide await the opening door,
Eager to tread the fairy-haunted floor
About the tree with goodly gifts for all,

And in the dark unto each other call—
  Trying to guess their happiness before,—
  Or of their elders eagerly implore
Hints of what fortune unto them may fall:

So wait we in Time's dim and narrow room,
  And with strange fancies, or another's thought,
    Try to divine, before the curtain rise,
The wondrous scene. Yet soon shall fly the gloom,
  And we shall see what patient ages sought,
    The Father's long-planned gift of Paradise.

Charles Henry Lüders

TIME AND ETERNITY

WHEN Life and Death clasp hands to part no more,
  When the wide wings of Earth no longer soar,
Time's pathway through the eternal heavens will gleam,
Brief as the passing of a meteor.

William Roscoe Thayer

PERFECTIBILITY

GOD first made man of common clay,
  And o'er the earth he brute-like went;
But deep within his bosom stirr'd
  A strange, unearthly discontent.

Woman God made a living soul—
  He made her fair, He made her sweet,—
Upon her with delight man look'd,
  And brought his conquests to her feet.

In her he found his heart's desire;
  He lov'd, and was no more a clod;
Subtly she purifies his soul,
  Surely she draws him up to God.

Helen Gray Cone

THE TORCH RACE

BRAVE racer, who hast sped the living light
　　With throat outstretched and every nerve a·strain,
Now on thy left hand labors gray-faced Pain,
And Death hangs close behind thee on the right.
Soon flag the flying feet, soon fails the sight,
With every pulse the gaunt pursuers gain ;
And all thy splendor of strong life must wane
And set into the mystery of night.

Yet fear not, though in falling, blindness hide
Whose hand shall snatch, before it sears the sod,
The light thy lessening grasp no more controls :
Truth's rescuer, Trust shall instantly provide :
This is the torch-race game, that noblest souls
Play on through time beneath the eyes of God.

A RESURRECTION

Neither would they be persuaded, though one rose from the dead.—Luke xvi. 31.

I WAS quick in the flesh, was warm, and the live
　　heart shook my breast ;
In the market I bought and sold, in the temple I
　　bowed my head.
I had swathed me in shows and forms, and was honored
　　above the rest
For the sake of the life I lived ; nor did any esteem
　　me dead.

But at last, when the hour was ripe—was it sudden-
　　remembered word ?
Was it sight of a bird that mounted, or sound of a
　　strain that stole ?
I was 'ware of a spell that snapped, of an inward
　　strength that stirred,
Of a Presence that filled that place ; and it shone, and
　　I knew my Soul.

And the dream I had called my life was a garment
about my feet,
For the web of the years was rent with the throe of
a yearning strong.
With a sweep as of winds in heaven, with a rush as
of flames that meet,
The Flesh and the Spirit clasped; and I cried, 'Was
I dead so long?'

I had glimpse of the Secret, flashed through the symbol
obscure and mean,
And I felt as a fire what erst I repeated with lips of
clay;
And I knew for the things eternal the things eye hath
not seen;
Yea, the heavens and the earth shall pass; but they
never shall pass away.

And the miracle on me wrought, in the streets I would
straight make known:
'When this marvel of mine is heard, without cavil
shall men receive
Any legend of haloed saint, starting up through the
sealèd stone!'
So I spake in the trodden ways; but behold there
would none believe!

Danske Carolina Dandridge

MAY

WHEN Eve went out from Paradise
With looks distraught and sad surmise,
And when she tried to make a home
For Adam in the thorny land,
By kinship I can understand
The homesick longing that would come,
The sad and lonely memories
Of Eden trees and Eden skies.

At sunset when her work was done,
Perchance she sat to muse alone,
And hear the Eden waters flow.
The birds might sing, but she was mute,
Still tasting in her mouth the fruit,
That sweet beginning of her woe.
Perchance some bird that she had fed
Would come to flutter overhead—
Some happy bird that built his nest
Within the cherub-guarded spot,
Would come to thrill her aching breast
With tender jargon, unforgot;
Or bring her in his beak a flower
She planted in a peaceful hour.

What heritage, O weeping Eve,
Your wistful daughters yet receive
Of yearnings, and of longing pain,
For that which may not come again!
What dim, inherited desire,
Still thwarted by the swords of fire!
Yet when the riot garden-close
Just hints the coming of the rose;
When sumptuous tulips burst apart,
And rock the wild bee, heart to heart;
When languid butterflies a-swing
From apple-blossoms droop the wing;
When purple iris, by the wall,
Imperial iris, proud and tall,
With Persian lilac is a-blow,
And nodding lilies, row by row;
When hoyden creepers run apace
To kiss the lime-rock's wrinkled face;
When snowball turns from green to white
And keeps the secret that she knows,
The pretty secret, out of sight,
Wherein the robin's household grows;
And when we pace the pleachèd aisles,
And share, with tender words and smiles,
The beauty of the summer feast,—
'Tis then we miss our Eden least.

THE SINGING HEART

THOU Heart! why dost thou lift thy voice?
  The birds are mute; the skies are dark;
Nor doth a living thing rejoice;
  Nor doth a living creature hark;
  Yet thou art singing in the dark.

How small thou art; how poor and frail;
  Thy prime is past; thy friends are chill;
Yet as thou hadst not any ail
  Throughout the storm thou liftest still
  A praise that winter cannot chill.

Then sang that happy Heart reply:
  'God lives, God loves, and hears me sing.
How warm, how safe, how glad am I,
  In shelter 'neath His spreading wing,
  And there I cannot choose but sing.'

WINGS

SHALL we know in the hereafter
  All the reasons that are hid?
Does the butterfly remember
  What the caterpillar did?
How he waited, toiled, and suffered
  To become a chrysalid.

When we creep so slowly upward;
  When each day new burden brings;
When we strive so hard to conquer
  Vexing sublunary things;
When we wait and toil and suffer,
  We are working for our wings.

THE STRUGGLE

'BODY, I pray you, let me go!'
  (It is a Soul that struggles so.)
'Body, I see on yonder height
Dim reflex of a solemn light;

A flame that shineth from the place
Where Beauty walks with naked face:
It is a flame you cannot see;—
Lie down, you clod, and set me free.

'Body, I pray you, let me go!'
(It is a Soul that striveth so.)
'Body, I hear dim sounds afar,
Dripping from some diviner star;
Dim sounds of holy revelry:
It is my mates that sing, and I
Must drink that song or break my heart;
Body, I pray you, let us part.

'Comrade! your frame is worn and frail;
Your vital force begins to fail;
I long for life, but you for rest;
Then, Body, let us both be blest.
When you are lying 'neath the dew
I'll come, sometimes, and sing to you;
But you will feel nor pain nor woe;
Body, I pray you, let me go!'

Thus strove a Being: Beauty-fain,
He broke his bonds and fled amain.
He fled: the Body lay bereft,
But on its lips a smile was left,
As if that Spirit, looking back,
Shouted upon his upward track,
With joyous tone and hurried breath,
Some message that could comfort Death.

ARE YOU GLAD?

ARE you glad, my big brother, my deep-hearted oak?
   Are you glad in each open-palm leaf?
Do you joy to be God's? Does it thrill you with living
    delight?
Are you sturdy in stalwart belief?
As you stand day and night,
As you stand through the nights and the days,
Do you praise?

O strenuous vine, do you run,
As a man runs a race to a goal,
Your end that God's will may be done,
Like a strong-sinewed soul?
Are you glad? Do you praise?
Do you run?
And shall I be afraid,
Like a spirit undone;
Like a sprout in deep shade;
Like an infant of days:

When I hear, when I see and interpret aright
The winds in their jubilant flight;
The manifest peace of the sky and the rapture of
    light;
The pæan of waves as they flow;
The stars that reveal
The deep bliss of the night;
The unspeakable joy of the air;
And feel as I feel,
And know as I know
God is there?

Hush!
        For I hear him—
Enshrined in the heart of the wood:
'Tis the priestly and reverent thrush,
Anointed to sing to our God:
And he hymns it full well,
All I stammer to tell,
All I yearn to impart.

Listen!
        The strain
Shall sink into the heart,
And soften and swell
Till its meaning is plain,
And love in its manifold harmonies, that shall remain,
Shall remain.

Katharine Lee Bates

UNDER THE SNOWS

UNDER the drifted snows, with weeping and holy
    rite,
For a little maid's repose lies the lonely bed bedight.
Cold is the cradle-cover our pitiful hands fold over
The heart that had won repose or ever it knew delight.

High are the heavens and steep to us who would enter in
By the fasts that our faint hearts keep and the thorn-
    set crowns we win.
Sweetly the child awaketh, brightly the day-dawn
    breaketh
On the eyes that fell asleep or ever they looked on sin.

Frank Dempster Sherman

EASTER

ACROSS the winter's gloom
    There falls a golden ray,
And from each wild-flower's tomb
    The stone is rolled away.

Once more to life and love
    The buds and leaves of spring
Come forth, and hear above
    The birds like angels sing.

In every wood and field
    Behold the symbol shown,—
The mystery revealed,
    The majesty made known.

Christ who was crucified
    Is risen! Lo, the sign!
The earth at Eastertide
    Touched by His hand divine.

ALLAH'S HOUSE

NÁNÁC the faithful pausing once to pray,
   From holy Mecca turned his face away;
A Moslem priest, who chanced to see him there,
Forgetful of the attitude in prayer,
Cried: 'Infidel, how durst thou turn thy feet
Toward Allah's house—the sacred temple seat?'
To whom the pious Nánác thus replied:
'Know'st thou God's house is, as the world is, wide?
Thou, turn them, if thou canst, toward any spot
Where mighty Allah's awful house is not.'

Louise Jmogen Guiney

SUMMUM BONUM

WAITING on Him who knows us and our need,
   Most need have we to dare not, nor desire,
But as He giveth, *softly* to suspire
Against His gift, with no inglorious greed,
For this is joy, tho' still our joys recede;
And, as in octaves of a noble lyre,
To move our minds with His, and clearer, higher,
Sound forth our fate; for this is strength indeed.

Thanks to His love let earth and man dispense
In smoke of worship when the heart is stillest,
A praying more than prayer: 'Great good have I,
Till it be greater good to lay it by;
Nor can I lose peace, power, permanence,
For these smile on me from the thing Thou willest!'

FLORENTIN

HEART all full of heavenly haste, too like the bubble
      bright
On loud little water floating half of an April night,
Fled from the ear in music, fled from the eye in light,
Dear and stainless heart of a boy! No sweeter thing
      can be
Drawn to the quiet centre of God who is our sea;
Whither, thro' troubled valleys, we also follow thee.

A TALISMAN

TAKE Temperance to thy breast,
    While yet is the hour of choosing,
As arbitress exquisite
Of all that shall thee betide;
For better than fortune's best
Is mastery in the using,
And sweeter than anything sweet
The art to lay it aside!

Langdon Elwyn Mitchell

SONG

MARY, the mother, sits on the hill
    And cradles child Jesu, that lies so still;
She cradles child Jesu, that sleeps so sound,
And the little wind blows the song around.

The little wind blows the mother's words,
' Ei, Jesu, ei,' like the song of birds;
' Ei, Jesu, ei,' I heard it still,
As I lay asleep at the foot of the hill.

' Sleep, babe, sleep, mother watch doth keep,
Ox shall not hurt thee, nor ass, nor sheep;
Dew falls sweet from Thy Father's sky,
Sleep, Jesu, sleep! ei, Jesu, ei.'

THE IMPERIAL SOUL

* * * * *

WHAT man can live denying his own soul?
    Hast thou not learned that noble uncontrol
Is virtue's right, the breath by which she lives?
O sure, if any angel ever grieves,
'Tis when the living soul hath learnt to chide
Its passionate indignations, and to hide
The sudden flows of rapture, the quick birth
Of overwhelming loves, that balance the worth

Of the wide world against one loving act,
As less than a sped dream; shall the cataract
Stop, pause, and palter, ere it plunge towards
The vale unseen! Our fate hath its own lords,
Which if we follow truly, there can come
No harm unto us.

*   *   *   *   *   *   *

Richard Hovey

BEETHOVEN'S THIRD SYMPHONY

PASSION and pain, the outcome of despair,
    The pang of the unattainable desire,
And youth's delight in pleasures that expire,
And sweet high dreamings of the good and fair
Clashing in swift soul-storm, through which no prayer
Uplifted stays the destined death-stroke dire.
Then through a mighty sorrowing, as through fire,
The soul burnt pure yearns forth into the air
Of the dear earth and, with the scent of flowers
And song of birds assuaged, takes heart again,
Made cheerier with this drinking of God's wine,
And turns with healing to the world of men,
And high above a sweet, strong angel towers,
And Love makes Life triumphant and divine.

Amélie Rives

DEATH

DEATH is but life's renewal; but the pause
    Between two great thoughts of a loving God,
Full of mysterious tenderness. The hush
That follows on some marvelous harmony;
The indrawn breath before a shout of joy;
The backward movement of God's tidal love,
Which, for its brief withdrawal to the deep,
Comes voluming in with mightier force of hope,
And vastlier floods the thirsty shore with peace.

UNTO THE LEAST OF THESE LITTLE ONES

(*From* HARPER'S MAGAZINE. *Copyright* 1889 *by* HARPER & BROTHERS)

O CHILDREN'S eyes unchildlike !—Children's eyes
   That make pure, hallowed age seem young indeed—
Wan eyes that on drear horrors daily feed ;
Learned deep in all that leaves us most unwise !
Poor wells, beneath whose troubled depths Truth lies,
Drowned, drowned, alas ! So does my sad heart bleed
When I remember you ; so does it plead
And strive within my breast—as one who cries
For torture of her first-born—that the day,
The long, bright day, seems thicker sown for me
With eyes of children than the heavens at night
With stars on stars. To watch you is to pray
That you may some day see as children see,
When man, like God, hath said, ' Let there be light.'

Dear Christ, Thou hadst Thy childhood ere Thy cross ;
These, bearing first their cross, no childhood know,
But, aged with toil, through countless horrors grow
To age more horrible. Rough locks atoss
Above drink-reddened eyes, like Southern moss
That drops its tangles to the marsh below ;
No standard dreamed or real by which to show
The piteous completeness of their loss ;
No rest, no hope, no Christ ; the cross alone
Borne on their backs by day, their bed by night,
Their ghastly plaything when they pause to weep,
Their threat of torture do they dare to moan :
A darkness ever dark across their light,
A weight that makes a waking of their sleep.

Father, who countest such poor birds as fall,
Count Thou these children fallen from their place ;
Lift and console them of Thy pity's grace,
And teach them that to suffer is not all ;
Hedge them about with love as with a wall,
Give them in dreams the knowledge of Thy face,
And wipe away such stains as sin doth trace,
Sending deliverance when brave souls call.

Deliver them, O Lord, deliver them!—
These children—as Thy Son was once a child!
Make them even purer than before they fell,
Radiant in raiment clean from throat to hem:
For, Lord, till Thou hast cleansed these sin-defiled,
Of such the kingdom, not of heaven, but hell.

A WINTER HYMN

OH, Spirit of Love and of Light,
  Thou, the Unknown whom I serve,
Be with me, make me Thine own!—
Drench all my being with Thine,
Like as the wild winter rain
Drenches the winter-wan grass;
Be to me like as the wind,
Heard in the plumes of the pines—
Swaying me; loosening my thoughts—
(Thought is the scent of the soul!)
Change, O Divine One, my mood,—
Heavy and mist-like and dark,
Like as the sunset the clouds,
Till in the golden delight
Clouds are more lovely than air.
Delicate secret withheld,
Once did I call Thee by name!
Once in a far-away world!—
Vaguer than perfume of flowers
Blossoming pale in a dream,—
(Flowers the dark earth never knew)
Softer than croon in rill
Heard 'neath its prison of ice;
Lovelier than musing on Love,
Sweeter than tears of a Bride,
Holier than joy for the Dead,
The waft of Thy once spoken name.
Oh, Spirit of Love and of Light,
Thou, the Unknown whom I serve,
Be with me, make me Thine own!

Y 2

Lizette Woodworth Reese

LORD, OFT I COME

LORD, oft I come unto Thy door,
  But when Thou openest it to me,
Back to the dark I shrink once more,
  Away from light and Thee.

Lord, oft some gift of Thee I pray;
  Thou givest bread of finest wheat;
Empty I turn upon my way,
  Counting a stone more sweet.

Thou bidst me speed; then sit I still;
  Thou bidst me stay; then do I go;
Lord, make me Thine in deed and will,
  And ever keep me so!

A RHYME OF DEATH'S INN

A RHYME of good Death's inn!
  My love came to that door;
And she had need of many things,
  The way had been so sore.

My love she lifted up her head,
  'And is there room?' said she;
'There was no room in Bethlehem's inn
  For Christ who died for me.'

But said the keeper of the inn,
  'His name is on the door.'
My love then straightway entered there:
  She hath come back no more.

Alice Brown

IN EXTREMIS

NOT from the pestilence and storm,—
  Fate's creeping brood,—the crouching form
Of dread disease, and image dire
Of wrack and loss, of flood and fire;

Not from the poisoned fangs of hate,
Or death-worm born to be my mate,
But from the fear that such things be,
    O Lord, deliver me!

Fear dogs the shadow at my side;
Fear doth my wingless soul bestride.
In the lone stillness of the night
His whisper doth mine ear affright;
His formless shape mine eye appals;
Under his touch my body crawls.
Now, from his loathsome mastery,
    O Lord, deliver me!

I would not loose me, if I might,
From touch, or sound, or taste, or sight,
Of all life's dread revealing. Nay,
Were I God's angel, I would stay
Here on this clod of crucial grief,
And learn my rede without relief;
But from this basest empery
    And last, I would be free.

My fiend hath poisoned even the cup
Of faith and love: I may not sup
But horror grins within the bowl,
And spectre guests affright my soul.
Yea, and the awful Sisters Three,
Spinning the web eternity,
Have lost their solemn state, and wear
    The Furies' snake-bound hair.

Out of the jaws of hell and night
Lead my sick soul, O Sovereign Light!
Let me tread shivering through the cold,
Despised, forsaken, hunted, old,
Unloved, unwept, beneath the ban
Of sharpest anguish laid on man;
But from the monster foul I flee,
    O God, deliver me!

THE SILENT WATCH

FULL-ARMED I fought the Paynim foe;
   Now palm to palm I lie;
My bed, of stone; my covering,
   The minster's vaulted sky.

Pilgrim and priest move softly here,
   On vain or holy quest.
Let me sleep on, and take the meed
   Of my appointed rest.

Let me sleep on, until my soul
   Hath made her strong again
To fight the fight of good with ill,
   Of peace with mortal pain.

For one day there shall come a voice
   Sounding from sky to sea:
'Arise, Sir Knight, before My face!
   Now I have need of thee.'

HORA CHRISTI

SWEET is the time for joyous folk
   Of gifts and minstrelsy;
Yet I, O lowly-hearted One,
   Crave but Thy company.
On lonesome road, beset with dread,
   My questing lies afar.
I have no light, save in the east
   The gleaming of Thy star.

In cloistered aisles they keep to-day
   Thy feast, O living Lord!
With pomp of banner, pride of song,
   And stately-sounding word.
Mute stand the kings of power and place,
   While priests of holy mind
Dispense Thy blessed heritage
   Of peace to all mankind.

I know a spot where budless twigs
    Are bare above the snow,
And where sweet winter-loving birds
    Flit softly to and fro ;
There with the sun for altar-fire,
    The earth for kneeling-place,
The gentle air for chorister,
    Will I adore Thy face.

Lord, underneath the great blue sky,
    My heart shall pæan sing,
The gold and myrrh of meekest love
    Mine only offering.
Bliss of Thy birth shall quicken me ;
    And for Thy pain and dole
Tears are but vain, so I will keep
    The silence of the soul.

Anne Reeve Aldrich

A WAYSIDE CALVARY

ITS shadow makes a sheltered place
    All through the burning summer day,
There at the foot, secure from sun,
    The ragged little children play.

And in the winter huddled birds
    Take refuge from the windward side,
When driving snows make bleak the plain,
    And herald holy Christmas-tide.

The bleeding Christ that hangs above
    To bid the passer stop and pray,
Smiles through His bitter agony
    On such small, tender things as they !

WRITTEN BENEATH A CRUCIFIX

HE hath not guessed Christ's agony,
    He hath not dreamed His bitterest woe,
Who hath not worn the crown of love,
    And felt the crown of anguish so.

Ah, not the torments of the cross,
Or nails that pierced, or thirst that burned,
Heightened the Kingly Victim's pain,
But grief of griefs,—His love was spurned!

A LITTLE PARABLE

I MADE the cross myself, whose weight
Was later laid on me.
This thought is torture as I toil
Up life's steep Calvary.

To think mine own hands drove the nails!
I sang a merry song,
And chose the heaviest wood I had
To build it firm and strong.

If I had guessed—if I had dreamed
Its weight was meant for me,
I should have made a lighter cross
To bear up Calvary!

THE ETERNAL JUSTICE

THANK God that God shall judge my soul, not man!
I marvel when they say,
'Think of that awful Day—
No pitying fellow-sinner's eyes shall scan
With tolerance thy soul,
But His who knows the whole,
The God whom all men own is wholly just.'
Hold thou that last word dear,
And live untouched by fear.
He knows with what strange fires He mixed this dust.
The heritage of race,
The circumstance and place
Which make us what we are—were from His hand,
That left us, faint of voice,
Small margin for a choice.

He gave, I took : shall I not fearless stand ?
Hereditary bent
That hedges in intent
He knows, be sure, the God who shaped thy brain,
He loves the souls He made ;
He knows His own hand laid
On each the mark of some ancestral stain.
Not souls severely white,
But groping for more light,
Are what Eternal Justice here demands.
Fear not ; He made thee dust.
Cling to that sweet word—' Just.'
All 's well with thee if thou art in just hands.

Katherine Eleanor Conway

IN THANKSGIVING

AT last ! at last ! Oh joy ! Oh victory !
   But not to me, my God, ah, not to me,
But to Thy Name the praise, the glory be !

At last ! at last ! but when was prayer unheeded ?
And more wouldst Thou have given, had more been
      needed,
For purer lips than mine my cause have pleaded.

O trust that trembled on the verge of failing !
O timid heart, at shadowy terrors quailing !
Spending thyself in conflict unavailing !

Dear God, forgive ! my fears are shamed to flight ;
O'ershadowed by Thy mercy and Thy might,
I rest in humble-hearted, still delight.

Oh teach me song to praise Thee gladsomely,
Whose strong hands cleared the tangled way for me,
And saved me from the snares I could not flee !

CHRIST AND THE MOURNERS

DOWN on the shadowed stream of time and tears,
  Voice of new grief and grief of ancient years—
Sad as when first from loving lips 'twas sighed —
'Hadst Thou been here, my brother had not died.'

Comfort us, Lord, who heardst poor Martha's plaint,
Heal the sore heart, uplift the spirit faint—
O Thou, the Peace that cometh after strife !
O Thou, the Resurrection and the Life !

Why didst Thou take the love we leaned on so ?
We know not, but hereafter we shall know.
Speaks now our faith, through tears Thou wilt not chide,
'Most wert Thou here when our belovèd died.'

Minnie Gilmore

ADIEU

ADIEU ! To God !
  In all love's mystic language
No word so sweet as this,
Wherein some dear, dear heart to God we tender
  Between the sob and kiss.

No song, no poem,
  No prayer, has its completeness,
Its pathos, faith, its love ;
Not one on earth is meet to guard our treasure,—
  Meet only God above !

O hearts ! O lips !
  Not for the common parting
Where no love is, nor pain—
Not for the farewells spoken 'midst light laughter,
  This holy word profane:

But hold in trust
  For life's sure Passion-hour,
When scourging fates beset,
And called our souls, to tender their best lovèd
  On Parting's Olivet.

O sundered breasts !
    O sore souls torn and bleeding !
O lonely hearts that ache !
Love is a bond earth's partings forge but firmer,
    Nor death itself shall break.

And each 'A Dieu,'
    As from faint lips it falters,
Has issue great and grand,
Our dear ones shrining surely in the hollow
    Of God's own guarding hand.

LIFE

A SONG of a White Throne circled
    By a girdle of white fire.—
Once on the flame God breathèd,
    Filled with divine desire.
Out, at His breath, there flickered
    A single tongue of flame,
Paling the golden planets,
    Putting the sun to shame.

It flashed thro' the flashing Saturn,
    It flamed thro' the flaming Mars,
Flooded the skies with glory,
    Glowed down the glowing stars ;
Burst on the six-day Eden,
    And since has the world been rife
With fruit of that flame from heaven —
    The God-breathèd flame of Life.

Hannah Parker Kimball

CONTRAST

R OUT and defeat on every hand,
    On every hand defeat and rout ;
Yet through the rent clouds' hurrying rack
    The stars look out.

Decay supreme from west to east,
  From south to north supreme decay;
Yet still the withered fields and hills
    Grow green with May.

In clod and man unending strife,
  Unending strife in man and clod;
Yet burning in the heart of man
    The fire of God.

LIGHT

HE wills we may not read life's book aright,
  Wrest from each awful line its meaning clear,
Till we have bowed to read it by the light
Of pallid tapers on some true love's bier.

LOVE'S MIRACLE

LOVE, work thy wonted miracle to-day.
  Here stand, in jars of manifold design,
Life's bitter waters, mixed with mire and clay,
  And thou canst change them into purest wine.

TWO POINTS OF VIEW

I

ALL this costly expense
  For a few white souls forgiven,
For a smiling throng of a few elect,
  White harpers harping in heaven.

II

Lord, Thy glance is wide,
  And Thy wide arms circle the whole;
Shall out of Thy net of loving glide
  One wand'ring human soul?

THE CHRIST-CHILD ALONE

IN the long pageant of man's destiny,
    A sweep of sunburnt country and a hill,
Where sits a little child to watch the sky.—
O little Jesus, wide-eyed, charmed, and still,
How doth Thy hushed, expectant, wondering will
Commune with blade, and flower, and startled thing
That flits across Thy path on timid wing?
What thoughts, what dreams, what hopes, what fantasies,
Doth yon vast sweep of radiant heavens bring?
In Thy child's brain loom what strange images?

THE REFUGE OF THE IDEAL

OUR souls are sick for permanence; this world
    Shifts wearily on creaking poles through space;
  No atom stays, no friend; there is no place
Where man may rest a heart through transience whirled.

And we are sick for permanence. We know
    Too well how cities sink upon the sands;—
    Yet far away one cloud-tipped city stands
Secure, and through it ever, to and fro,

Surges a voice that cries: 'Ye sons of care,
    Frequent, with hearts appeased, my gleaming walls;
    Tread my white streets, and hear your sad footfalls
Rise deathless music through my radiant air.'

    Oh to attain this city of our quest,
    This luminous shelter for our souls' unrest!

William Hunter Birckhead

ASPIRATION

HIGHER, higher,
    Purified by suffering's fire,
Rise, my soul, until thy flight
Pierce its way to heaven's light.

Clearer, clearer,
Until, ever drawing nearer,
There shall burst upon thy sight,
Through the darkness of earth's night,
All the eye of faith may see,
Set in God's eternity.

R. T. W. Duke

LOST HOURS

THEIR advent is as silent as their going,
 They have no voice nor utter any speech,
No whispered murmur passes each to each,
As on the bosom of the years' stream flowing,
They pass beyond recall, beyond our knowing,
Farther than sight can pierce or thought can reach,
Nor shall we ever hear them on Time's beach,
No matter how the winds of life are blowing.

They bide their time, they wait the awful warning
Of that dread day, when hearts and graves unsealing
The trumpet's note shall call the sea and sod,
To yield their secrets to the sun's revealing:
What voices then shall thrill the Judgment morning,
As our lost hours shall cry aloud to God?

Paul Lawrence Dunbar

CONSCIENCE AND REMORSE

'GOOD-BYE,' I said, to my conscience—
 'Good-bye for aye and aye,'
And I put her hands off harshly,
 And turned my face away;
And conscience, smitten sorely,
 Returned not from that day.

But a time came when my spirit
 Grew weary of its pace;
And I cried: 'Come back my conscience,
 I long to see thy face,'
But conscience cried: 'I cannot,
 Remorse sits in my place.'

Ellen Sturgis Hooper

DUTY

I SLEPT, and dreamed that life was Beauty;
 I woke, and found that life was Duty.
Was thy dream then a shadowy lie?
Toil on, sad heart, courageously,
And thou shalt find thy dream to be
A noonday light and truth to thee.

Joseph Brownlee Brown

'THALATTA'

Cry of the Ten Thousand

I stand upon the summit of my years.
Behind, the toil, the camp, the march, the strife,
The wandering and the desert; vast, afar,
Beyond this weary way, behold! the Sea!
The sea o'er-swept by clouds and winds and wings,
By thoughts and wishes manifold, whose breath
Is freshness and whose mighty pulse is peace.
Palter no question of the dim Beyond;
Cut loose the bark; such voyage itself is rest;
Majestic motion, unimpeded scope,
A widening heaven, a current without care.
Eternity!—Deliverance, Promise, Course!
Time-tired souls salute thee from the shore.

EPILOGUE

———◆———

THE POETS

*W*HEN *this young land has reached its wrinkled*
  prime,
And we are gone, and all our songs are done,
And naught is left unchanged beneath the sun,
What other singers shall the womb of Time
Bring forth to reap the sunny slopes of rhyme?
For surely till the thread of life be spun
The world shall not lack poets, though but one
Make lovely music like a vesper chime
Above the heedless turmoil of the street.

 Those unborn poets! What melodious breath,
What larger music, shall be given to these?
Shall they more closely lie at Nature's feet,
Reading the volume of her mysteries?
Shall they new secrets wring from darksome Death?

     Thomas Bailey Aldrich.

NOTES

BIOGRAPHICAL AND EXPLANATORY

PAGE

1. John Pierpont, b. Litchfield, Conn., Apr. 6, 1785. Graduated Yale ; admitted to the bar 1812, retired on account of conscientious scruples. Entered Harvard Divinity School, 1818. Held pastorates at Hollis Street Church, Boston ; Troy, N.Y. ; and Medford, Mass. When more than 70 years of age became Chaplain of a Massachusetts regiment in the Civil War—this proved too much for his strength. He then undertook the vast work of indexing the decisions of the Treasury Department at Washington, which he completed before his sudden death, Aug. 27, 1866. His poetic works were *Airs of Palestine*, 1816 ; *Collected Poems*, 1840.

'Universal Worship'—written for the opening of the Congregational Church in Barton Square, Salem, Mass., Dec. 7, 1824— is the earliest really great hymn I have found by an American writer.

3. Andrews Norton, b. Hingham, Mass., 1786. Graduated Harvard. Librarian, Lecturer, and Professor of Sacred Literature at Harvard, 1819-30. Well known for his *Historical Evidences of the Genuineness of the Gospels.* d. 1853.

3. Written for the dedication of the First Church, Cambridge, Mass.

4. Charles Sprague, b. Boston, Oct. 25, 1791. (His father was one of those who, in resistance to British taxation, threw overboard the tea in Boston Harbor, 1773.) For the greater part of his life cashier in the Globe Bank, Boston. *Poems* appeared 1841. d. 1875.

'The Winged Worshippers' was addressed to two swallows that flew into Chauncy Place Church during divine service— see *Monthly Magazine* for May, 1870.

5. Nathaniel L. Frothingham, D.D., b. Boston, July 23, 1793. Graduated Harvard, 1811, with distinguished honor. When 19 years of age he became Instructor in Rhetoric and Oratory in Harvard. Studied theology, and was ordained pastor of the First Church, Boston, 1815, where he remained till failing sight, which ended in blindness, obliged him to resign, 1850. Much of his best poetic work was done after he had become blind. d. Apr. 4, 1870.

'A Lament,' for the Rev. Wm. Parsons Lunt, D.D., who died at Akabah, the ancient Ezion-Geber, on the Red Sea, Mar. 20, 1857, on his way to the Holy Land.

7. **William Cullen Bryant,** b. Nov. 3, 1794. Son of a highly cultured physician, to whose training he owed much. Before he was ten years old some of his verses appeared in the *Hampshire Gazette* for 1807. For two years a student at Williams College. Then studied law, and practised until 1825, first at Plainfield, Mass., and next at Great Barrington. Removing to New York became the editor of the *New York Review*. In the following year he joined William Coleman in conducting the New York *Evening Post*, assuming its entire editorial charge a year after. d. New York, 1878. Bryant was the first of American poets whose fame reached out to all English-speaking lands. Lowell describes him thus—

'He 's a Cowper condensed, with no craziness bitten,
And the advantage that Wordsworth before him has written.
* * * * * * * * *
He is almost the one of your poets that knows
How much grace, strength, and dignity lie in repose.'

For a long period his poetry held a very high place on account of its finish, and fidelity to nature, but the rise of the Impressionist School in poetry has made critics a little impatient of what they deem his over-elaboration.

'Thanotopsis,' written when he was only seventeen or eighteen years old, appeared in the *North American Review* in 1817. 'He had been engaged, as he says, in comparing Blair's poem of "The Grave," with another of the same cast by Bishop Porteus; and his mind was also considerably occupied with a recent volume of Kirke White's verses—those "Melodies of Death," to use a phrase from the Ode to the Rosary. It was in the autumn; the blue of the summer sky had faded into gray, and the brown earth was heaped with sere and withered emblems of the departed glory of the year. As he trod upon the hollow-sounding ground, in the loneliness of the woods, and among the prostrate trunks of trees that for generations had been mouldering into dust, he thought how the vast solitudes about him were filled with the same sad tokens of decay. He asked himself, as the thought expanded in his mind, What, indeed, is the whole earth but a great sepulchre of once living things, and its skies and stars but the witness and decorations

of a tomb? All that ever trod its surface, even they who
preceded the kings and patriarchs of the ancient world, the
teeming populations of buried cities that tradition itself has
forgotten, are mingled with its soil. All who tread it now, in
the flush of beauty, hope, and joy, will soon lie down with
them, and all who are yet to tread it in ages still unknown . . .
will join the innumerable hosts that have gone the dusky way.
While his mind was yet tossing with the thought, he hurried
home, and endeavoured to paint it to the eye, and render it in
music to the ear. This poem, for which he coined a name
from the Greek, was, says the poet Stoddard, "the greatest
poem ever written by so young a man." And as it came out of
the heart of our primæval woods, so it first gave articulate voice
to the genius of the New World, which is yet, as the geologists
tell us, older than the Old.'

9. 'Ode to a Waterfowl.' 'Written in his very early years, when
about to begin his work as a lawyer at Plainfield. He went over
to the place to make the necessary inquiries. He says in a letter
that he walked up the hills very forlorn and desolate indeed, not
knowing what was to become of him in the big world, which
grew bigger as he ascended, and yet darker with the coming on
of night. The sun had already set, leaving behind it one of
those brilliant seas of chrysolite and opal which often flood the
New England skies; and while he was looking on the rosy
splendor with rapt admiration, a solitary bird made wing along
the illuminated horizon. He watched the lone wanderer until
it was lost in the distance, asking himself whence it had come,
and to what home it was flying. When he went to the house
where he was to stop for the night, his mind was full of what he
had seen and felt, and he wrote these lines, as imperishable as
our language.'

Students of Robert Browning will note the striking similarity
of thought in the last verse of this poem and the following lines
in 'Paracelsus'—the favorite passage of General Gordon :—

> ' I go to prove my soul!
> I see my way as birds their trackless way.
> I shall arrive! what time, what circuit first,
> I ask not; but unless God send His hail,
> Or blinding fire-balls, sleet, or stifling snow,
> In some time, His good time, I shall arrive:
> He guides me and the bird. In His good time!'

Bryant's *Hymns* were not included in his *Poems*, but
published separately.

12. 'The Mother's Hymn,' written at the suggestion of the

Rev. Samuel Osgood, D.D., and included in the Service-book entitled *Christian Worship*, which he and the Rev. F. A. Farley, D.D., compiled.

14. **Henry Ware, jun., D.D.**, b. Hingham, Mass., Apr. 21, 1794. Son of Henry Ware, D.D., Hollis Professor of Divinity at Cambridge. Graduated with high honor at Harvard, 1812. Ordained minister of the Second Church of Boston in 1817. On account of ill-health resigned in 1828 ; the church, unwilling to accept his resignation, appointed Ralph Waldo Emerson to be his assoœiate. The same year he was appointed Professor of Pulpit Eloquence and Pastoral Care in the Harvard Divinity School. d. Sept. 25, 1843.

15. **William Augustus Mühlenberg**, grandson of Henry Melchior Mühlenberg, the patriarch of Lutheranism in America. b. Philadelphia, 1796. Graduated at the University of Pennsylvania, 1814. He was greatly beloved as the Rector of the Church of the Holy Communion in New York, and as the founder of philanthropic institutions, of which St. Luke's Hospital, in New York, is chief. d. 1877. His poem, 'I would not live alway,' attained great popularity in America. In an abbreviated form it was included in the hymnal of the Protestant Episcopal Church, but was omitted from the last edition. Dr. Doane, the Bishop of Albany, told me that the author expressed his gratification at its omission, since the hymn had been the outcome of a morbid mood.

16. **William Bourne Oliver Peabody, D.D.**, b. Exeter, N. H., July 9, 1799. Graduated Harvard, 1817. Studied theology at the Harvard Divinity School. Ordained pastor at Springfield, Mass., Oct., 1820, where he died, May 28, 1847.

16. **George Washington Doane**, b. Trenton, May 27, 1799. Educated at Union College. For 27 years Bishop of New Jersey. d. Apr. 27, 1859. Father of Dr. W. Croswell Doane, the present Bishop of Albany.

17. **Lydia Maria (Francis) Child.** b. Medford, Mass., Feb. 11, 1802. m. 1828, David L. Child. Wrote in 1833 appeal ' For that Class of Americans called Africans,' said to be the first anti-slavery book in America; and many stories. d. Wayland, Mass., Oct. 20, 1880.

18. **Louisa Jane Hall**—daughter of John Park, a physician —b. Newburyport, Mass., Feb. 2, 1802. During her long life she contributed much, both in prose and poetry, chiefly of a religious character, to the papers and magazines. Published a volume under the title of *Verse and Prose* in 1850. d. 1892.

19. **William Henry Furness, D.D.**, b. Boston, Apr. 20, 1802. Graduated at Harvard, 1820, and the Harvard Divinity School,

PAGE

1823. Ordained pastor, 1825. Author of many theological works. d. 1896. One of the most beautiful and venerable figures of America.

20. Ralph Waldo Emerson, b. Boston, Mass., May 25, 1803. Entered Boston Latin School, 1813, and Harvard, 1817. Colleague, and afterwards successor, of Henry Ware, jun., in the Second Church of Boston. Resigned on account of scruples concerning the Communion. Thenceforward he devoted himself to literature and lecturing. He was at once the moving spirit and the severe critic of the so-called Transcendentalists. d. Concord, Mass., Apr. 27, 1882. Emerson's fame rests on his prose writings, which are poetic in all save their form. Lowell describes him as

'A Greek head on right Yankee shoulders, whose range
   Has Olympus for one pole, for t'other the exchange.'

And of his verse he says—

'In the worst of his poems are mines of rich matter,
   But thrown in a heap with a crash and a clatter.'

His is the poetry of ideas, but often the ideas are so penetrating that we can forgive the poorness of their vesture. He once said to his close friend, Elizabeth Peabody, 'I am not a great poet— but whatever is of me, *is poet!*' Earl Lytton very happily describes his poems thus—'They are not Hebrew Psalms attuned to the harp, but Delphic oracles, or sunny meditations of a serene Pan delivered in broken snatches to faint sounds of sylvan flutes.' And yet every now and then we may say of some of his poems what John Ruskin sometimes says of his own writing—'This could not be better expressed.' Like Robert Browning, caring chiefly for ideas, yet every now and then he struck out passages exquisite in their lyric beauty.

27. 'The House of God.' Written in 1833 for the ordination of Rev. Chandler Robbins, who succeeded Emerson as minister of the Second Church, Boston.

28. William Croswell, b. Hudson, N. Y., Nov. 7, 1804. d. Boston, 1851. The founder, and for seven years Rector, of the Church of the Advent in that city. His *Poems*, edited by Bishop Coxe, appeared in 1861.

29. Frederic Henry Hedge, D.D., b. Cambridge, Mass., Dec. 12, 1805. After studying at Ilfeld and Schulpforte, graduated at Harvard, 1825, and Harvard Divinity School three years later. Held pastorates at West Cambridge, now Arlington; Bangor, Me.; Providence, R.I.; and Brookline, Mass. Professor of Ecclesiastical History in the Harvard Divinity School, and Professor of German Literature in Harvard. d. 1890.

31. Henry Wadsworth Longfellow, b. Portland, Me., Feb. 27, 1807. Entered Bowdoin College, 1822. After graduating in 1825, visited Europe to prepare himself for the chair of Modern Languages at that College. Entered upon the Professorship, 1829. Called to a similar post at Harvard, which he held from 1836 to 1864. LL.D. at Cambridge, Eng., and D.C.L. at Oxford, 1868. His bust placed in the Poets' Corner, Westminster Abbey, 1884. d. Cambridge, Mass., Mar. 24, 1882. His Life, followed by *Final Memorials*, edited by his brother Samuel. He is one of the most widely read of American poets. Unfortunately, some of his least worthy poems are the best known, such as 'The Psalm of Life.' This has tended to depreciate him somewhat in the eyes of the cultivated.

34. Written for Samuel Longfellow's ordination, 1848.

35. 'Nature' is by many regarded as the finest of American sonnets. It reminds one somewhat of Filicaja's lovely sonnet translated by Leigh Hunt.

> 'Just as a mother, with sweet, pious face,
> Yearns towards her little children from her seat,
> Gives one a kiss, another an embrace,
> Takes this upon her knees, that on her feet;
> And while from actions, looks, complaints, pretences,
> She learns their feelings and their various will,
> To this a look, to that a word, dispenses,
> And, whether stern or smiling, loves them still;—
> So Providence for us, high, infinite,
> Makes our necessities its watchful task,
> Hearkens to all our prayers, helps all our wants,
> And even if it denies what seems our right,
> Either denies because 'twould have us ask,
> Or seems but to deny, or in denying grants.

37. Sarah Elizabeth (Appleton) Miles, b. Boston, Mass., Mar. 28, 1807. Her verse, written mostly at a very early age, was sent to the printer by her father. Her finest hymn, given here, appeared in the *Christian Examiner* in 1827, and is remarkable for so young a writer.

38. Nathaniel Parker Willis, b. Portland, Me., Jan. 20, 1807. Graduated Yale, 1827. Founded the *American Monthly Magazine,* 1829, which in 1831 became the *New York Mirror.* Made a tour through Europe and the East, 1831, of which he sent accounts to his paper. Reports of private conversations in these led to a duel with Captain Marryat. Leaving the *Mirror* in 1839 he established *The Corsair,* to which Thackeray contributed. In 1846 started *The Home Journal,* with which he was connected till his death.

Jan. 20, 1867.   Best known by his poems on Scripture Events, which, though rather inflated, were once very popular.

38. Written for the consecration of Hanover St. Church, Boston, 1826.

38. Ray Palmer, D.D., b. Little Compton, R.I., Nov. 12, 1808. Graduated Yale, 1830.   Held pastorates in Bath, Maine, and Albany, N.Y.   d. 1887.

'My faith looks up to Thee' is probably the best-known of American hymns.   Written in 1830, when its author was between his college and theological studies—in poor health and teaching in a girls' school. He says, 'I gave form to what I felt by writing with little effort the stanzas.   I wrote them with very tender emotion, and ended the last line with tears.'   The manuscript was then placed in a pocket-book until Lowell Mason asked young Palmer if he had not some hymn to contribute to his new book.   The hymn was produced, and Dr. Mason asked for a copy ; they stepped together into a store and the copy was made and taken away ; on examining the hymn at home Dr. Mason was so much pleased that he wrote for it the tune Olivet. A few days after he met the author and said, 'Mr. Palmer, you may live many years and do many good things, but I think you will be best known to posterity as the author of ' My faith looks up to Thee.'   A true prophecy.   It has been translated into Arabic, Tamil, Tahitian, Mahratta, Chinese, to say nothing of the European languages.   It consisted originally of six stanzas, but in Ray Palmer's *Poetical Works* it stands as in the text.

41. John Greenleaf Whittier, b. Haverhill, Mass., Dec. 17, 1807.   Brought up on his father's farm till his twentieth year, when verses of his having appeared in the Newburyport *Free Press*, its editor, William Lloyd Garrison, urged his father to give him a better education.   As a result he went for two terms to the Haverhill Academy, the funds being provided by the youth's own work at slipper-making and teaching.   When he was 21 he edited at Boston the *American Manufacturer*.   From 1830 to 1832 he edited successively the *Haverhill Gazette* and the *New England Weekly Review*.   From 1832 to 1837 he was occupied in managing the family farm and writing for the anti-slavery press.   In 1837 he removed to Philadelphia, where, for two years, he edited the *Pennsylvania Freeman*.   In 1840 he made his home at Amesbury, Mass., but during his latest years he resided at Oak Knoll, Danvers.   From 1847 to 1857 the greater part of his writing appeared in the *National Era* of Washington, D.C., an anti-slavery paper.   When the *Atlantic Monthly* was founded in 1857, most of his work appeared first

PAGE

in its pages. His first volume, *Legends of New England in Prose and Verse*, appeared in 1831; his last, *St. Gregory's Guest and Recent Poems*, in 1886. A posthumous volume, *At Sundown*, was published in 1892. His complete writings in prose and verse were published in 7 vols. by Houghton, Mifflin & Co. in Boston, and Macmillan & Co. in London (1888-9). Whittier is one of the few poets who belonged to the Society of Friends, and, strange to say, his muse was kindled by a volume of Robert Burns's poetry left at his father's house by a travelling pedlar; but the muse was in him, and the marvel is that, with so slender an education, it gave forth notes so rich. Had he been blessed with the opportunities of culture which fell to the lot of Longfellow, Holmes, and Lowell, he would, I think, have outdistanced them all in lyric work. Lowell says:—

> 'There was ne'er a man born who had more of the swing
>   Of the true lyric bard and all that kind of thing;
> And his failures arise (though perhaps he don't know it),
> From the very same cause that has made him a poet—
> A fervor of mind which knows no separation
> 'Twixt simple excitement and pure inspiration.'

Opportunities for culture would have taught him to know that difference. His poem 'Snow-bound' is worthy of a place beside Goldsmith's *Deserted Village* and Gray's *Elegy*, and is as perfect a picture of American as these are of English village life. In pathetic expression his religious verse has few equals in English poetry.

51. Written for the opening of Plymouth Church, Minnesota, 1872.

52. 'The Voice of Calm' from 'The Brewing of Soma.'

56. **Oliver Wendell Holmes**, b. Cambridge, Mass., Aug. 29, 1809. For a year at Phillips Academy in Andover. Graduated Harvard, 1829. After a year's study of law he turned to medicine, which he studied at Harvard, Edinburgh, and Paris, taking his medical degree in 1836. Appointed Professor of Anatomy and Physiology at Dartmouth, 1839. In 1840 began practice in Boston. Seven years later appointed Parkman Professor of Anatomy at Harvard. d. 1894. His professional works were numerous and valuable, but his fame rests on his literary writings both in prose and verse. His first poem— a protest against the breaking up of the worn-out frigate *Constitution*, appeared in the Boston *Advertiser* in 1830. On the founding of the *Atlantic Monthly* in 1857 he contributed the papers afterwards known as *The Autocrat of the Breakfast Table*, followed in 1860 by *The Professor*, and in 1873 by *The Poet at the Breakfast Table*. In these some of his finest verse first

appeared. From time to time he gathered his fugitive verse for publication in book-form—the last of these being *Before the Curfew*, in 1888. His complete poetical works were issued by Houghton, Mifflin & Co. He was one of the most delightful characters of America, and beloved on both sides of the Atlantic. Best known though he is by his prose, especially *The Autocrat*, his poems are full of fancy, fun, kindly satire, but sometimes they are marked by the tenderest pathos, and in a few cases they rise to grandeur, as in certain verses of 'The Chambered Nautilus' and 'The Living Temple.'

57. ' The Chambered Nautilus,' from *The Autocrat of the Breakfast Table*, 1857-1858.

60. 'A Sunday Hymn' is introduced with these words at the conclusion of *The Professor at the Breakfast Table :*—'They will, doubtless, forget for the moment the difference of the hues of truth we look at through our human prisms, and join in singing (inwardly) this hymn to the Source of the light we all need to lead us, and the warmth which alone will make us all brothers.'

61. ' Hymn of Trust' is also from *The Professor at the Breakfast Table*.

62. Stephen Greenleaf Bulfinch, b. Boston, June 18, 1809. (His father, Charles Bulfinch, was the designer of the National Capitol at Washington.) Graduated at Columbia College, 1827, and at the Harvard Divinity School in 1830. Held pastorates at Pittsburgh, Pa.; Washington, D.C.; Nashua, N.H.; Dorchester, and at East Cambridge, Mass., where he died, Oct. 12, 1870. His verse—*Poems*, 1834 ; *Lays of the Gospel*, 1845 ; Editor of *The Harp and the Cross*. 1857.

64. Edgar Allan Poe, b. Boston, Mass., Jan. 19, 1809. Educated at Manor House School near London, Eng., 1815-20, and for a few months in 1826 at the University of Virginia. After a changeful and somewhat wayward life, d. Baltimore, Oct. 7, 1849. Remarkable for his weird stories and such poems as ' The Raven,' ' The Bells,' and 'Annabel Lee.'

64. James Freeman Clarke, b. Hanover, N.H., Apr. 4, 1810. Graduated at Harvard, 1829, and in its Divinity School, 1833. Held pastorates at Louisville and Boston. Professor of Natural Theology and Christian Doctrine at Harvard. For six years a member of the State Board of Education. d. 1888. Author of numerous and valuable theological works.

65. Theodore Parker, b. Lexington, Mass., Aug. 24, 1810. His father was a farmer and mechanic, but the son managed to teach himself during the winter months. Entered Harvard, 1830, at the same time working on a farm. From 1837 to 1845 minister at West Roxbury, and from 1846 to 1859 of an independent religious society organized in Boston. Compelled to resign from failure of health. d. Florence, Italy, May 10, 1860. An ardent abolitionist and eloquent preacher and writer. His works, published in 14 vols. after his death, edited by Frances Power Cobbe.

'Jesus' expresses his earlier view.

66. Chandler Robbins, b. Lynn, Mass., 1810. Graduated at Harvard, 1829, and Harvard Divinity School, 1833. Minister of Second Church, Boston, 1833–1874. d. 1882. This hymn was contributed to Dr. George E. Ellis's *Psalms and Hymns for the Sanctuary*, 1845.

66. Edmund Hamilton Sears, b. Sandisfield, Mass., 1810. Graduated Union College, 1834 ; Harvard Divinity School, 1837. Minister of churches in Lancaster, Wayland, and Weston, Mass. d. Weston, 1876. Author of *The Fourth Gospel—the Heart of Christ*, and other works.

'Peace on Earth' was first published in the *Christian Register*, Boston, 1849.

68. 'Ideals' appeared in the *Christian Register*, Jan. 3, 1889.

69. William Henry Burleigh, b. Woodstock, Conn., 1812. Harbor Master and afterwards Port Warden of New York, 1853–70. d. 1871, in which year his poems were published at New York.

72. Samuel Dowse Robbins, brother of Chandler Robbins, b. Lynn, Mass., 1812, where he was ordained in 1833. After three pastorates in other towns, he retired from active work in 1873. d. recently.

73. Robert Cassie Waterston, b. Kennebunk, Me., 1812. Lifelong resident in Boston, where, beside pastoral charges, he was largely interested in educational and philanthropic work. Contributed to the *North American Review*. d. recently.

74. Harriet (Beecher) Stowe, b. Litchfield, Conn., June 14, 1812. Daughter of Rev. Lyman Beecher, D.D. m. 1836 the Rev. Calvin E. Stowe, D.D., Professor first at Bowdoin College and then at Andover Theological Seminary. Best known as the authoress of *Uncle Tom's Cabin*, which first appeared in the *National Era*, of Washington, D.C., 1851–52, followed by many other works. d. 1896. The verses quoted are from *Religious Poems*, 1865.

77. One verse omitted from 'When I awake I am still with Thee.'

78. Christopher Pearse Cranch, b. Alexandria, Va., 1813. Studied art in Europe. Afterwards lived at Cambridge, Mass., and New York. Beyond his work as an artist, published *Æneid of Virgil in English Verse* (1872), *The Bird and the Bell*

(1875), and *Ariel and Caliban* (1877).   d. Cambridge, Mass., Jan. 20, 1892.

81. Jones Very, b. Salem, Mass., Aug. 28, 1813. Early left fatherless. At fourteen errand boy, occupying spare time in self-education, and then tutor in a private school. Entered Harvard, 1834; two years later graduated with honors and appointed tutor in Greek—was spoken of as an ideal instructor 'who fairly breathed the spirit of the Greek language and its literature, surrounding their study with a charm which his pupils declare vanished from Harvard with him.' Many of the verses that flowed from his pen appeared first on the backs of young men's Greek exercises, as 'Incentives to a nobler life.' In 1838 he gave up his classical work and retired to Salem. Regarded by many as insane, but Dr. James Freeman Clarke said it was a case of *monosania* rather than *monomania*, and Emerson wished the whole world were as mad as he. He was most modest, and deemed himself only a reed through which the Spirit might breathe a music of its own. He said, 'I value these verses not because they are mine, but because they are not.' A fellow-clergyman said, 'To have walked with Very was truly to have walked with God'; and a sportsman once remarked, 'I don't set up to be a religious man, but you could not meet Very in the field without feeling the better for it somehow.' 'Rapt, twirling in his hands a withered spray, and waiting for the spark from heaven to fall, it seemed as if a gentle presence had wandered from another world than ours.' d. May 8, 1880. His collected works were published, with a portrait, and biographical sketch by Dr. James Freeman Clarke, 1886.

84. 'Labor and Rest.' Not included in the complete edition of the works of Jones Very, but in the volume edited by W. P. Andrews.

85. Cyrus Augustus Bartol, b. Freeport, Me., Apr. 30, 1813. Graduated Bowdoin, studied Harvard Divinity School. Colleague pastor of the West Church, Boston, 1837. Pastor, 1861. Philanthropist and social reformer. Close friend of Dr. Horace Bushnell, in whose *Life* many of his letters appear.

86. Charles Timothy Brooks, b. Salem, Mass., June 20, 1813. Graduated Harvard. Pastor of church in Newport, R. I., 1837-73, where he died June 14, 1883. Issued many translations from the German, and several volumes of poems.

87. James Thomas Fields, b. Portsmouth, N. H., Dec. 31, 1816. Was editor of the *Atlantic Monthly*, 1862-70. His work as a publisher in the well-known house of Ticknor and Fields brought him into intimate relations with many eminent writers, of whom he has written in *Yesterdays with Authors*. d. Boston, Mass., Apr. 24, 1881.

87. **Charles Gamage Eastman**, b. Fryeburg, Me., June 1, 1816. Graduated University of Vermont. Journalist. Member of the Vermont Senate, 1851–2. d. Montpelier, Vt., 1860. His poems published 1848, revised ed. 1880.

88. **Henry David Thoreau.** b. Concord, Mass., July 12, 1817. Graduated Harvard, 1837. In 1845 he built, with an outlay of a few dollars, a hut on the edge of Walden Pond, in Concord, on ground belonging to Emerson, and lived there for two and a quarter years, sustaining himself by a little farming and doing odd jobs for neighbors. See *Walden, or Life in the Woods*, 1854. Dr. O. W. Holmes thinks that from companionship with Thoreau, Emerson derived a deeper interest in the common things of nature. d. Concord, Mass., May 6, 1862.

89. **Arthur Cleveland Coxe**, D.D., b. Mendham, N.J., May 10, 1818. Graduated University of New York, rector of various Protestant Episcopal Churches, appointed Bishop of Western New York. 1864. d. July, 1896. Published *Advent—a Mystery*, 1837, and *Christian Ballads*, 1840.

89. **Thomas William Parsons**, b. Boston, Mass., Aug. 18, 1819. Educated Boston Latin School, studied Italian in Italy and translated Dante's *Inferno*. Practised Dental Surgery at Boston, which he afterwards pursued in England. Returned to Boston in 1872. d. Scituate, Mass., Sept. 3, 1892. Issued *Ghetto di Roma*, 1854; *Magnolia and other Poems*, 1867; *The Old House at Sudbury*, 1870; and *The Shadow of the Obelisk*, 1872. Best known by his stately 'Lines on a Bust of Dante.'

91. **Julia (Ward) Howe**, b. New York, May 27, 1819. m. 1843, Dr. Samuel Gridley Howe, the philanthropist, distinguished by his work for the blind. She visited Europe and became fluent in Italian, French, and Modern Greek. Issued many volumes of poems, but is best known by her 'Battle Hymn of the Republic,' written when the Civil War broke out. Deeply moved by the sight of troops starting for the seat of war, she penned these remarkable verses.

92. **Josiah Gilbert Holland**, b. Belchertown, Mass., July 24, 1819. Graduated Berkshire Medical College, but devoted himself to educational and literary pursuits. Planned and became the editor of the monthly journal originally known as *Scribner's*, but subsequently and now as the *Century*. d. New York, Oct. 12, 1881. His poetical works were *Bitter-Sweet*, 1855; *Kathrina*, 1867; *The Marble Prophecy*, 1872; and *The Mistress of the Manse*, 1874.

94. **James Russell Lowell**, b. Cambridge, Mass., Feb. 22, 1819.

Graduated Harvard, 1838. In 1855 succeeded to Longfellow's chair at Harvard. Appointed Minister to Spain, 1877; transferred to London, 1880, a post he held till 1885, during a part of which time he was rector of St. Andrew's University; D.C.L. Oxford, 1873; LL.D. Cambridge, Eng., 1874. His poetical works were *A Year's Life*, 1841; *A Legend of Brittany*, 1844; *The Vision of Sir Launfal*, 1845; *A Fable for Critics*, which came out anonymously, 1848; *Under the Willows*, 1869; *Heartsease and Rue*, 1888. The *Biglow Papers* first appeared in the Boston *Courier*, 1846-48, and the second series in the *Atlantic Monthly* during the Civil War. d. 1891. Mr. Lowell's range in his poetic work is very wide; there we find the broad humor of the *Biglow Papers*, the exquisite tenderness of *The Changeling*, the stateliness of *Bibliolatres*. It is often said by critics that he will be longest remembered by the *Biglow Papers* as being the most racy of the soil. I take leave to differ from this dictum, and to express the conviction that many of Mr. Lowell's serious poems will be treasured as long as the *Biglow Papers*.

103. I question whether anything finer can be found in the poetry of America than ' All Saints.'

105. Samuel Longfellow, brother and biographer of H. W. Longfellow, b. Portland, Me., June 18, 1819. Graduated Harvard. Minister of various churches until 1882, when he settled at Cambridge, Mass. d. 1892. Joint compiler with Samuel Johnson of *A Book of Hymns*, 1846, and *Hymns of the Spirit*, 1864. Editor, with T. W. Higginson, of *Thalatta*. Some of the finest of American hymns are from his pen.

109. Walt(er) Whitman, b. West Hills, Long Island, N.Y., May 31, 1819. In his early days a printer in summer and school-teacher in winter. From 1862-65 served as an army nurse in Washington and Virginia, which impaired his constitution. Then appointed clerk in the Interior Department, Washington; deposed by a superior who did not approve of his poetry, but shortly afterwards made a Clerk in the Attorney-General's Office—a post he held for eight years. A stroke of paralysis in 1873 led to his retirement to Camden, N.J. His poetical works were *Leaves of Grass*, 1855, of which he was his own compositor; *Drum Taps*, 1865; *Passage to India*, 1870; *After All not to Create only*, 1871; *As a strong bird on pinions free*, 1872; *November Boughs* and *Sands at Seventy*, 1888.

Concerning no American poet are the estimates so diverse—some regarding him as the greatest of the company, others denying to him even the name of poet. His influence on some eminent men has been very powerful, notably John Addington

PAGE

Symonds, witness his *Study of Whitman*. Probably the sanest estimate of his work is by Robert Louis Stevenson.

109. The 'Sea of Faith'— concluding stanzas of 'Passage to India.'

The 'Prayer of Columbus,' 8th, 9th, and 10th stanzas.

111. 'The Mystic Trumpeter,' closing stanzas.

111. **Alice Cary**, b. April 20, 1820, Miami Valley, nr. Cincinnati, d. 1871, is scarcely separable from her younger sister Phœbe. Under great difficulties, caused by an unsympathetic step-mother, who would not permit them even a light to read by, they studied at home, and when about eighteen years old began writing poems and stories for the press. In 1852 they removed to New York City, where the reputation of their writings and the charm of their manners made their home a centre for many of the chief persons of note in letters, art, and philanthropy. Their complete poems were published by Houghton, Mifflin & Co., with a delightful sketch of their lives by Mary Clemmer.

121. An able critic of poetry declares this 'Dying Hymn' to be as fine as anything in William Blake. In moments of deepest agony during her last illness she repeated it to herself.

121. **Anne Charlotte (Lynch) Botta**, b. Bennington, Vt., 1820. m. Prof. Vincenzo Botta, 1855. Her receptions in New York City were attended by the most distinguished people in art and letters. d. 1896. Published *Poems*, 1848 and 1884, and *Handbook of Universal Literature*, 1860 and 1887.

122. **Sarah (Knowles) Bolton**, dr. of John S. Knowles; at the age of fifteen went to reside with her uncle, Col. H. L. Miller, at Hartford, where his extensive library and the literary folk who frequented his house furnished means of culture. m. C. E. Bolton, a graduate of Amherst College, and removed to Cleveland, Ohio. An ardent worker in the temperance cause. For a time one of the editors of *The Congregationalist*. With her son, Charles Knowles Bolton of Harvard College, published *From Heart and Nature* (Thomas Y. Crowell & Co., 1887).

123. **Maria (White) Lowell**, b. Watertown, Mass., July 8, 1821. m. James Russell Lowell, 1844. d. Cambridge, Mass., Oct. 27, 1853. Her poems privately printed, 1855.

124. **Eliza Scudder**, niece of Dr. E. H. Sears, b. Boston, Nov. 14, 1821. Until recently lived in Boston. Her verse published in a tiny volume with the title *Hymns and Sonnets*, by E. S., 1880. The quantity small, the quality high.

129. **Samuel Johnson**, b. Salem, Mass., Oct. 10, 1822. Graduated, Harvard, 1842, and Harvard Divinity School, 1846. Pastor of a Free Religious Society at Lynn, Mass., 1853-70. d. North Andover, Mass., Feb. 19, 1882. Author of *Oriental*

PAGE

Religions. Compiled, with Samuel Longfellow, *A Book of Hymns*, 1846; *Hymns of the Spirit*, 1864.

130. **Caroline Atherton (Briggs) Mason**, b. Marblehead, July 27, 1823. Her father was Dr. Calvin Briggs, an eminent physician. It was of her paternal grandfather, the Rev. James Briggs, for 45 years minister at Cummington, that William Cullen Bryant, one of his parishioners, wrote 'The Old Man's Funeral.' She was the youngest of seven sisters who, when at the Bradford Academy, were called 'The Pleiades.' It was of her elder sister Harriet, who became the wife of David T. Stoddard, and, after five years' devoted service in her mission to the Nestorians, died of cholera at Trebizond, that she wrote 'Aroma' and 'The Grave by the Euxine.' In 1853 she became the wife of Charles Mason, a lawyer at Fitchburg. d. June 13, 1893. To her husband I am indebted for a copy of her poems, *The Lost Ring*, with an introduction by Charles G. Ames, and portrait, published in 1892.

134. **David Atwood Wasson**, b. Brookville, Me., May 14, 1823. Studied at Bowdoin College. In 1865-66 was minister to Theodore Parker's congregation in Boston. Subsequently accepted a post in the Boston Custom House. d. West Medford, Mass., Jan. 21, 1887. His poems published in the following year.

139. **Thomas Wentworth Higginson**, b. Cambridge, Mass., Dec. 22, 1823. Graduated Harvard. Minister of non-denominational churches in Newburyport and Worcester, Mass.; raised two companies for the Civil War, and was appointed Colonel of the first regiment recruited from the negroes. Wounded in October, 1864, and obliged to resign. In 1889 appointed State Historian of the soldiers and sailors of Mass. in the Civil War. His poems and translations collected and published in the *Afternoon Landscape*, 1889, a small but very charming book.

141. 'To my Shadow.' Compare Virgil, *Aen.* vi. 743 :—

'Quisque suos patimur Manes.'

142. 'Vestis Angelica.' 'It was the custom of the early English Church for pious laymen to be carried in the hour of death to some monastery, that they might be clothed in the habit of the religious order, and might die amid the prayers of the brotherhood. The garment thus assumed was known as the *Vestis Angelica.*' See Moroni, *Dizionario di Erudizione Storico Ecclesiastica*, ii. 78 ; xcvi. 212.

144. **Sarah Hammond Palfrey**, daughter of John Gorham Palfrey, the historian of New England, b. Boston and lives in

PAGE

Cambridge. Contributed many articles and poems to magazines, and published a volume of verse, *Prémices*, under the *nom de plume* of E. Foxton.

145. George Henry Boker, b. Philadelphia, Penn., Oct. 6, 1823. Graduated Princeton ; studied law. Appointed Minister to Constantinople, 1871. and to Russia, 1875. Resigned 1879. d. Philadelphia, Penn., Jan. 2, 1890. Possessed great dramatic faculty, as seen in his tragedies and comedies, which were collected in *Plays and Poems*, 1856. His *Poems of the War*, 1864, contain some of the most noted lyrics of that conflict. His best-known work is the *Book of the Dead*, from which extracts have been taken.

146. Phœbe Cary, b. Miami Valley, nr. Cincinnati, Sept. 24, 1824. The inseparable companion of her sister Alice, whom she survived only a few months. d. July 31, 1871. Their ability had much in common, though the elder sister wrote more verse, and, taken as a whole, of a finer kind. Phœbe was less strenuous than Alice, but possessed more humor.

149. 'Field Preaching,' says an able critic, ' has something of the charm of Christina Rossetti.'

150. 'Nearer Home,' though by no means equal to her sister's 'Dying' Hymn,' is the best-known verse associated with the name of Cary.

151. Adeline D. (Train) Whitney, b. Boston, Mass., Sept. 15, 1824. Writer of books for the young. Her poems are *Pansies*, 1872; *Daffodils* and *Bird-talks*, 1887; *Holy Tides*, 1886 (Houghton, Mifflin & Co.). All the poems given are from *Pansies*, save 'Kyrie Eleison,' which is from *Daffodils*.

155. Lucy Larcom, b. Beverly, Mass., 1826. Worked in a mill at Lowell, where, however, she managed to cultivate her mind ; afterwards studied at Monticello Seminary, Illinois, and became a teacher. Gradually, however, she came to devote herself to literature. Editor of *Our Young Folks*, 1866-74. d. 1893. Her poems—*An Idyl of Work*, 1875 ; *Wild Roses of Cape Ann*, 1880 ; *Childhood Songs*. Collected edition of her poems, 1885 (Houghton, Mifflin & Co.), from which extracts are taken. Her life written by Daniel Dulany Addison. A woman greatly beloved, whose verse, especially when the scantiness of her early education is remembered, must be pronounced remarkable. Had her work been condensed somewhat her place would have been still higher. The present selections represent her at her best, and are noteworthy for their freshness of thought and vigor of expression.

161. Richard Henry Stoddard, b. Hingham, Mass., July 2, 1825. Early years spent in an iron foundry ; spare time given

PAGE

to self-culture. Held government appointment at New York, 1853-73. Literary editor of the *New York World*, 1860-70, and of the *New York Mail and Express* in 1880. A collected edition of his poems appeared in 1880. For an interesting account of Mr. Stoddard see *American Authors at Home* (Cassell & Co.).

'Adsum' was suggested by the sudden death of William Makepeace Thackeray on Dec. 24, 1863.

162. **Bayard Taylor**, b. Kennett Square, Chester Co., Penn., Jan. 11, 1825. The greater part of his life spent in travel as a correspondent of important newspapers. Secretary of U.S. Legation at St. Petersburg, 1862. Soon after presenting his credentials as U.S. Minister to Germany, died at Berlin, Dec. 19, 1878. His most important work a translation of *Faust* in the original metres. A collected edition of his poems published 1880.

'Thou who sendest sun and rain' is the closing lyric of the third, and 'God, to whom we look up blindly,' of the second, evening of *The Poet's Journal*.

163. 'Wait' has been attributed to Bayard Taylor, but I am in some doubt whether it is actually from his pen. I do not find it in his works. It appeared in the *Boston Transcript* about twenty years ago, signed B.T., which may or may not have stood for Bayard Taylor.

163. **Julia Caroline (Ripley) Dorr**, b. Charleston, S.C., Feb. 13, 1825. m. in 1847 Seneca R. Dorr, of Rutland, Vt. Published *Poems*, 1871; *Friar Anselmo*, 1879; *Daybreak*, 1882; *Afternoon Songs*, 1885.

166. **Horatio Nelson Powers**, b. Amenia, Dutchess Co., N.Y., Apr. 30, 1826. Graduated Union College. Rector of various Episcopal churches. President of Griswold College (1864–67). In 1885 became rector at Piermont-on-the-Hudson, where he remained till his death, 1891. For many years American correspondent of the French Review *L'Art*. His verse—*Early and Late*, 1876; *A Decade of Song*, 1885. A memorial introduction was prefixed to a posthumous volume of his poems by Oscar Fay Adams.

167. 'My Walk to Church' is from *Harper's Monthly Magazine*.

169. **John Townsend Trowbridge**, b. Ogden, Monroe Co., N.Y., Sept. 18, 1827. Remarkable as a delineator of New England life. His poetical works—*The Vagabonds*, 1869; *The Emigrant's Story*, 1885; and *The Lost Earl*, 1888; *A Home Idyl* (Houghton, Mifflin, & Co.).

172. **Rose (Terry) Cooke**, b. West Hartford, Conn., Feb. 17, 1827. Educated at the Female Seminary there. m. and removed to Winsted, Conn., 1873. d. 1892. Collected edition of her poems published 1888.

PAGE

173. 'Rest' appeared in the New York *Independent*.

175. Ellen Clementine (Doran) Howarth, b. Cooperstown, N.Y., May 17, 1827. Employed as a calico-printer. m. Joseph Howarth, of the same occupation, lived in humble circumstances at Trenton, N.J., until assisted by appreciative friends. Her *Poems of Clementine*, from which two stanzas of ' The Passion Flower ' are taken, were edited by Richard Watson Gilder, 1867.

175. Charles Gordon Ames, b. Oct. 3, 1828. Unitarian minister in Philadelphia, now in Boston, sometime editor of the *Christian Register*, Boston. Much absorbed in various lines of public work, and consequently his publications, for the most part, are of fugitive nature, as sermons, addresses, &c.

178. Albert Laighton, b. Portsmouth, N.H., Jan. 8, 1829, privately educated there. His *Poems* published in 1859. Another edition in 1878—dedicated to his cousin, Celia Thaxter.

178. Martha (Perry) Lowe, b. Keene, N.H., Nov. 21, 1829. After travel in the West Indies and Europe, m. in 1857 Rev. Charles Lowe, a man of singularly beautiful character. Her poetical works are *The Olive and the Pine*, and *Love in Spain*.

179. Emily Dickinson, b. Amherst, Mass., Dec. 10, 1830. d. there, May 13, 1886. Wrote much in verse but only two or three poems printed during life. Occasionally she sent a poem to a friend ; great was the surprise to find after her death her portfolio full of poems, written in continuous lines like prose. These were entrusted to Mabel Loomis Todd and Thomas Wentworth Higginson, who issued them in two series (Roberts Brothers). Her verse is bold and unconventional, sometimes faulty, but sometimes well-nigh perfect in form. Her poetry needs to be looked at in the light of her life. I gather from a sketch prefixed to her poems that in her earlier days she mixed much in society, but found it utterly unsatisfying, and then entered on a hermit-like life, even restricting her walks to her father's grounds. Thus her ideas and thoughts were only known to a few close friends. Naturally of an introspective nature, she little needed the ordinary amusements of the world around ; her world was within. Storm, wind, the wild March sky, sunsets and dawns, birds, bees, butterflies and flowers, with a few trusted friends, were a sufficient companionship.

179–182. The first eight pieces are from the First Series.

182–183. The remaining five are from the Second Series.

184. Elizabeth (Lloyd) Howell, b. Philadelphia, Penn., 1830. m. Robert Howell, 1853. d. 1878. Her poems appeared in the *Wheatsheaf* for 1852. Best known by poem here given, which on its first appearance created a great impression, and was

thought to be a newly-discovered poem of Milton's. Canon Wilton says he remembers the stir caused by the publication of this poem.

185. **Paul Hamilton Hayne**, b. Charleston, S.C., Jan. 1, 1830. Graduated University of South Carolina. Gave up the practice of law for literary pursuits, editing various periodicals. Served in the Southern Army during the Civil War till obliged to resign on account of failing health. House and all his property destroyed at the bombardment of Charleston. Later years overshadowed by poverty and ill-health. d. Copse Hill, Forest Station, Ga., July 6, 1886. Author of *Poems*, 1855: *Sonnets and other Poems*, 1857; *Legends and Lyrics*, 1872; *The Mountain of the Lovers*, 1873. Complete edition of his poems, 1882.

186. **Helen Hunt (Fiske) Jackson**, better known as ' H. H.,' b. Amherst, Mass., Oct. 18, 1831. m. early to Capt E. B. Hunt of the U.S. army, who d. Oct. 1863. m. in 1875 W. S. Jackson. d. San Francisco, Aug. 12, 1885. A warm friend of the Indians, on behalf of whom she wrote *A Century of Dishonor*, 1881, and *Ramona*, 1884. Her poetic work is included in *Verses* by H. H., 1870, enlarged edition, 1874, and *Sonnets and Lyrics*, 1876. The extracts given are from *Verses* (Roberts Brothers, 1886).

189. **Saxe Holm**. While this *nom de plume* has not been wholly cleared of mystery, I am disposed by internal evidence to agree with the suggestion that the writer is none other than the above.

' The Angel of Pain' is from 'The One-legged Dancer.'

191. ' The Gospel of Mystery' is from ' The Elder's Wife.'

193. **Louisa May Alcott**, b. Germantown, Penn., Nov. 29, 1832. Educated by her father, influenced by Thoreau. Occupied first with teaching, then as a hospital nurse in Washington. Her *Little Women*, 1868, and *Little Men*, 1871, are known in all English-speaking countries. At the age of thirteen she wrote the remarkable hymn 'A little kingdom I possess.' Cf. No. 1184 in *The Treasury of Hymns*. d. March 6, 1888. The poem given appeared in an anonymously edited collection, *A Masque of Poets*.

194. **Edmund Clarence Stedman**, b. Oct. 8, 1833, Hartford, Conn. Educated at Yale ; class of 1853. Member of the New York Stock Exchange. His poems—*The Diamond Wedding; Poems Lyric and Idyllic.* 1860 ; *Alice of Monmouth*, 1864 ; *The Blameless Prince*, 1869; *Lyrics and Idylls*, 1879 ; *Hawthorn and other Poems*, 1877; *Collected Poems*, 1873, and subsequently with additions. His war poems and *Pan in Wall Street* have gained most popularity. He is even better known as a critic of poetry, through his *American Poets* and *Victorian Poets*, and his lectures at the Johns Hopkins University on 'The Art of

PAGE

Poetry.' In recognition of his work as a critic, Yale conferred on him the degree of LL.D.

196. Nancy Priest Wakefield, b. Royalston, Mass., 1834, though Winchendon, the adjoining town, claims her, since for five or six generations her family resided there. d. 1870. Her *Over the River* attained great popularity.

197. Phillips Brooks, D.D., b. Boston, 1835. Graduated Harvard, 1855; Preacher to the University, 1886-91; Rector of Holy Trinity, Philadelphia, 1859-69; Trinity Church, Boston, 1869-91; Bishop of Massachusetts, 1891-93. d. 1893. One of America's greatest preachers and most catholic-minded men. Spent Christmas, 1866, at Bethlehem; on return wrote for Christmas festival, 1868, of the Sunday School of Holy Trinity, Philadelphia, the Carol here given.

198. George Arnold, b. June 24, 1834, New York. Brought up at the Fourierite Settlement, at Strawberry Farms, N.J. Studied painting at the age of eighteen, but soon turned to literature. Served in the army during the Civil War. d. Nov. 3, 1865. His poems, *Dress—a Sea-shore Idyl*, 1866; *Poems Grave and Gay*, were edited, with a memorial Introduction, by William Winter, in 1866.

'"In the Dark" was written within a few days of his death, when the shadow of the night that knows no earthly dawn was already closing round him.'

199. Harriet McEwen Kimball, b. Portsmouth, N.H., Nov. 2, 1834. Chief founder of Cottage Hospital at Portsmouth. Her works—*Hymns*, 1867; *Swallow-Flights of Song*, 1874; *The Blessed Company of all Faithful People*, 1879; *Poems*, complete, 1889.

201. 'All's Well,' one of the favorite hymns of John Bright.

201. John James Piatt, b. James' Mill, now Milton, Ind., Mar. 1, 1835. Educated at Kenyon College. In 1861 appointed clerk in U. S. Treasury at Washington; 1870, enrolling clerk to U. S. House of Representatives; 1871, its librarian. U. S. Consul, Cork, Ireland, 1882, through two administrations. His works—*Poems by Two Friends*. in conjunction with W. D. Howells, 1860; *The Nests at Washington* (with his wife), 1864; *Poems in Sunshine and Firelight*, 1866; *Western Windows*, 1869; *Landmarks*, 1871; *Poems of House and Home*, 1879; *Idyls and Lyrics of the Ohio Valley*, 1884; *At the Holy Well*, 1887.

202. 'Transfiguration,' from *Idyls and Lyrics of the Ohio Valley*, 1881, seems to be the original version of 'A Dream of Church Windows,' the title poem of the volume published in 1888.

203. Sarah Margaret (Bryan) Piatt, b. Aug. 11, 1835, Lexington, Ky. Educated at Henry Female College, Newcastle, Ky. m. John James Piatt, 1861. First poems published in *Louisville Journal*. Her works—*A Woman's Poems*, 1871 ; *A Voyage to the Fortunate Isles*, 1874 ; *That New World*, 1876 ; *Poems in company with Children*, 1877 ; *Dramatic Persons and Moods*, 1880 ; *An Irish Garland*, 1884 ; *The Witch in the Glass*, 1889 ; *Child-World Ballads*, first series, 1887 ; second series, 1895.

204. ' Faith ' is a short extract from *An Irish Fairy Tale*.

' When saw we Thee ' is taken from *Child-World Ballads*, second series.

206. Louise (Chandler) Moulton, b. Pomfret, Conn. Educated at Mrs. Emma Hart Willard's Seminary at Troy, N. Y. m. to W. A. Moulton, Boston, 1855. Paid frequent visits to France and England, accounts of which she communicated to American journals. Literary executor of Philip Bourke Marston, whose poems she edited. Author of many stories. Her poetical works—*Poems*, 1877 ; *Swallow Flights*, 1878 ; *In the Garden of Dreams*, 1890. Her poems, especially her sonnets, are among the most artistic produced in America. Like much of the finest poetry of our time, touched with a deep sadness, but in her case relieved by a buoyant hope. Her sonnets bear not a little likeness to those of Mrs. Browning.

206-209. The first six poems are from *Swallow Flights*.

209-212. The next seven from *In the Garden of Dreams*.

212-213. The last three sonnets were sent me in MS. by Mrs. Moulton.

214. Harriet Elizabeth (Prescott) Spofford, b. Calais, Me., Apr. 3, 1835. Graduated Pinkerton Academy, Derry. N. H. m. R. S. Spofford, 1865, who died 1888. Since his death she has lived in Boston and Washington. Wrote early for periodicals. Popularity began with a story, ' In a Cellar,' in the *Atlantic Monthly*, 1859. She has since written much fiction. Her poetical works—*Poems*, 1882 ; *Ballads about Authors*, 1887. The extracts are from *Poems* (Houghton, Mifflin & Co.).

216. Theodore Tilton, b. Oct. 2, 1835. Graduated at the University of the City of New York. Journalist and lecturer. His verse—*The Sexton's Tale*, 1867 ; *Thou and I*, 1879 ; *Swabian Stories*, 1882 ; *The Chameleon's Dish*, 1893.

216. Washington Gladden, b. at Pitts Grove, Penn., Feb. 11, 1836. Educated at Williams College. Minister of Congregational churches at Brooklyn, New York City, North Adams, Springfield, Mass., and Columbus. For a time editor of the New York *Independent* and the *Sunday Afternoon*. In the latter his well-known hymn, ' O Master, let me walk with Thee,' appeared.

217. Thomas Bailey Aldrich, b. Portsmouth, N. H., Nov. 11, 1836. Early life spent in Louisiana. The death of his father prevented his entering college, and led to his taking a post in the counting-room of an uncle in New York. Success in writing for periodicals, followed by his appointment as reader in a publishing house. After various editorial connections, succeeded William Dean Howells as editor of *The Atlantic Monthly*, 1881. His poetical works — *The Bells*, 1854; *The Ballad of Babie Bell*, 1856, which started his poetic reputation; *Pampinea*, 1861; *Cloth of Gold*, 1874; *Flower and Thorn*, 1876; *Friar Jerome's Beautiful Book*, 1881; *Mercedes* and later *Lyrics*, 1884; *Wyndham Towers*, 1889. His work is characterized by great delicacy of finish. No writer in America has ever told stories in verse more exquisitely.

219. Celia (Laighton) Thaxter, b. Portsmouth, N. H., June 29, 1836. m. Levi Lincoln Thaxter, 1851—well-known as an interpreter of Browning's poetry. d. 1894. Her poetical works—*Among the Isles of Shoals* (off Portsmouth, where a large part of her life was spent), 1873; *Poems*, 1874; *Drift Weed*, 1878; *Poems for Children*, 1884; *The Cruise of the Mystery*, 1886.

'A Song of Easter' is from *Poems for Children*.

220. 'The Sunrise never failed us yet' is from *Drift Weed*.

'The Sandpiper,' a perfect gem, from *Poems*. All these published by Houghton, Mifflin & Co.

221. William Winter, b. Gloucester, Mass., July 15, 1836. Graduated Harvard Law School—admitted to, but did not practise at Bar. Devoted himself to lecturing and literature. His poetic works—*The Convent*, 1854; *The Queen's Domain*, 1858; *My Witness*, 1871; *Thistledown*, 1878; *Wanderers*, a selection from his poems, 1888.

223. Mary Frances Butts, b. Hopkinton, R.I., 1837. Resident at Westerly, R.I. Contributor to current literature.

224. William Dean Howells, b. Martin's Ferry, Belmont Co., O., Mar. 1, 1837. Compositor at Hamilton, O. Wrote for his father's journal. The writing of a Campaign Life of President Lincoln led to a Consular appointment at Venice, 1861-1865, which furnished materials for *Venetian Life*, 1866, and was followed by *Italian Journeys*, 1867. Assistant Editor of the *Atlantic Monthly*, 1866. Chief Editor, 1871-1881. Formed connection with firm of Harper Brothers, 1886, writing 'The Editor's Study' in their Magazine. Author of many novels, and books of descriptive travel. His poetic works—*Poems of Two Friends* (with J. J. Piatt), 1860; *No Love Lost—a Poem of Travel*, 1868; and recently, *Stops of Various Quills* (Harper Brothers).

225. **Francis Bret Harte**, b. Albany, N. Y., Aug. 25, 1839, successively teacher, miner, printer's apprentice, express messenger, then obtained editorial position on *The Golden Era* (San Francisco), afterwards editor of *The Californian.* First Editor of *The Overland Monthly*, where his most popular poem 'The Heathen Chinee,' appeared Sept., 1870. U. S. Consul, Crefeld, Germany, 1878, and Glasgow, 1880–1885. Author of many popular novels. His poetical works—*Poems*, 1870; *East and West Poems*, 1871; *Poetical Works*, 1873.

'The Two Ships'—the reference of this line is to the "Golden Gate" which connects the land-locked bay of San Francisco with the Pacific Ocean.

The 'Angelus' refers to an old Spanish Mission in San Francisco.

226. **John Burroughs**, b. Roxbury, N.Y., Apr. 3, 1837. Brought up on his father's farm, then became teacher. In Treasury Department, 1863. Various posts in connection with banks. Later occupied himself with a fruit farm at West Park on the Hudson, and with literature. Contributor to *Atlantic Monthly*, *The Century*, and other journals. An enthusiastic admirer of Walt Whitman, on whom he wrote *Notes*.

227. **Seth Curtis Beach**, b. Marion, N.Y., 1837. Graduated Union College, 1863. Harvard Divinity School, 1866. Minister at Bangor, Me.

This hymn written for Visitation Day, Harvard Divinity School, 1866.

228. **Edna Dean Proctor**, b. Henniker, N.H., Oct. 10, 1838. Resided first at Concord, N. H. afterwards at Brooklyn, N.Y. Travelled much in Europe. *Poems*, 1866, revised and enlarged 1890, Houghton, Mifflin & Co., from which extracts are taken.

229. **Henry Ames Blood**, b. Temple, N.H., June 7, 1838. Graduated Dartmouth. A teacher and afterwards in the Department of State at Washington. Verse contributed to periodicals. Author of *How much I Loved Thee*, a play privately printed.

230. **Mary (Mapes) Dodge**, b. New York, 1838. m. William Dodge, a well-known New York lawyer; on his early death devoted herself to literature, especially for children. Her 'Hans Brinker, or the Silver Skates,' a great success and translated into the principal European languages. Editor of *St. Nicholas* from foundation in 1873. Her verse—*Rhymes and Jingles*, 1874; *Along the Way*, 1879.

'The Two Mysteries' was suggested by the following incident: In the middle of the room, in its white coffin, lay the dead child, nephew of the poet. Near it, in a great chair, sat

PAGE

Walt Whitman, surrounded by little ones, and holding a beautiful little girl in his lap. The child looked curiously at the spectacle of death, and then inquiringly into the old man's face. 'You don't know what it is, do you, my dear?' said he, 'We don't either.'

231. Margaret Elizabeth (Munson) Sangster, b. New Rochelle, N. Y., Feb. 22, 1838. m. George Sangster, 1858. Engaged in various editorial work; now Editor of *Harper's Bazar*. Her verse — *Poems of the Household*, 1883; *Home Fairies and Heart Flowers*, 1887.

231. Charlotte Fiske (Bates) Rogé, b. New York, Nov. 30, 1838. m. M. Rogé. Assisted Longfellow in editing *Poems of Places*, for which she made several translations. Editor of the *Cambridge Book of Poetry*, 1882. Author of *Risk and other Poems*, 1879; *The Seven Voices of Sympathy*, 1881.

233. John White Chadwick, b. Marblehead, Mass., Oct. 19, 1840. Graduated Harvard Divinity School. Minister of Second Unitarian Church, Brooklyn. His verse—*A Book of Poems*, 1876; *In Nazareth Town*, 1883.

'A Prayer for Unity,' written for the Graduating Class of the Divinity School, Harvard, June 19, 1864.

235. William Channing Gannett, son of the revered Dr. Ezra Stiles Gannett, junior Pastor with Dr. Channing and his successor. b. Boston, Mar. 13, 1840. Graduated Harvard, 1860; Divinity School, 1868. For three and a half years at work among the freedmen during the Civil War. Pastor at Milwaukee, 1868–70. Then resided in Boston. Since 1889 minister at Rochester, N.Y. Joint author with F. L. Hosmer (see next note) of *The Thought of God in Hymns and Poems*, first series, 1886; second series, 1894 (Roberts Brothers)—small books, but full of verse of great tenderness and beauty, which richly deserve wider recognition.

240. Frederick Lucian Hosmer. b. Framingham, Mass., 1840. Graduated Harvard, 1862; Divinity School, 1869. Minister Unity Church, Cleveland, 1878–1892; Church of the Unity, St. Louis, 1894.

Poems taken from *The Thought of God*, mentioned above.

246. Charlotte Mellen Packard, b. Hamilton, Ohio, 1839. The lines here given first published in the *Monthly Religious Magazine*, edited by Dr. E. H. Sears, Dec., 1862.

247. George McKnight, b. Sterling, N.Y., 1840, where he practises as a physician. Author of *Firm Ground: Thoughts on Life and Faith*, a series of sonnets, 1877; revised edition, 1878, from which extracts are taken.

249. Sophie Winthrop (Shepherd) Weitzel, b. Nov. 20, 1840.

m. Rev. Charles T. Weitzel, 1872. d. Santa Barbara, California, June 1, 1892. Under the name of Sophie Winthrop she contributed much to the religious press, both in prose and verse. Author of several stories and historical studies. Rendered into modern English many Latin and old English hymns under the title *Hymns to Jesus*. Her verse collected and published under the title *From Time to Time*, by A. D. F. Randolph & Co., N.Y.

250. Nora Perry, b. Dudley, Mass., 1841. Contributor to *Harper's Magazine*, Chicago *Tribune*, and *Providence Journal*. d. 1896. Her verse—*After the Ball*, 1875; *New Songs and Ballads*, 1886 (Houghton, Mifflin & Co.) From the last of these 'A Prayer' is taken.

251. Minot Judson Savage, b. Norridgewock, Me., June 10, 1841. Graduated Bangor, Me. Pastor of the Church of the Unity, Boston, 1874; Church of the Messiah, N.Y., 1896. *Poems*, 1882.

252. James Herbert Morse, b. Hubbardston, Mass., Oct. 8, 1841. Graduated Harvard. Established a university school in New York. Author of *Summer-Haven Songs*, 1886.

253. Mary Anne Lathbury, b. 1841. I have been unable to find any particulars of the life of the author of these two exceedingly fine hymns. The first I discovered in a book sent me by Miss F. E. Willard; the second in the *Savoy Hymn Book*.

254. Edward Rowland Sill, b. Windsor, Conn., April 29, 1841. Graduated Yale. Professor of English Literature, University of California, 1874–1882. d. Cleveland, O., Feb. 27, 1887. His verse—*The Hermitage*, 1867; *Venus of Milo*, 1883. An edition of his poems issued posthumously, 1888. A writer of much force and beauty, from whom, had his life been spared, still greater things might have been expected.

258. Cincinnatus Hiner Miller, usually known as Joaquin Miller, b. Wabash District, Ind., Nov. 10, 1841. Gold miner in California. Studied law and admitted to Bar of Lane County. Judge of Grant County, Oreg., 1866–1870. Journalist at Washington, D.C. His poetical works—*Songs of the Sierras*, 1873; *Songs of the Desert*, 1875; *Songs of Italy*, 1878; *Songs of the Mexican Seas*, 1887.

259. Sidney Lanier, b. Macon, Georgia, Feb. 3, 1842. Graduated Oglethorpe College 1860. At the outbreak of the Civil War joined the second Georgia battalion of the Confederate Volunteers, and served in Virginia. Attempted to run the blockade, was captured and imprisoned for five months at Point Lookout. Here the weakness of lungs which troubled,

PAGE

and at last ended, his life, arose. A chequered career followed—at first a clerk, then a teacher, then studied law and practised with his father at Macon (1868-1872), then removed to Baltimore, where he afterwards chiefly resided, and became first flute-player at the Peabody Symphony Concerts. Literature and music now occupied his time. 1879-1881 Lecturer on English Literature at Johns Hopkins University, where he set forth his theory as to the relations between music and verse. Harassed by poverty and ill health till death came at Lynn, N. C., Sept. 7, 1881. Attention first called to his poetic ability by 'Corn,' in *Lippincott's Magazine*, 1874, which led to his selection as the writer of the words of the cantata for the Centennial Exhibition, 1876. His Poems were published in 1877, and a complete edition edited by his wife with a memorial sketch by William Hayes Ward in 1884 (Scribner's Sons, New York; Gay and Bird, London). Held by some, and with good ground, as extracts given will show, to be the most original poet of America. *The Spectator* said, concerning his work, that nothing so original had appeared either in America or England for thirty years. Highly regarded by Mr. Robert Bridges, who desires his works to be better known in Great Britain.

263. **May Louise (Riley) Smith**, b. Brighton, Monroe Co., N.Y., May 29, 1842. m. Albert Smith, of Springfield, Ill., now of New York City. Her verse—*A Gift of Gentians*, 1882; *The Inn of Rest*, 1888.

264. **Charles Munroe Dickenson**, b. Louisville, Lewis Co., N.Y., Nov. 15, 1842 Admitted to the bar 1865, and practised law in New York City until 1878. Editor and proprietor of the Binghamton *Republican*. Author of *The Children and other Verses*, 1889.

264. **Francis Howard Williams**, b. Philadelphia, Penn., Sept. 2, 1844. A literary critic. Resides at Germantown, and is now devoting himself to poetry. Author of *The Princess Elizabeth—a Dramatic Poem*, 1880; *Theodora—a Christmas Pastoral; The Flute Player and other Poems* (G. P. Putnam's Sons), 1894, from which extracts are taken.

265. **Richard Watson Gilder**, b. Bordentown, N.J., Feb. 8, 1844. Began life as a clerk in a railroad office. Served in the artillery in the Civil War. Then editor of the *Newark Morning Register*, and at the same time of *Hours at Home*—a New York monthly. Then chosen by Dr. Holland as assistant editor of *Scribner's Magazine*, which afterwards became *The Century*, of which, on Dr. Holland's death, he became the editor—a position he still holds with distinguished ability. Author

of *The New Day*, 1875; *The Poet and his Master*, 1878;
Lyrics, 1885: *The Celestial Passion*. 1885. Mr. Gilder has
gathered into *Five Books of Song*, 1895, all his previously
published poems. For strength, beauty, and variety his verse
has rarely been surpassed in America.

270. **John Banister Tabb**, b. 1845. A priest of the Roman
Catholic Church, whose tiny volume of striking verse was
published by Copeland and Day, in Boston, and John Lane,
in London, 1894.

273. **Elizabeth Stuart (Phelps) Ward**, b. Andover, Mass.,
Aug. 13, 1844, daughter of Prof. Austin Phelps of the Andover
Theological Seminary. m. Herbert D. Ward, of New York
City, 1888. Became known by *The Gates Ajar*, 1868. Her
verse—*Poetic Studies*, 1875 ; *Songs of the Silent World*, 1885.
Poems given are from *Poetic Studies* (Houghton, Mifflin & Co.).

274. **Sarah Chauncey Woolsey**, usually known as Susan Coolidge,
b. Cleveland, O. Niece of Theodore D. Woolsey, President of
Yale College. Writer of books for children. *Verses*, 1880.

276. **Edgar Fawcett**, b. New York, May 26, 1847. Graduated
Columbia College, N. Y. Author of many novels and plays.
His verse—*Short Poems for Short People*, 1871 ; *Fantasy and
Passion*, 1878 ; *Song and Story*, 1884 ; *The Buntling Ball*, 1884 ;
Romance and Revery, 1886 (Houghton, Mifflin & Co.).

276. **Henry Augustin Beers**, b. Buffalo, N. Y., July 2, 1847.
Graduated Yale, where he was first tutor and then assistant
Professor of English, 1865, full Professor, 1880. His verse—
Odds and Ends, 1878 ; *The Thankless Muse*, 1885.

277. **John Vance Cheney**, b. Groveland, Livingston Co., N.Y.,
Dec. 29, 1848. First a teacher, then admitted to the Bar and
practised at New York. Ill-health drove him to a warmer
climate, and he became Librarian of the Free Public Library,
San Francisco, 1877. He is now Librarian of the Newberry
Library, Chicago. His verse—*Thistle-drift*, 1887 ; *Wood-blooms*
(F. A. Stokes & Co.), 1888.

278. **Emma Lazarus**, b. New York, July 22, 1849, of Jewish
parents. An ardent Semite, who cared more for her race in
a national than a religious sense. She was deeply influenced
by Emerson, who encouraged her in her writing. She travelled
much in Europe in search of health. Her sufferings were
great. d. New York, 1887. Her verse—*Poems and Translations*
(written when from 14 to 17 years of age), 1867 ; *Admetus*, 1871 ;
Poems and Ballads of Heine, 1881 ; *Songs of a Semite*, 1882.
Her collected poems brought out posthumously 1888 (Houghton,
Mifflin & Co.), from which extracts are taken.

280. **Arlo Bates**, b. East Machias, Me., Dec. 16, 1850. Graduated

PAGE

Bowdoin College. Editor of various papers. His verse—*Berries of the Brier*, 1886 ; *Sonnets in Shadow*, 1887, a memorial volume to his wife, who died in 1886.

280. **Mary (Woolsey) Howland,** b. 1832; m. Rev. R. S. Howland of New York; d. 1864. This touching little poem, which has borne various names—'Requiescam,' 'In Hospital,' and 'Rest'—is said to have been found under the pillow of a wounded soldier near Port Royal, South Carolina, 1864.

281. **Oscar Fay Adams,** b. Worcester, Mass. Taught in various places. First venture in literature was with a story in the N. Y. *Independent*. In 1882 began to write verse. Published *Poet Laureate Idyls* in 1886. In same year edited *Through the Year with the Poets*, 12 vols. Wrote Memorial Introduction to his friend Horatio Nelson Powers' last volume of poems, 1891. Now resides at Cambridge, Mass.

282. **Nathan Haskell Dole,** b. Chelsea, Mass., Aug. 31, 1852.

283. **Eugene Field,** b. St. Louis, Mo., Sept. 2, 1850. Studied at the University of Missouri. A journalist by profession. d. 1896. His verse—*Culture's Garland*, 1887 ; *Little Book of Profitable Tales*, 1889 ; *Little Book of Western Verse*, 1889 ; *Second Book of Verse*, 1892 ; *With Trumpet and Drum*, 1892 ; *Holy Cross*, 1893 ; *Love Songs of Childhood*, 1894. Since his death his works have been published in ten volumes :—*The Writings in Prose and Verse of Eugene Field*. Blended with virile strength, 'there was in Field's nature,' says a reviewer, 'a genuine child-like element—great simplicity, affection and tenderness.' Says another, 'Of all American poets Field, it seems to me, best understood the heart of a child.'

287. **Charles Francis Richardson,** b. Hallowell, Me., May 29, 1851. On editorial staff of the N.Y. *Independent*, 1872–1878. Professor of Anglo-Saxon and English Literature at Dartmouth College. Author of *A Primer of American Literature*, 1876. His verse is contained in a tiny book, *The Cross*, 1879, consisting of short but vigorous pieces, from which the extracts are taken.

289. **Maurice Francis Egan,** b. Philadelphia, Penn., May 24, 1852. Graduated La Salle College. Professor of English Literature, Georgetown College, 1878. Editor of the N.Y. *Freeman's Journal*, 1881–88. Professor of English Literature in University of Notre Dame. His verse—*Songs and Songs*, 1886 ; *Lyrics and Sonnets*, 1895, from which extracts are taken.

291. 'Perpetual Youth.' Flower-land, i. e. Florida, a Spanish name.

292. **Annie (Trumbull) Slosson,** b. Stonington, Conn. m. Edward Slosson, of New York. Author of *Seven Dreamers*, which includes the well-known 'Fishin' Jimmy.' The two

delightful poems for children, included, printed on leaflets, were
sent me by her friend, the late lamented J. Ashcroft Noble.

295. **James Whitcomb Riley** (Benjamin F. Johnson), b.
Greenfield, Ind., 1853, son of a leading attorney.   First a sign-
painter, then a strolling actor, then on the staff of the *Indianapolis
Journal*.   Reciter of his own verse.   His poems in the Hoosier
dialect became very popular.   His verse—*The Old Swimmin'-
Hole*, 1883 ; *The Boss Girl*, 1886; *Character Sketches and Poems*,
1887 ; *Afterwhiles*, 1888 ; *Pipes o' Pan at Zekesbury*, 1889—
published by the Bowen Merrill Company.

295. ' The Prayer Perfect' is from *Rhymes of Childhood*, 1891.

' The Kingly Presence' is an extract from ' Das Krist Kindel'
in *Old-Fashioned Roses*.

296. ' The Beautiful City' is from the same work.

297. ' The Dead Wife' is from *Poems Here and There*, 1893.
All the extracts are from British editions of Mr. Riley's poems
published by Longmans, Green & Co.   It would seem that this
writer's poems are issued in England in differently arranged
collections from those published by the Bowen Merrill Company
in America.

298. **Ellen Mackay Hutchinson.**   Joint editor with Edmund
Clarence Stedman of *The Library of American Literature*.

From *Songs and Lyrics* (J. R. Osgood & Co.), 1881, now
published by Houghton, Mifflin & Co.

298. **Edith Matilda Thomas**, b. Chatham, Ohio, Aug. 12, 1854.
When at school contributed poetry to newspapers, some of which
caught the eye of Mrs. Helen Hunt Jackson, who introduced
her to the editors of the *Atlantic Monthly* and *The Century*, and
this led to her writing for those magazines.   Her poems at once
became popular.   Her verse—*A New Year's Masque*, 1885 ;
The Round Year, 1886 ; *Lyrics and Sonnets*, 1887 ; *The Inverted
Torch*—published by Houghton, Mifflin & Co.

300. **William Ordway Partridge**, a sculptor of high merit,
b. 1861.   Resides at Milton. Mass.   His verse—*The Song-Life
of a Sculptor*, 1894 (Roberts Brothers).

301. **Carl Spencer.**   I have failed to find any particulars of this
writer beyond the fact that he was born about 1854.

302. **George Edward Woodberry**, b. Beverly, Mass., May 12,
1855.   Graduated Harvard.   Professor of English Literature in
the State University of Nebraska, and then in Columbia College.
Contributor to *Atlantic Monthly* and *Nation*, New York.   Author
of a Life of Poe ; and *Studies in Letters and Life*.   Published *The
North Shore Watch and other Poems*, 1890, from which our striking
extract is taken.   Canon Wilton tells of a similar experience
after looking at a picture with the same subject in the Louvre.

PAGE

303. **Willis Boyd Allen.** Author of *In the Morning* (A. D. F. Randolph & Co.), 1890.

303. **Anna Jane Granniss,** b. 1856. Resides at Plainville. Conn. Said to have been, for the greater part of her life, a worker in a factory. Author of *Skipped Stitches* (Darling & Co., Keene, N.H.. 1894, fourth edition). I am indebted to Mrs. Tileston for bringing this remarkable little book under my notice. Read in the light of the fact stated above it is very significant.

306. **Margaretta Wade (Campbell) Deland,** b. Allegheny, Penn., Feb. 23, 1857. Studied at the Cooper Union in New York. m. Lorin F. Deland, of Boston, 1880. Well known by her theological novel, *John Ward, Preacher.* Her poems—*The Old Garden and other Verses* (Houghton, Mifflin & Co., 1886), of which an edition, with illustrations by Walter Crane, has been issued.

308. **Ina Donna Coolbrith,** b. near Springfield, Ill., c. 1858. Now resides at San Francisco. Since 1874 Librarian to the Oakland Free Library. Contributor to magazines. Published in 1881 *A Perfect Day and other Poems ; Songs from the Golden Gate,* 1896 (Houghton, Mifflin and Co.), from which 'A Prayer' is taken.

310. **Tudor Jenks,** on editoral staff of *The St. Nicholas Magazine.* Poem published in *The Outlook,* Christmas, 1895.

310. **Charles Henry Crandall,** b. Greenwich, Washington Co , N.Y , June 19, 1858. Journalist. His verse—*Wayside Music ; Lyrics, Songs, and Sonnets* (G. P. Putnam's Sons, 1893), from which extract is taken.

311. **Charles Henry Lüders,** b. Philadelphia, Penn., June 25, 1858. Studied at the University of Pennsylvania. Contributor of verse and prose to magazines. Joint author with S. D. Smith, jun., of *Hallo my Fancy,* 1887.

From *The Dead Nymph and other Poems* (Charles Scribner's Sons, 1892).

311. **William Roscoe Thayer,** b. Boston, Jan. 16, 1859. Graduated Harvard. Editorial work, 1882–5. Instructor in English. Harvard, 1888. His verse—*Confessions of Hermes,* 1884 ; *Hesper,* 1888.

From *Poems New and Old* (Houghton, Mifflin & Co.), 1894.

312. **Helen Gray Cone,** b. New York, Mar. 8, 1859. Instructor in English Literature, Normal College, New York. Author of *Oberon and Puck,* 1885 ; *The Ride to the Lady and other Poems* (Houghton, Mifflin & Co.), 1891, from the latter extracts are taken.

313. **Danske Carolina (Bedinger) Dandridge,** b. Copenhagen, Denmark, c. 1860, where her father was U.S. Minister. m. in

1877 Stephen Dandridge, of Shepherdstown, W. Va., now her home. Her verse—*Joy and other Poems*, 1888; *Rose Brake* (G. P. Putnam's Sons), 1890. From the latter the poems given are taken.

318. **Katherine Lee Bates**, b. Falmouth, Mass. Graduated Wellesley College, at which she became Associate Professor of English Literature. Author of *The College Beautiful*.

318. **Frank Dempster Sherman**, b. Peekskill, N.Y., May 6, 1860. Studied at Harvard; Fellow of Columbia, where he became Instructor in Architecture. Author of *Madrigals and Catches*, 1887, and *Lyrics for a Lute*, 1890, from which poems given are taken.

319. **Louise Imogen Guiney**, b. Boston, Jan. 7, 1861. Graduated Elmhurst Academy, Providence. Her poems—*Songs at the Start*, 1884; *The White Sail*, 1887; *A Roadside Harp*, 1893 (Houghton, Mifflin & Co.), from which extracts are taken.

Thanks are due to this writer for stirring up the lovers of Henry Vaughan, the Silurist, to restore his desecrated grave.

320. **Langdon Elwyn Mitchell (John Philip Varley)**, b. Philadelphia, Feb. 17, 1862. Studied at Harvard Law School, admitted to the Bar, New York. Author of *Sylvian and other Poems*, 1885; *Poems*, 1894. Poems given are from *Sylvian and other Poems*.

321. **Richard Hovey**. Author of *The Marriage of Guenevere*, a Drama; *Seaward*, an elegy on the death of Thomas William Parsons; Joint-Author with Bliss Carman of *Vagabondia*. Translator of *The Plays of Maurice Maeterlinck*.

321. **Amélie Rives (Princess Troubetzköy)**, b. Richmond, Va., Aug. 23, 1863. m. Prince Troubetzköy, a brilliant portrait painter. Has written several novels of a striking character. Her poems contributed to magazines and as yet uncollected.

'Death' appears in this work for the first time.

322. 'Unto the least of these little ones' appeared in *Harper's Monthly Magazine*, and is inserted here by the permission of the proprietors and the Author. A worthy companion to 'The Cry of the Children,' by Elizabeth Barrett Browning.

323. 'A Winter Hymn' also appears here for the first time.

324. **Lizette Woodworth Reese**, b. Waverly, Md. c. 1860. Removed to Baltimore. Author of *A Branch of May*, 1887; *A Handful of Lavender* (Houghton, Mifflin & Co.), 1891, from which extracts are taken.

324. **Alice Brown**. Author of *The Road to Castaly* (Copeland & Day, Boston), 1896, from which extracts are taken.

327. **Anne Reeve Aldrich**, b. 1866. Author of *Songs about Life, Love, and Death* (Charles Scribner's Sons, 1892). d. 1892.

PAGE

This volume prepared for publication before beginning of her fatal illness. 'Death at Daybreak,' included in it, was dictated by her just before her death.

329. Katherine Eleanor Conway, b. Rochester, N.Y., Sept. 6, 1853. Educated St. Mary's Academy, Buffalo N.Y. Joined the editorial staff of the *Boston Pilot* as associate editor with James Jeffrey Roche, 1883, a post she still retains. Author of *The Sunrise Slope*, 1883.

330. Minnie Gilmore, b. Boston, Mass., daughter of S. P. Gilmore, the well-known musician. Has written novels—*A Son of Esau* and *The Woman that Stood Between*. Her verse—*Pipes from Prairie Land* (Cassell & Co., Ld., New York).

'Life' is from 'A Quintette of Song,' contained in the above volume.

331. Hannah Parker Kimball. b. 1861. Author of *Soul and Sense*, published by Copeland & Day, Boston, 1896, from which extracts are taken. I am indebted to this firm for bringing this striking little book under my notice.

333. William Hunter Birckhead. From *Changing Moods* (George H. Carr), 1888.

334. R. T. W. Duke, b. Charlottesville, Virginia, 1855. Educated University of Virginia. Practised law. Now Judge of Charlottesville Corporation. Has contributed verse to *The Century*, *Lippincott's*, and other magazines.

334. Paul Lawrence Dunbar, b. Duyton, Ohio, June 27, 1872. A negro, whose book, *Majors and Minors*, printed by Hadley & Hadley, Toledo, Ohio, was reviewed at great length by W. D. Howells, in *Harper's Weekly*, June 22, 1896. Most of the poems are in dialect, and give a vivid picture of negro life.

335. Ellen (Sturgis) Hooper. m. Dr. Hooper, of Boston. Both she and her sister, Caroline Sturgis, wrote many short poems for *The Dial*, the short-lived magazine edited by Margaret Fuller, to which Ralph Waldo Emerson and other distinguished writers of the so-called Transcendentalists contributed. Ellen's were reprinted after her death, at the age of forty, for private circulation only.

'Duty' was published anonymously in the first number of *The Dial*, July, 1840. A like idea finds expression in the well-known lines :—

> Curved is the line of beauty,
> Straight is the line of duty,
> Walk by the last, and thou shalt see
> The former ever follow thee.

335. Joseph Brownlee Brown, b. Charleston, S.C., Oct. 4, 1824. Graduated at Dartmouth. Studied law, but became a teacher.   Belongs to the Transcendentalist school influenced by Emerson.   A confirmed invalid after 1865.   d. 1888.

Concerning 'Thalatta,' Thomas Wentworth Higginson says, in *The New World and the New Book*—' Who knows but that, when all else of American literature has vanished in forgetfulness. some single little masterpiece like this may remain to show the high-water mark, not merely of a single poet but of a nation and a generation.'

INDEX OF AUTHORS

INDEX OF FIRST LINES